15/4/92

NET PROFITS

NET PROFITS
The Story of National Sea

Stephen Kimber

NIMBUS PUBLISHING LIMITED

Copyright © 1989 by National Sea Products Ltd.

All rights reserved. No part of this publication may be reproduced or transmitted in any form or by any means, electronic or mechanical, including photocopying, recording, or any information storage and retrieval system, without the prior written permission of the publisher.

Nimbus Publishing Limited
P.O. Box 9301, Station A
Halifax, Nova Scotia
B3K 5N5

Design: GDA, Halifax
Copy-editing, Photo Research: Elizabeth Eve
Printing and Binding: Tri-Graphic, Ottawa

Canadian Cataloguing in Publication Data

Kimber, Stephen

Net Profits: The Story of National Sea

ISBN 0-921054-08-4

1. National Sea Products Ltd. — History.
2. Fisheries — Nova Scotia. I. Title.

HD9464.C24N386 1989   C89-098533-2
338.7'63922'09716

The publisher is grateful to the following people for their assistance in collecting the illustrations for this publication: Wilf Eisnor, Knickle's Studio, Lunenburg; Heather-Anne Risser, Fisheries Museum, Lunenburg; H.D. Pyke, Lunenburg; Dorothy MacLaren, Mahone Bay; Margaret Campbell, Public Archives of Nova Scotia.

Printed and Bound in Canada

Contents

Foreword *vii*
Acknowledgements *ix*

Part I — Crisis at National Sea
Chapter One   Big Fish, Big Pond *3*
Chapter Two   The No-Solution Solution *14*

Part II — Major Players in the Fish Business
Chapter Three   Setting the Scene *29*
Chapter Four   The Smith Brothers *38*
Chapter Five   Can-Do Connor *46*
Chapter Six   Buccaneering Boutilier *51*
Chapter Seven   W.C. Smith in Transition *54*
Chapter Eight   Ralph Pickard Bell *64*
Chapter Nine   One Company from Many *75*
Interlude   Cap'n High Liner *84*

Part III — The Rise and Fall of National Sea
Chapter Ten   An Era Ends, An Era Begins *117*
Chapter Eleven   Expansion and Consolidation *124*
Chapter Twelve   Transition — 1960-1969 *133*
Chapter Thirteen   The Third Generation *155*
Chapter Fourteen   The Nickerson Return *168*
Chapter Fifteen   Caught in the Nickerson Net *178*
Interlude   "Have you ever been to sea, Billy?" *196*

Part IV — Back on Course
Chapter Sixteen   The Private-Sector Solution *235*
Chapter Seventeen   Rescue at (National) Sea *256*
Chapter Eighteen   The Factory Freezer Trawler *269*
Chapter Nineteen   High on the High Liner *282*

To the fishermen past, present and future

Foreword

IT IS a singular and quite unexpected honor to have been invited to write a foreword to *Net Profits*. The families of the principals of National Sea Products Ltd. have been friends and associates of my own family for four generations. I therefore embark on this effort with both delight and pride.

As a Lunenburger whose forebears established a family firm in the saltfish business in 1789, and successfully pioneered the artificial drying of the product in the late 1930s, I am fiercely proud that another Lunenburg family established a corporate entity whose commercial enterprises today exert worldwide influences.

Our famous Lunenburg schooner the *Bluenose* is proof that a small town can produce an international racing champion. The chronicles of the growth of National Sea Products to a world-class corporation offer like evidence of how a handful of citizens from the same small town have, with vision and dedication, provided the entrepreneurship to create yet another international champion. Indeed, mighty oaks from little acorns grow.

Not unlike Bill Morrow, I spent many of my childhood hours on the Lunenburg waterfront. I haunted the shipyard and the sail loft, the rigging loft and the cooper shop, the blacksmith shop and the dory shop. My young eyes witnessed the transitions from the sailing ship to the auxiliary motor vessel, to the diesel trawler. Mine was a wonderful and never-to-be-forgotten youth. For me, and, I am sure, for Bill as well, Lunenburg was, is and always will be the fishing capital of Canada.

One usually suspects that corporate histories are rather dry affairs, but the readers of *Net Profits* need not have such fears. While it is, of course, basically the story of a business venture, it is also far more than that. It is a drama of the lives of men, which is what all true sagas are. It is a story of faith and dedication, of hope and despair, of tragedy and triumph. It is a tale of suspense and intrigue. Each chapter is chock-full of swashbucklers, visionaries, conciliators, philosophers, schemers, gamblers and pioneers, each with a role to play, each with a contribution to make.

Most of all, there are the fishermen themselves. As Bill Morrow so sagely observes, "It all starts with the fishermen. Without them, there would be no National Sea."

Though few except the skippers are named, the fishermen are indeed the true heroes of the story. Their courage, their faith and dedication, is the cornerstone of this and any other successful fishing venture.

Stephen Kimber makes the corporate life of National Sea come alive. Under his skillful pen, the peaks and valleys, the trials and tribulations, of the fishing industry leap from the pages to fire the reader's imagination, so that he or she almost becomes part of the high drama as it proceeds. From the thwarts of the dory to the seats of the mighty in the Parliament of Canada, from the stormy seas of the Grand Banks to the treacherous waters and shoals of the financial negotiations of 1983, the tale unfolds.

The fortunes of the fishery have always ebbed and flowed like the tides. Its history has traditionally been one of feast or famine, and like the fabled phoenix, it has never failed to rise from its ashes.

No fictional creation of the most imaginative screenwriter could epitomize life in the corporate boardroom, on the assembly line or on the rolling deck in a more exciting manner, but truth is always stranger than fiction. The writer of this most fascinating story of key players in Canada's oldest primary industry over the past 90 years holds the reader's attention from chapter one through to its conclusion. I, for one, could not put it down, devouring the text the day I received it. Having read it, I am convinced that every skipper and every deckhand, every plant worker and every office clerk, will feel some "pride of ownership" in having been a part of this remarkable story.

Wives and sweethearts have played a leading role as well. As John Milton observed in his "Ode on Blindness": "They also serve who only stand and wait." Without their love, understanding and strength, men would never have gone to sea. Now, of course, with the advent of the *Cape North,* women go to sea as well.

Stephen Kimber's own short voyages to the Banks on the pride of the fleet, the *Cape North,* and her smaller sister ship, the *Cape Ballard,* have given him some insight into the love-hate relationship that fishermen have with their trade. It is a mystery not at all understood by landsmen — and probably not entirely by those who have heard the siren's call, the fishermen themselves. The poet Masefield may have captured a sense of mystery in his poem "Sea Fever" when he wrote, "... for the call of the running tide,/is a wild call and a clear call that may not be denied."

I approach the end of the foreword with two personal notes. Firstly, I still possess and treasure a single-shot 22-calibre Remington rifle that my father purchased from Ralph Bell and gave me as a Christmas present in 1944. Secondly, I am most pleased that one of my children works for National Sea: my younger daughter Andrea is employed in the Marine Department of the High Liner Division.

I conclude with a toast frequently used in Lunenburg: "Success to the fishery." I would like, of course, to add, "and to National Sea."

Sherman Zwicker
Lunenburg, N.S.

Acknowledgements

WRITING a commissioned history is fraught with almost as many dangers for a journalist as sailing into a North Atlantic storm is for a fisherman.

The biggest danger, of course, is that the company commissioning its own history may not be interested in "history" at all, but simply looking to pay public tribute to their own gussied-up version of a grand and glorious past that may or may not have ever happened.

To their credit, National Sea officials made my job a lot easier by being as willing to answer my questions about the "other stuff" — the family feuds, the boardroom battles, the political punch-ups, the financial finagling that help to make its real fish-and-guts success story such a fascinating one — as they were eager to talk about plant openings and profit margins.

That's not to suggest that this book will tell you everything you ever wanted to know about National Sea Products Ltd. or the east coast fishing industry. The more I got involved in the project the more convinced I became that there are any number of fascinating books just waiting to be written — about what it's really like to live in a fishing community, for example, or the unfathomable but seemingly unending boom-and-bust cycles of the fishing industry, or the complexities of fishery politics, or the relationships between the company and its unions.

Although I touch on all of those subjects, the book I've chosen to write is mostly a chronology of one company and how it evolved from a fishermen's grocery store into one of the world's largest fishing enterprises.

As with any such undertaking, there are many people who deserve special thanks.

Much of the material used in my account of the events from the time of National Sea's founding on December 12, 1899, to C.J. Morrow's purchase of Ralph Bell's shares in 1953 comes from an earlier, unpublished history of the company, which Jack Wilcox wrote and generously made available to me while I was preparing my book. I thank him for that.

During the process of gathering material for the book, many people allowed me to interview them at length. They included Steve Comeau, Harold Connor, Perry Conrad, Gordon Cummings, Earl Demone, Earl Foster, Alec Green, Peter Green, Terry Hayward, David Hennigar, John Kelly, Senator Michael Kirby, Henry Kohler, Ian Langlands, Romeo LeBlanc, John Leefe, Charles MacFadden, John Maloney, Roland Martin, Willoughby Mills, Chris Morrow, C.J. Morrow, J.B. Morrow, W.O. Morrow, Charles Moulton, Peter John Nicholson, Eric Nowe, Morris Nowe, Tom Pittman, Jr., Kathleen Pittman, Doug Pyke, Abe Ryoichi, Robbie Shaw, David Smith, Roger Stirling and Judge Gordon Tidman. I thank them all for their patience, their insights and their very important contributions to my understanding of the company and the industry.

I'm especially grateful as well to the captains and the crews of the National Sea trawlers *Cape Ballard* and *Cape North* for allowing me to spend some time at sea with them during my research. In the process, I began to appreciate why successful fishermen are so well respected in their communities. My own respect for the ways of men who go down to the sea in ships was strengthened even more by my experiences aboard the *David Melgueiros,* the Portuguese side trawler that ferried me from the Grand Banks to St. Pierre. I thank Captain Antonio Fonseia and his crew for their kindness.

I'd also like to thank Peter MacLellan from Corporate Communications Ltd. During this book's long voyage from conception to completion, Peter served as the able and easy-going navigator. And copy editor Elizabeth Eve, who not only diligently rooted out errors, inconsistencies or omissions in the text, but who also took responsibility for tracking down the fascinating photographs that accompany it.

Finally, a special thanks to my wife, Jean, and to my family, who endured the many hours I spent researching and then writing this book with more good grace than anyone has a right to expect.

Stephen Kimber
Halifax, N.S.

Part I
Crisis at National Sea

1
Big Fish, Big Pond

APPEARANCES sometimes deceive.

The man standing in the line at the Air Canada ticket counter at the Halifax International Airport on this chilly November 1986 afternoon doesn't look at all like you'd expect the chairman of the board of a successful multinational corporation to look. He has a barrel chest, meaty workingman's hands and a ruddy complexion that would seem far more fitting for a deckhand on a fishing trawler than for a decision-maker in the boardroom of a major fishing corporation. Although he wears an expensive well-tailored Italian suit and carries a leather briefcase, his body language suggests he'll never be truly at home with either of them. But then, when he makes small talk with the ticket taker, the image changes. His face softens and he displays an unexpected salesman's charm, a quick smile and an easy laugh. The twinkle in his blue eyes transforms his appearance into that of perhaps the owner of a small rural hardware store, the kind where the owner knows his customers as well as he knows his business, and he knows his business inside out.

If the man still seems an unlikely fit in the sophisticated world of international high finance, so, at first blush, does the company he heads.

It's easy to understand how an outsider might put together some of the more obvious "facts" about the company — that it is in the traditionally unglamorous fish business, for example, that its head office is on the chronically economically depressed east coast of Canada, and that the man who heads the company is a member of the third generation of the company's founding family, as is the company's executive vice president — and conclude that the company itself is a conservatively managed, small local enterprise.

Appearances really do deceive.

William O. Morrow, the man who doesn't look like an international corporate executive, is, in fact, on his way to Montevideo, Uruguay, to attend a meeting of the board of directors of Astra Pesquerias Uruguayas S.A., a vertically integrated South American fishing company that is the largest fish exporter in Uruguay.

Its investors include two of Uruguay's most powerful business and political families, important private Danish investors, the Danish government's development agency, the International Finance Corporation (the commercial arm of the World Bank) and National Sea Products Ltd. of Halifax, Nova Scotia, Canada. NatSea is — not coincidentally — the company of which Bill Morrow is chairman of the board.

National Sea owns a 10-percent stake in Astra, a company that was set up in the 1970s to take economic advantage of Uruguay's 200-mile fishing zone. Despite the small percentage of the company it owns, National Sea is a pivotal partner in the operation. National Sea's willingness to become an investor and "technical partner" in Astra, in fact, was a key consideration in convincing the International Finance Corporation to provide capital for the company.

W.O. Morrow, Chairman of the Board of Directors

During this week's board meeting in Montevideo, National Sea — and Bill Morrow — will again play a pivotal role in determining Astra's future. Astra is currently looking for a grant from CIDA, the Canadian International Development Agency, to finance an experimental project to catch anchovita, a plentiful species in South American waters, using Canadian herring-seining technology. If the scheme works, the company will have found a way to produce fish meal and oil — the commercial fish products it makes from the anchovita — far more cheaply than previously believed possible. CIDA's experts are coming to Uruguay this week to discuss the project, and Astra officials want Morrow present for the sessions, not only to help answer technical questions but also to demonstrate that Canada's largest and most successful fish company is a full and active partner in the venture.

And it is.

The Uruguayan deal is just one of many international projects National Sea Products has on its corporate plate these days. The company that Bill Morrow's grandfather, a fishing captain named Smith, helped launch at the turn of the century as a humble little "grocery store" for fishermen in his home port of Lunenburg, Nova Scotia, has now become a massive international enterprise with tentacles reaching from the northernmost parts of the North Atlantic to the Far East.

On this day, for example, as Bill Morrow wings his way to Uruguay — he flies Air Canada from Halifax to Toronto to Miami and then switches to Pan Am for the overnight flight from Miami to Rio and then on to Montevideo, where he will arrive at 1:20 p.m., just over 20 hours after leaving Halifax — other National Sea executives are busy playing their own variety of jet-lag hopscotch around the globe. Company president Gordon Cummings is bouncing back and forth between sales meetings in Toronto and Boston; Executive Vice President for Finance and Administration Rod McCulloch is in Chicago to meet with officials from a major U.S.-based company National Sea has recently purchased; Executive Vice President for International and Trading Henry Demone is in China talking with officials there about a possible joint venture; Vice President for Fleet Earl Demone (Henry's father) is in Norway scouting a good deal on a new scallop vessel; and recently appointed executive vice president Robbie Shaw is in Ottawa for talks with Canadian federal fisheries officials.

But the company's corporate executives are not the only members of the NatSea family operating far from the corporate home base today. While Bill Morrow is waiting at the Miami Airport to board his flight to Montevideo, workers at the company's plant a few hundred miles to the northwest, in Tampa — many of them blacks and Hispanics who have never even seen the company's head office in Halifax — are busy processing another load of shrimp for the American market. And several thousand miles to the north, the skipper and the mate of National Sea's factory freezer trawler — both German born and trained — are scrounging the deep waters off Labrador in a frustrating search for codfish.

Today's National Sea Products Ltd. is, in fact, a huge, vertically integrated multinational company that employs just under 7,000 people; operates a fleet of 59 fishing vessels, including Canada's first fully equipped factory freezer trawler; owns its own shipyard; runs 14 fish-processing plants scattered along the Atlantic coast of North America from Tampa, Florida, to La Scie, Newfoundland; maintains an international trade division that ranges the world in search of sources of more and new fish to market and process; has corporate links with other major fish companies in Uruguay and Australia that allow it to acquire even more fish while giving it access to even more markets; operates two European procurement marketing and sales offices in Portugal and France, and Far Eastern sales offices in Tokyo, Hong Kong and Seattle; and even owns its own research and development firm that helps it develop products for today's marketplace as well as seeking new and better ways to catch and process fish in order to grab an even bigger share of tomorrow's marketplace.[1] Over at Fisheries Resource Development Ltd., the company's research and development arm, for example, engineers and scientists are not only busy trying to come up with new and interesting recipes for fish but also attempting to transform the traditional fishing master's art of fish-finding into a modern science based on oceanography, water temperature and the collection and interpretation of satellite data.

Besides introducing new fish products — the company launched five new frozen seafood entrées on supermarket shelves in 1986 — National Sea is also attempting to increase its overall international market share by buying up other seafood producers. During 1986, for example, the company spent $6 million (U.S.) to buy two major American labels, Booth and Fisherboy, which themselves already sold a combined total of $30 million worth of seafood a year on the U.S. market.

National Sea hasn't limited itself to seafood. Its first non-fish consumer product, a line of pre-formed, frozen chicken pieces was first marketed in 1987 under the brand name "Captain's Chicken" and promoted by the company's popular fish products advertising spokesman, the avuncular Captain High Liner. It was so successful that it captured one-quarter of the Canadian frozen-chicken market after only five months on supermarket shelves.

In fact, the 1986 National Sea Products Ltd. Annual Report, which is still in the early planning stages as Bill Morrow flies to Uruguay today, will pointedly describe the company as "a North American-based *food* company" instead of as a Halifax- or even Canadian-based fishing company. That annual report will also announce that the company's 1986 sales — $516,415,000 — increased 14 percent over the previous year; that its before-tax return on sales was 8.6 percent

---

1. How big is National Sea Products? Big enough to attract the interest of the lunatic fringe. In the mid-1970s, Sandra Good, a cult follower of American mass murderer Charles Manson, told a Canadian national radio audience that an ecological guerilla organization called the International People's Court of Retribution planned to carry out sabotage and assassinations against what she called major polluting companies. Good, who also described herself as chief lieutenant to Lynette "Squeaky" Fromme, another Manson disciple convicted of attempting to assassinate U.S. president Gerald Ford, told *As It Happens* host Barbara Frum that one of the organization's definite targets was a "very large fish packaging plant on the island of Nova Scotia that has been destroying our oceans. They manufacture fish sticks and frozen foods." Although the RCMP discreetly watched National Sea's Lunenburg plant as well as the homes of several company executives for six months after the threat, nothing ever came of it.

R.A. McCulloch, Executive Vice President, Finance and Administration

Henry Demone, Executive Vice President, International and Trading

Earl Demone, Executive Vice President, Fleet

L.R. Shaw, Executive Vice President
(CARLOS PHOTO)

compared to just two percent a year earlier; and that its net income had jumped from a little over $10 million in 1985 to more than $36 million in 1986. What all of that means for company shareholders is an income per common share of $2.30 in 1986 compared with just $0.61 a year earlier.

"Your company experienced a much more satisfactory year in 1986," the Directors' Report to Shareholders will modestly understate, adding, "It was a period during which primary emphasis moved beyond the successful process of recovery, to addressing the emerging role of National Sea Products in a changing world food market."

But that snippet of formal annual reportese will hardly begin to put the flesh of drama, tension and excitement on the skeleton of what one Canadian business magazine called "one of the most remarkable corporate turnarounds of 1985."

Although most of the participants have their own, often very different views on how and when that turnaround began, Bill Morrow can trace its beginnings to a meeting in a Halifax hotel meeting room on the night of Sunday, October 16, 1983, when there not only did not appear to be much hope for a turnaround but there didn't appear to be anything much worth turning around either. For starters, National Sea then owed a whopping $244 million, its warehouses were full to bursting with $80 million worth of fish it couldn't sell, it was about to record a stunning $17.3 million loss for 1983 and its future prospects, if it was possible to conceive of such a thing, looked even bleaker. The Bank of Nova Scotia was even threatening to call more than $100 million in outstanding loans, and some of the company's traditional suppliers were becoming so skittish about its fortunes they were beginning to demand cash on the table before they would agree to supply any more goods or services.

At its simplest level, National Sea Products was caught in what Bill Morrow later ruefully described as a "triple whammy" — high interest rates, low prices and far too many unsold fish — that came together to trigger the worst crisis in the company's 83-year history.

Because of the increasing value of the U.S. and Canadian dollars against European currencies, Canadian fish had suddenly become much more expensive than its competition in the vital American market. That meant no one was buying the fish National Sea was selling. At the same time — thanks to the quirks of a kindly Mother Nature and the realities of a catch-as-catch-can harvesting-oriented industry — National Sea had more fish to sell than ever in its history.

To complicate and compound its problems, the company suddenly got smashed by a tidal wave from another direction when 1981's worldwide recession washed interest rates up over the 20-percent high-water mark. As bad as that was for business in most of the western world, it was that much worse for the Canadian fishing industry, and especially for National Sea Products Ltd.

When Canada declared a 200-mile coastal fishing zone in 1977, most observers expected Canadian fishing companies would soon harvest an oceanful of profits. After years of indiscriminate overfishing by foreign fleets, Canada finally controlled the resource off its shores, and Canadian companies would get first crack at harvesting it. There developed what one analyst today calls a "Klondike mentality" in which fish-company executives decided they must immediately stake their claim to the gold of the ocean by building more and more new fishing boats and processing plants.

Because inflation was spiralling upward so quickly at the time that it was creating what effectively amounted to "negative" interest rates, borrowing to finance this massive expansion of catching and processing capacity not only seemed prudent but downright good business as well. Canada's chartered banks, awash in excess petro-dollars they needed to redeploy, willingly, almost eagerly, agreed to finance the industry's rapid expansion.

For their part, the Canadian federal government and the four Atlantic Canadian provincial governments, which all saw a newly energized fishing industry as a convenient, politically attractive vehicle to kickstart the sluggish east coast economy, egged them all on. When the industry eventually collapsed, the Nova Scotia government alone was left holding $51 million worth of loans to National Sea and its associated companies.

Although it was clear even at the time that the industry's long-term debt-to-equity ratio was getting seriously "out of whack" — especially for an industry as traditionally cyclical and risky as the fishery — "no one paid much attention to the conventional warning signals at the time," explains an industry analyst today, "because no one thought of the times as conventional." By the time 1980's muted warning signals turned into 1981's clanging alarm bells, it seemed almost too late to prevent the entire east coast fishing industry, including National Sea Products Ltd., its biggest and best-known corporate fish, from being beached by the recession.

National Sea, which had traditionally been the most stable company in the Atlantic fishery, faced the same kinds of economic problems that were creating havoc in the rest of the industry, but its financial problems were magnified because its major shareholder, H.B. Nickerson & Sons Ltd. of North Sydney, N.S., was not only a fish company itself but had also — ironically — borrowed all of the money it needed to finance its multimillion-dollar purchase of National Sea's shares in 1977. The result was that National Sea's own serious financial situation was inextricably linked with Nickerson's calamitous one.

By early 1982, Nickerson was drowning in debt and threatening to pull National Sea under with it. At the same time, Atlantic Canada's two other major fishing companies — the Lake Group Ltd. and Fishery Products Ltd. of Newfoundland — seemed on their way to the corporate sea bottom too. Given that reality, Ottawa and the provincial governments suddenly had to come face to face with the awful prospect that a major industry — one that provided 44,000 jobs in one of the country's economically weakest regions — was about to collapse.

To understand the implications of that, it's important to recognize that the fishery is more than just another industry in Atlantic Canada. Exploiting the bounty of the ocean had been the historical *raison d'être* for much of the region's coastal settlement and development — early Nova Scotia currency, in fact, even featured an engraving of a cod with the motto "Success to the Fisheries" on one side. The industry's complex, interdependent web of independent inshore fishermen, locally owned, seasonal fish-processing plants and large, vertically integrated regional and national fishing corporations has become the crucial economic underpinning for an entire rural way of life.

That government saw the fishery as an integral part of the region's social fabric, rather than as just another business, had actually contributed to the industry's current financial woes. Because the fishing industry is so heavily regulated — fish don't "belong" to any one company or individual, so it only makes sense that someone has to dictate who catches what, when and where — governments could, and often did, use their vast powers to manage the industry to encourage small inshore fishermen at the expense of their larger and perhaps more efficient corporate cousins, for example, or to force the companies to keep open uneconomic small local processing plants in order to preserve important jobs in isolated rural communities.

During periods of rapid growth and expansion such as occurred during the late 1970s, the industry could ignore such government meddling as the cause of little more than an inconvenient case of corporate hiccups. But when the industry fell upon hard times, as it did so dramatically in the early 1980s, the executives of the large fish companies began to argue urgently that using the fishing industry to achieve social-policy objectives would have the effect of completely choking off their economic air supply. All of which raised important public-policy questions. Should the fishery be regarded as simply an economic enterprise like any other, or should it be seen as an instrument of social policy? And how could the volatile industry be managed in the future to prevent it from smacking into another, perhaps worse financial crisis a few years down the road?

In an attempt to find answers to these and other similar questions, the federal government appointed a special high-powered task force in February 1982. As if to emphasize its importance, Prime Minister Pierre Trudeau appointed one of his own closest advisors, a brilliant former Halifax-based academic and later senator named Michael Kirby, to head up the task force.

In many ways the task force's report, *Navigating Troubled Waters: A New Policy for the Atlantic Fishery*, was a dazzling political *tour de force*. The task force not only completed its assigned work in less than a year, but — unlike most other task forces and royal commissions whose recommendations are ignored by politicians and bureaucrats and whose reports are left to gather dust on academics' shelves — Kirby convinced his political masters to specifically accept, reject or put over for further study each of its 57 recommendations *before* the report was even released.[2]

Although the report established a new and businesslike framework for the *future* management of the industry — clearly placing economic viability ahead of social-policy objectives, which the report conceded "would be universally regarded as a definite change in government policy" — it did little to resolve the current crisis.

Drawing on some of the best and brightest members of his original task force, Kirby put together a new committee in the spring of 1983 to tackle the increasingly more urgent and basic question of what to do to prevent the region's major fishing enterprises from collapsing.

Its members included Peter John Nicholson, a Stanford-educated former Liberal member of the Nova Scotia legislature who'd worked as a lobbyist and spokesman for H.B. Nickerson & Sons Ltd. before joining Kirby's task force. Within the task force, he was known as the "bionic pen."

"He's the best, fastest synthesizer of information I've ever met," Kirby says. Nicholson was fond of joking that the fishing industry was the "quicksand of the intellectual," meaning that the more you become involved in attempting to analyze its labyrinth ways, the deeper you become drawn into it.

Jack Hart, a partner in Price Waterhouse, was the committee's "numbers guy who came up with the computer models," Kirby says, "but in this situation his 'clients' — Peter Nicholson and myself — also had PhD's in the same area. We worked very well together."

The fourth member of the team was David Mann, a well-connected Liberal lawyer from Halifax "who worked virtually full time for the task force and seemed like a logical guy to help out with the restructuring too."

The restructuring committee's mandate was to bring together all the important players — the major fishing companies, the banks to whom they owed so

---

2. The federal government, in fact, accepted 50 of the report's 57 recommendations.

much money and the federal and provincial governments for whom their collapse would have been a political and economic disaster of Dome-like proportions — to try and cobble together a deal that would keep the fishery, though not necessarily the fishing companies and their current managements, afloat.

Kirby was attempting to do exactly that when he flew to Halifax on October 16, 1983, for a special meeting — the one that Bill Morrow would later regard as pivotal — with the executive committee of National Sea's board of directors, representatives of its major creditors and invited officials from both the federal and provincial governments.

As the 14 invitees[3] shuffled into a meeting room in the Citadel Inn, a modern hotel in downtown Halifax, Michael Kirby had good reason to feel pleased with himself. After five intense, difficult months of haggling, he was sure he and his three-member restructuring team had finally pieced together a deal that would allow National Sea to continue to operate — albeit as a pseudo-nationalized rather than privately owned company.

His scheme already had the blessing of the Bank of Nova Scotia, the company's main creditor, and both the federal and Nova Scotia governments. The purpose of tonight's meeting was simply to explain the deal to National Sea's executive committee and convince them to recommend it to their full board at another meeting the next day.

Michael Kirby didn't expect the National Sea officials he was meeting tonight to be happy with what he was about to propose. Like them, he would have preferred a private-sector solution. But Kirby, who prided himself on his ability to apply logic to the solution of virtually any problem, had carefully analyzed the company's situation, played out all the various scenarios and come to the inevitable conclusion that there were no private Canadian entrepreneurs willing or able to inject the kind of cash National Sea Products needed, and so there simply was no choice but for the government to step in and take control of National Sea.

Michael Kirby had underestimated — perhaps even overlooked — the possibility that Bill Morrow might come up with a realistic alternative to a government takeover. At one level that was because Kirby simply lumped Morrow in

---

3. They included restructuring-task-force members Kirby, Nicholson, Mann and Hart; National Sea's executive committee of Bill Morrow, his brother Jim, Jerry and Harold Nickerson and board executive committee chairman Bill Mingo, a Halifax lawyer; George Hitchman, the Bank of Nova Scotia's chief negotiator; George Buckrell, the senior regional vice president of the Royal Bank of Canada, National Sea's traditional banker; Danny Gallivan, a Halifax lawyer representing the federal government; Jack McClure, an assistant deputy minister in the federal department of fisheries; and Sandy MacLean, the deputy minister of the Nova Scotia department of fisheries.

with all the other fishing-industry executives he believed had been largely to blame for the crisis in the first place. At another, Kirby — like others before and since — found it difficult to take the easy-going, ever-friendly and hail-fellow-well-met Morrow seriously.

That was a mistake.

What Michael Kirby did not know as he organized his papers for his meeting with National Sea's executive committee this evening was that Bill Morrow was also busy behind the scenes applying logic to the same problem as Kirby and, having carefully analyzed his company's situation and played out all the various scenarios himself, had come to the no-less inevitable conclusion that there were private-sector solutions including — most promising — a Canadian entrepreneur who would be willing and able to inject the kind of cash National Sea needed, and so there was, after all, a choice other than a government takeover.

2

The No-Solution Solution

BILL MORROW knew he wasn't going to like what he was about to hear tonight. Ever since the first Kirby Task Force report was released in mid-February, the newspapers had been full of seemingly endless rumors and speculations concerning how and when Canada's "Big Four" east coast fishing companies would be restructured.

According to a March 9, 1983, Canadian Press story, for example, the federal cabinet was expected to reach a final decision within weeks, after considering "at least eight proposals for dealing with the companies.... While solutions range from nationalization of the major companies to letting the weakest fail," the report noted, "sources say the option that seems to be gaining support was first advanced in the mid-1970s by then fisheries minister Romeo LeBlanc. The plan ... would see the government buy the fishing vessels of the troubled companies and then help fishermen take them over."

As if that was not enough to send shudders down Bill Morrow's capitalist spine, Newfoundland premier Brian Peckford weighed in with an equally drastic proposal of his own. On March 29 Peckford called a press conference in St. John's to announce that his province wanted to amalgamate the entire offshore trawler fleet into one super-company to be owned and controlled by the federal and provincial governments, the banks and the 27,000-member Newfoundland Fishermen, Food and Allied Workers Union. As for the current shareholders of the big fish companies, Peckford gave them the back of his hand. He argued that those shareholders had not reinvested their profits in plant modernization and upgrading and had tolerated poor management practices, so they "should not be rewarded for their failures." Peckford called his scheme a "revolutionary way of looking at the fishing industry."

In public, Bill Morrow contented himself with a pointed but polite rejoinder that Peckford was "putting together some strange bedfellows. It won't work."

In private, he worried that federal Fisheries Minister Pierre DeBané's views on how best to restructure the fishing industry were probably not that much different from Peckford's.

In June the *Financial Post* reported that "a preliminary announcement [of the terms of the restructuring] is expected within weeks...." Pointing out that there "have been rumors afoot in recent months of a power struggle within cabinet" between proponents of creating a Crown corporation to run the entire fishery and supporters of continuing with some form of private ownership, the *Post* concluded: "As for public sector ownership, this is [also] likely an inevitable part of the so-called 'private sector solution,' since [the restructured companies] will probably need an infusion of government equity."

If there was little dispute over the need for some infusion of government money into the companies, there was plenty over the ultimate role that Ottawa should play in the fishery. "Kirby's group had three or four proposals they were pushing," remembers Joe Zatzman, the chairman of the Nova Scotia Resources Development Loan Board, a provincial government agency that lent money to the fishing industry. Zatzman himself was the key provincial negotiator in the restructuring process. "The one they pushed hardest was what I call the 'whale approach.' They wanted to take all the companies and the plants and everything and roll them into one big company for the whole east coast, a company that the feds would finance and control. But we didn't like that one — we felt Nova Scotia's interests wouldn't be very well looked after if the Newfoundland companies were involved. A large percentage of the fish that were being caught, even by Nova Scotia-based companies, was coming from off Newfoundland. And since fishing represented a larger percentage of Newfoundland's gross provincial product than ours, we were afraid we'd be dragged down by them in a company in which the federal government was involved and calling the shots."

While Zatzman negotiated, Bill Morrow read his newspapers and tried to divine the meaning of the political and fishing-industry gossip he was hearing, but he could do little more than worry about his — and his company's — future.

Michael Kirby, on the other hand, was very much involved in the real-life negotiations as he jetted from Toronto to Ottawa to St. John's to Halifax on what began to seem like a never-ending but never-successful round of bargaining.

Failure was not a word that slipped easily from Michael Kirby's lips. A Montreal-born minister's son — and the grandson of a Newfoundland fisherman — Kirby had spent most of the first 40 years of his life playing upwardly mobile, ever-successful political hopscotch between the intellectual groves of academe and the strategic trenches of politics.

Michael Kirby, Chairman, Task Force on the Atlantic Fishing Industry
(CP PHOTO)

Before being named to head up the task force, Kirby had been a university mathematics professor, the principal assistant to the premier of Nova Scotia, an assistant principal secretary to the prime minister of Canada, a member of a vital provincial regulatory agency known as the Nova Scotia Public Utilities Board, the president of an influential national think tank called the Institute for Research on Public Policy, the secretary to the federal cabinet for federal-provincial relations and the deputy clerk of the privy council.

At the time of his appointment to the task force, in fact, Kirby, who had just recently helped Pierre Trudeau mastermind the patriation of Canada's constitution, was widely regarded as "the second most important non-elected official in the federal civil service." What made Kirby so important — and so successful — was not his detailed understanding of specific issues so much as his ability to cut through to the essence of any problem and, more importantly, to solve it. Although opponents sometimes called him Machiavellian and a "bloodless, calculating manipulator," he was also, everyone agreed, "a devastatingly well-informed, brilliantly analytical, hard-headedly pragmatic problem-solver."

When his appointment to head the fishery task force was announced, Kirby was quick to admit to stunned reporters that he didn't know the difference between a halibut and a cod. "I wasn't a constitutional lawyer either," he noted simply. As he did with whatever job he took on, however, Kirby quickly made himself an expert on the issues as well as the options. By the time that the restructuring committee succeeded the task force, Kirby and his colleagues had concluded that there were only three real options available for saving the region's major fish companies.

The first, outright grants to the companies, had been ruled out immediately as politically unacceptable to both federal and provincial governments because it smacked of a government "bailout" of corporations that hadn't been able to manage their own affairs.

The second, providing more loans or guarantees to the companies, was also considered and dismissed because it would mean increasing the debt burden that had been at the heart of the current crisis, and could only increase the risk that the companies would collapse anyway.

In the end, the committee decided the only way to get the companies back on their feet with any expectation that they would remain standing was to inject new equity capital into them.

Kirby insists there never was any disagreement among the restructuring team or their federal masters over whether that new money should come from the public or private sector. As he explained the position in a paper presented later to the Max Bell Program in Business-Government Studies at York University, the federal objective "was to retain control of the restructured companies within the private sector, providing this could be done while meeting the primary objective of long-term commercial viability and certain other policy constraints." But it is also clear, in retrospect, that the committee concluded early on that no private entrepreneur in his right mind would be prepared to risk his capital in such an apparent sinkhole.

"We had our doubts that anyone would come along," admits Peter Nicholson, one of the restructuring committee's key strategists. "I talked with a number of possibilities myself, and there were some half-hearted attempts by investment dealers to come up with a private investor, but we didn't want to end up with a chewing-gum and bailing-wire solution that would fall apart again in a few years, so that meant that anyone who came in would have to bring a lot of capital with them. But there was a feeling that the only outsider likely to come forward in those circumstances was going to be a foreigner who wanted to make a strategic investment in the industry, something that wouldn't have been acceptable either."

As a result, Kirby and his committee assumed from the beginning of their negotiating that the real wheeling and dealing would have to take place among the federal and provincial governments and the banks, especially the Bank of Nova Scotia, which was on the hook for close to $400 million worth of loans to the industry.[1]

---

1. The Bank of Nova Scotia's role as banker to much of the east coast fishing industry "is explicable in purely historical terms," says Peter Nicholson, a member of the Kirby Task Force and now a vice president at the Bank of Nova Scotia. "The bank was always heavily involved in the east coast fishery through the Caribbean fish trade. That was one of the reasons the bank opened offices down there. It was also the dominant bank on the east coast at the same time that it didn't have a strong corporate portfolio elsewhere. That made the fishing industry very attractive, especially in the years after the 200-mile limit and during the era of recycled petro-dollars."

Kirby's strategy was simple enough: "We decided we would deal with the bank first, then, after we got an agreement there, we could go to the provinces to try and lay off part of the federal cost on them. After that, we could deal with the companies themselves.

"With the bank, we began by estimating its position in the event of the worst possible scenario, which would be bankruptcy. If the companies went under, what did the bank stand to lose? We took that figure, then added a sweetener for their troubles and took a proposal to them."

The negotiations were complex and difficult. In the beginning, the committee's view of the bank's potential losses and the bank's view of those losses were millions of dollars apart. At one point, in fact, George Hitchman, the bank's curmudgeonly chief negotiator, ended a negotiating session with a curt reminder that they were still $70 million apart. "Seventy million," he repeated, then added dryly, "It's too much to flip for, boys."

At another point near the end of the negotiations, when Kirby thought that the bankers still weren't giving enough ground, he decided to play a game of bargaining "chicken." Just before a scheduled meeting with Hitchman, Chairman of the Bank Cedric Ritchie and Deputy Chairman Gordon Bell at the Four Seasons Hotel in Ottawa, Kirby warned his committee colleagues — Nicholson and Mann — that he intended to throw a tantrum and walk out if the bankers didn't move from their opening position early in the meeting. The bankers didn't, so Kirby left in his strategic huff. The other members of his team followed a few minutes later.

"Two hours after that," Kirby recalled with satisfaction, "I got a call from the bank asking if we could get together to talk again."

Both sides, of course, had powerful reasons to want to strike a deal. "This was the Bank of Nova Scotia's Dome Petroleum," says Kirby of the huge losses the bank would face if it ended up with $400 million worth of worthless loans, but he's quick to admit that "there would have been incredible political fallout too if the federal government had just walked away and left the companies to go under."

All of that was cold comfort for Bill Morrow back in Halifax. In August — the same month in which the restructuring committee was officially supposed to report but didn't — Morrow released his company's third-quarter results: National Sea had lost nearly $2 million more between April and the end of June. As a result, he was forced to announce that the company was laying off 1,500 workers, closing five processing plants, slowing down production at a sixth and tying up 23 deep-sea trawlers.

Still there was no word from Ottawa.

Finally, on September 26, officials of the Newfoundland and Ottawa governments announced they had struck the first of the deals required to restructure the east coast fishing industry. They'd agreed to create a new Newfoundland super fish-company that would put together the assets of seven troubled Newfoundland fish companies with Nickerson's Nova Scotia-based scallop fleet. The new company would be 60 percent owned by the federal government, which agreed to contribute $75.3 million in new cash; 25 percent by the provincial government, which agreed to convert $31.5 million worth of debt to equity; and 15 percent by the Bank of Nova Scotia, which agreed to do the same with its $44.1 million worth of loans to the companies.

The deal-makers were careful not to use the word nationalization. "Governments and the banks have simply become the buyers of last resort," Michael Kirby told a reporter from the Toronto *Globe and Mail*, adding, "It's pretty foolish to use the word nationalization unless we've nationalized the Bank of Nova Scotia without my noticing."

Still, Bill Morrow couldn't help but notice that the existing owners of the Newfoundland fish companies had pointedly not been included in the new deal.

Even though the Newfoundland agreement was difficult to achieve — it was reached after a marathon week of secret negotiations in Montreal that followed months of public haggling between Newfoundland premier Brian Peckford and federal fisheries minister Pierre DeBané, during which Ottawa even threatened to impose its own unilateral restructuring deal and Newfoundland threatened to retaliate by refusing the new company a fishing license — Kirby says negotiating with the Newfoundland government was a piece of cake compared to the problems his committee encountered in dealing with the Nova Scotia government. "In Nova Scotia," Kirby says today, "we got caught up talking frigging ideology. Ideologically, Nova Scotia didn't want to take an equity position; they only wanted to deal with debt. But, we said, 'Look, debt is what created the problem in the first place and the only way to solve it is to convert that debt to equity.'"

Nova Scotia's chief negotiator, Joe Zatzman, says it was never quite that simple. "The banks just wanted to find a way so they could be paid out and walk away. But we had $50 million involved in those two companies, so we had an interest too. We had to have a deal that protected the province's interests."

Zatzman, who at one point referred to Bank of Nova Scotia chairman Cedric Ritchie and president Gordon Bell as "Jesse Jameses without guns," admits those negotiations were "as tough as any I've ever been involved with." Contrary to the popular perception that Nova Scotia Conservative premier John Buchanan's own ideological antipathy to government involvement was at the heart of the delay in reaching an agreement, Zatzman claims the problem was really his own very pragmatic fear that the province would end up signing a bad deal. There were times, in fact, Zatzman says, when he had to "talk to the premier to toughen his spine" during the negotiations. "I used to say that it's a good thing the premier's not a girl," Zatzman jokes. "He never liked to say no to anybody."

In the end, it took 11 straight hours of face-to-face negotiations between DeBané and Buchanan, followed by an all-day cabinet meeting, to finally win the grudging and — as it later developed — temporary approval of the province.

Under the terms of the arrangement, H.B. Nickerson & Sons Ltd. would be dismantled and its assets split between a number of independent operators and a restructured National Sea, which would get Nickerson's key assets, including two large processing plants, 14 trawlers and two scallop draggers.

National Sea would then be refinanced, with both the Bank of Nova Scotia and the provincial government agreeing to convert some of their debts into stock in the new company, and with the federal government agreeing to provide some initial financing as well.

No one mentioned what would happen to the company's existing shareholders, and neither Buchanan nor DeBané would release any specific figures about the refinancing until it had been presented to — and approved by — National Sea's board of directors.

But no one seemed unduly concerned that the board would stand in the way of a deal. "Observers say the company's precarious financial position will leave them little choice [but to approve the deal]," the *Financial Post* explained in an October 8 report.

But the *Post*'s observers clearly didn't reckon on Bill Morrow, who had, in fact, already quietly set in motion the biggest, most dangerous gamble of his corporate life. He knew his audacious scheme might very well not work, and even if it did, that it could get him into trouble with the corporate regulators at the Ontario Securities Commission, who might conceivably argue he was violating stock exchange rules against disclosing confidential company information to one group of shareholders that wasn't available to all the others. But he also knew that the best way to protect the interests of National Sea's minority shareholders — the real purpose behind those OSC regulations — was to ignore what could only be technical breeches of the rules.

After National Sea's financial problems first became the stuff of newspaper speculation and its future the subject of cocktail-party gossip, however, Bill outline the details of the restructuring package. Quite simply, his plan was to create a new holding company with the federal government, the Nova Scotia government and the Bank of Nova Scotia as shareholders. That new company would buy out Nickerson's slightly more than 50 percent interest in National Sea and replace the Nickerson directors on the company's board of directors with its own appointees. In addition, National Sea would issue $45 million worth of new shares, which the federal government would own. The result would be that the new consortium would own 75 percent of the restructured National Sea.

The existing minority shareholders, Kirby said, would be permitted to retain their current percentage interest in the company but only if they could come up with 49 percent of the necessary $45 million to buy the new shares. Otherwise, they would end up owning a grand total of only 6.8 percent of the company they had previously controlled.

Good God, Morrow said to himself, it's worse than I expected. It would be virtually impossible, he knew, for the minority shareholders to come up with enough cash to maintain their position, meaning that those shareholders would be forced into a position of controlling only a small number of effectively "locked-in" shares in perpetuity. Morrow had little faith in Kirby's assurance that the government's shares would be sold back to private interests as soon as practicable. From Morrow's perspective, the only small ray of sunshine in the evening's gloomy news was the suggestion from Hitchman that, if the company decided not to accept the Kirby proposal, it had better have its own viable alternative in order to avoid what he called its "anticipated default," and George Buckrell's swift rejoinder that the Royal stood ready to assist the company if it chose to pursue such alternatives.

Morrow knew he might very soon be taking Buckrell up on his offer.

Finally it was over. Jerry Nickerson thanked Hitchman and Kirby for their presentations and told them that the company would be asking the Toronto Stock Exchange tomorrow to suspend trading in the company's stock pending an announcement. The board, he added, would probably want to hire a consultant to evaluate their proposal.

Morrow was sure Nickerson didn't mean that the company would hire a consultant to evaluate the merits of the Kirby proposal so much as to figure out if the price being offered was fair.

As he watched Nickerson tonight, Morrow couldn't help but wonder — with some regret and not a little bitterness — what might have happened if Jerry Nickerson hadn't managed to get control of the company in a coup that the then premier of Nova Scotia, Gerald Regan, had likened to "a horse swallowing an elephant." Now the horse was about to be shot and put out of its misery, while the elephant....

But it was best not to think of that.

Back in 1899, Bill Morrow's grandfather, a crusty sea captain named Ben Smith, had been one of the founders of the company that became National Sea Products Ltd. His father, Clarence J. Morrow, his uncle, Wallace Smith, and his cousin, William Smith, had taken that small ship's chandlering company and built it into a major fishing enterprise. And Bill Morrow, who grew up in the fish business and began working summers in the family's Lunenburg fish plant when he was just 13, had taken that company and devoted his adult life to building and expanding its horizons still more.

Just because there were problems now — Bill Morrow knew from experience the fishery was a cyclical business and there would always be troubled times among the prosperous ones — didn't mean he could simply walk away from 85 years of family history.

Bill Morrow did not stick around for the usual post-meeting pleasantries. Instead he hurried off to find a telephone to call David Hennigar. They had a company to save.

Part II
Major Players in the Fish Business

3
Setting the Scene

YOU can trace the corporate genealogy of today's National Sea Products Ltd. — a company that is the end product of a whole series of often unlikely and sometimes almost accidental corporate couplings, marriages, divorces, buyouts, sellouts, takeovers, reverse takeovers, even reverse-reverse takeovers involving some of Nova Scotia's most legendary wheelers and dealers — all the way back to the December 12, 1899, incorporation of a small Lunenburg, Nova Scotia, schooner outfitting and supply enterprise called W.C. Smith and Company Ltd.

Its 11 shareholders, seven of them members of the Smith family, set up their new company partly because they were tired of seeing all the money they spent to equip and provision their own fishing vessels each year winding up in someone else's pocket. Given that four of the Smith brothers were themselves sea captains, as were three of the company's four non-Smith shareholders, they began their little venture with the decided advantage of a built-in, loyal customer base. But the opportunities to attract other customers to their fledgling business seemed almost limitless too. Besides the more than 200 offshore vessels registered in Lunenburg County's fishing fleet in 1900, for example, there were another 35 sail-powered wooden vessels currently under construction at various local boatyards. If the new firm could sweeten its pot by convincing just a few of those ship owners to buy from them too, well, W.C. Smith and Company could become a profitable venture for all its shareholders.

As they gathered in a classroom in the recently completed Lunenburg Academy for their first directors' meeting on the night of January 4, 1900, the new shareholders fairly bubbled with enthusiasm for the future.

With good reason. At the beginning of the century that Laurier predicted would belong to Canada, Lunenburgers could have been forgiven for believing their community's ship had already come in.

Thanks to the recently developed Grand Banks cod fishery and the increasingly profitable trade in salt cod it spawned with the West Indies, this picturesque little shiretown of just 3,000 people had become so prosperous some said there was more wealth per capita here than in any Canadian centre east of Montreal, including Halifax.[1]

Ironically, the fishery that was Lunenburg's *raison d'être* by 1900 had had very little to do with Nova Scotia governor Edward Cornwallis' decision to establish a permanent settlement there in 1753.

Cornwallis wasn't unaware of the area's incredible fishing riches. After visiting Lunenburg briefly in 1749, Cornwallis wrote glowingly of a harbor "full of all kinds of fish.... A man may catch as much fish in two hours as will serve six or seven people for a whole week, such as cod, halibut, turbot, salmon, skate, haddock, herrings, smelts and lobsters; and they lie as thick as stones in Cheapside, so that Billingsgate is but a fish stall in comparison to it."

Despite that, Cornwallis — like most members of the British colonial establishment of the day — saw Lunenburg less as a potential source of good and plentiful fish and more as a potential pawn to be placed on the French-English chessboard of colonial North America.

Originally known as Merliguesche, an Indian name of indeterminate origin,[2] Lunenburg was only an incidental part of the "country, coasts and islands" between Forchu (Yarmouth) and Merliguesche that Sir William Alexander of Scotland deeded to French fur trader Charles de La Tour and his father in 1630 in the fond expectation that they would "build towns and forts" there. Although de La Tour, who was named a Knight Baronet of Scotland for his assistance to that short-lived Scottish dream of empire, never did build a fort or town at Lunenburg — he paid an annual rent of 20 beaver skins and 20 moose skins for the privilege of being permitted to do so — a group of about 50 Acadians eventually did establish a subsistence farming community in what is now Lunenburg during the early 1700s.

Cornwallis visited them during his 1749 stopover. He described their community as "but a few families with tolerable wooden houses, covered with bark." More importantly, as he noted in a letter back to England, "[the Acadians] seem to be very peaceable, say they always looked upon themselves as

---

1. See *Halifax, Warden of the North* (Revised Edition) by Thomas H. Raddall (McClelland and Stewart Limited, 1971).
2. In his *History of the County of Lunenburg* (Mika Publishing, 1980), nineteenth-century historian Mather B. DesBrisay quotes suggestions by a variety of authorities on the possible origins of the name, as well as the following lament by a Reverend Dr. Rand: "Let anyone who does not understand Indian, attempt to collect Indian names or words from an Indian who does not understand English, and see what blunders he will make."

English subjects; have their grants from Colonel Mascarene, the Governor of Annapolis; and showed an unfeigned joy to hear of the new settlement [at Halifax]. They assure us the Indians are quite peaceable and not to be feared."

That may help explain why Cornwallis, soon after he had established his main base at Halifax, settled on Lunenburg as one of six appropriate locations for establishing additional English settlements to help solidify Britain's still rather tenuous hold on Nova Scotia. His original plan was to intersperse new settlers among the loyal Acadians already at Lunenburg and the other places, thereby creating thriving new communities loyal to England that could serve to counterbalance the existing French fact at Louisbourg and Quebec City.

Things didn't work out exactly as Cornwallis planned. For starters, French-inspired Indian attacks on existing British settlements soon stretched the capabilities of the colony's small defence forces to their limits, meaning that Cornwallis had no soldiers to spare to protect new settlements in other parts of the colony. At the same time, British colonial officials began to re-interpret the Acadians' apparent neutrality as disloyalty and were therefore reluctant to allow them to be part of any new English settlements.

In 1752, the new British governor, a man named Hopson who had replaced Cornwallis the year before, finally decided to begin the process of consolidation by establishing just one new community.

"I propose to send out the foreigners in three days," he wrote on May 26, 1753. "They go to Merliguesche ... where there has formerly been a French settlement, by which means there is between three and four hundred acres of cleared land, which is to be equally divided amongst the settlers who consist of upwards of 1,600 persons."

In the end, 1,453 would-be settlers, along with 92 regular troops[3] and 66 Rangers under the command of Colonel Charles Lawrence, set out from Halifax in 14 transport vessels on May 28, 1753, for the 60-mile voyage down the coast of Nova Scotia to Merliguesche.

Because most of the new settlers were German-speaking Protestants from southwestern Germany and the Montbéliard district of France and Switzerland, the new community was renamed Lüneburg after the German royal house of Brunswick-Lüneburg, the area from which many of the settlers had come and which had produced England's King George I.

Given Lunenburg's later international fame as home to the famous fishing and racing schooner *Bluenose* and to the world's largest fish-processing plant, it is ironic that the first Lunenburgers should have been landsmen instead of fishermen.

---
3. Among those soldiers was James Smith, whose descendants established W.C. Smith and Company Ltd.

Many of the settlers who came to carve out a new life for themselves in this often harsh and unaccommodating part of North America were farmers who had been lured to Nova Scotia mainly by the promise of free town-and-garden lots with additional farm acreage nearby.

That's not to say that the early settlers didn't fish at all. "In those days," reported local historian Mather DesBrisay in 1895, "the [LaHave River near Lunenburg] teemed with fish. In [March], nets were set through holes cut in the ice and the fishermen were accustomed to say that if they did not get more fish than they could carry home without their ox-carts, it was not worthwhile to go to the river."

Still, most settlers clearly considered fishing as little more than a helpful larder-filling supplement to their real job of farming the land. "If men had then laid out for fishing as they do now," marvelled 91-year-old Lunenburger Peter Zink in an interview with DesBrisay in 1878, "they would have caught more fish than they could put away.... A man could catch three or four quintals [a quintal equals 170 pounds of wetfish or about 112 pounds of dried fish] of codfish in a day. Mackerel were very abundant — good large ones and fat. My brother and me, with four nets, caught 110 barrels from the last of June till September, and attended to the farming besides."

Lunenburg's transformation from a primarily agricultural economy, supplemented here and there with a little fishing, into a prosperous, principally fishing community was slow. In 1825, the newly arrived rector of St. John's Anglican Church, the Reverend James C. Cochran, described Lunenburg as not a very prosperous community, little known except for its production of potatoes and cabbages.

In fact, it wasn't until the mid-1800s, when local shipbuilders began building bigger and more efficient ships and local fishermen began experimenting with new fishing techniques in fishing grounds they hadn't previously exploited, that the fishing industry finally began to assume pre-eminence in the local economy.

These new fishing grounds — the Grand Banks — weren't really new, of course. The 36,000 square miles of ocean territory known as the Grand Banks had been prime fishing territory for Europeans since John Cabot discovered the cod-filled waters in 1497.

The Grand Banks are actually a range of underwater plateaus that extend along the Continental Shelf near the south and east coasts of Newfoundland. The meeting of the warm Gulf Stream and the cold Labrador Stream currents on the Grand Banks not only produces the dense fog that has been the bane of the existence of fishermen for generations but also the rich and varied vegetation that helps to support what is still among the world's largest and richest fishing grounds.

Although English fishermen did follow Cabot's lead and came out to fish off Newfoundland — they used small open boats, fished close to shore and then dried their catch in the sun along the shore — the first Europeans to successfully exploit the bounty of the Banks were the French, who came in massive, square-rigged vessels of 130 tons or more and carried crews of 15 to 20. The French — as well as the Basques, Spanish and Portuguese, who all also fished the Banks — preserved their catch during their four-to-six-month voyages by gutting and salting the fish before stowing it in the ship's hold. Because their catch was still moist, or "green," when they returned home to Europe months later, the fishery became known as the "greenfishery."

During the 1700s, the Europeans were joined by English colonists from New England who took advantage of their proximity to the fishing grounds and developed a smaller, faster vessel — the schooner — that required fewer crew members, was easier to handle and could make three or four trips to the Banks each year. During the fishing season, the schooners were based at Canso, Nova Scotia, which was also where they dried their catch.

After the American Revolution, the British North American ports were suddenly closed to the New England fishermen and, as a result, Nova Scotia slowly, tentatively, began to develop its own Banks fishery in the early 1800s.

Although they were soon to become the most famous and successful of the Banks fishermen, Lunenburgers were initially slow to take advantage of the opportunity.

Even Benjamin Anderson, the prominent Lunenburg sea captain who pioneered the Grand Banks fishery in 1873, allowed in an interview in the Lunenburg *Progress* in 1888 that, "Comparatively speaking, this town had no fish business 40 years ago. There were scarcely 10 fishing vessels sailing out of this port in 1850, and if I remember aright, they did not average over 45 tons each, nor did they carry more than 10 men and two boats."

The first significant improvement in fishing technology, according to Anderson, occurred in about 1870 when a local fish-boat owner suggested his crew begin using seine nets — huge baglike affairs that hung vertically in the water and trapped schools of fish inside them whenever their ends were pulled together — instead of sticking to their traditional but far less certain method of fishing from the sides of their vessels with handlines and baited hooks. "The advice was acted upon," Anderson told the newspaper, "resulting in a big catch the first season."

Incidentally, perhaps in response to the fishermen's success, Anderson added, the fish soon stopped "schooling," and the fishermen were forced to switch to using "traps," ordinary nets with gateways into which the fish would swim and then become trapped when the mesh bottoms of the nets were raised. That too worked for a while, but then the fish became "frightened of the trap and we discarded it."

In 1871, a Lunenburg schooner called the *Union* became the first local vessel to adapt a French innovation called the "bultow," or trawl, system. Trawling involved using a mile-long line that was anchored and set with thousands of baited hooks. The line was tended to by fishermen using small two-man dories that were carried on the decks of the main fishing vessel.

By using dories — each vessel carried up to a dozen of the small, flat-bottomed boats that stacked easily out of the way during trips to and from the fishing grounds — a schooner could cover a far greater territory than it had been able to do when fishermen simply handlined from the sides of the vessel. At the same time, by using hundreds of baited hooks on trawl lines instead of fishing with single lines and hooks, the fishermen could dramatically increase their catches of fish.

To give some idea of the differences between trawling and single-hook fishing, consider this description of the trawling process from a schooner captain of the day: "We rig up three tubs to a man. Two men go in each dory, which makes six tubs to a dory. Each tub [consists of] about 670 hooks, so that when we sets out four tubs of this trawl as we call it, bending the end-line of each trawl to the other as we set it out, that means we have 1,400 fathoms of line with about 2,700 baited hooks in the water. Multiply that number of hooks by nine — which is the number of dories we'll run this trip — and you'll have somewheres around 24,000 hooks in the set."

Thanks to that combination of dory fishing and the use of longline trawling, the 1880s eventually came to be regarded as the Golden Age of the Saltbank Fishery.

Even as the fishermen were experimenting with new ways of catching more fish, local shipbuilders were refining and modifying the design of their fishing vessels so they could travel greater distances and carry more fish with fewer crew members. By the late 1800s, the vessel of choice was the bank schooner, a fast but sturdy ship of about 100 tons and 100 feet in length with topmasts of more than 100 feet and more than 8,500 square feet of sail. Although one writer admiringly described them as "among the most beautiful vessels in the world," fishing skippers prized the schooners for far more than their beauty. They were able to operate with crews of only about two dozen men, so there was more room for storing fish aboard. That, in turn, encouraged local fishermen to test new and more distant fishing grounds.

Ben Anderson, in fact, was one of five Lunenburg skippers who decided to fish the waters of the Grand Banks off Newfoundland in the spring of 1873. "At first the effort was not crowned with success," Anderson allowed in that interview with the Lunenburg newspaper. "In fact, by the first of June, four of the five [skippers] had become so thoroughly disheartened that they set sail for Labrador [the traditional offshore fishing grounds for Lunenburg fishermen], leaving me on the Grand Banks in command of a 58-ton schooner, the *Dielytris*, four boats and 13 men." But when Anderson finally did return home with 1,850 quintals of dried fish (more than 300,000 pounds) compared with 1,200 quintals at Labrador in the same time and with the same appliances, "we reckoned that great things had been accomplished."

Two years later, 10 Lunenburg skippers made the trip and, Anderson noted, "all hands reap[ed] a rich reward." After that, the "bankers," as the Grand Banks schooners were called, became the backbone of a successful and increasingly famous local fishing fleet.

Lunenburg fishermen even developed their own unique system for building and owning their fishing vessels. It became known as the "famous Lunenburg-64" system. In her 1934 book, *The Canadian Atlantic Fishery* (Ryerson Press), writer Ruth Fulton Grant described it as a "type of cooperative enterprise [in which] each schooner is ordinarily divided into 64 shares, which may be owned by the builders, the chandlers, the fishermen, or the townspeople who may wish to invest — there are possibly 40 or 50 people share owners in one vessel. Credit is obtained from outfitting companies, which, in turn, are financed by local banks."

At the same time, largely because fishing was still considered such an unpredictable enterprise, the fishermen who worked on the vessels became "co-adventurers" with the vessel's skipper and the shore-bound owners rather than working as employees in the conventional sense. That meant that they weren't paid a salary but that they shared in the work, the risks and the profits — if any — from each fishing trip.

By the late 1800s, fishing had become exceedingly profitable as well as increasingly vital to the local economy.

In 1888, the Lunenburg fishing fleet consisted of 193 offshore vessels valued at $564,700 and 1,931 smaller boats valued at $34,366. The fleet, which provided steady work for some 4,842 fishermen that year, also accounted for more than 10 percent — nearly $2 million — of Canada's $17.5 million worth of fish sales in 1888.

Much of that came from export sales. By the turn of the century, in fact, Lunenburg's Montague Street, which ran alongside the harbor, was home to more than a dozen bustling shipping businesses, ranging from the venerable Zwicker and Company, the oldest fish company in Canada — it had been founded in 1789 to export "fish, lumber and staves" to the West Indies — to the upstart Adams and Knickle, another exporting firm established in 1897 to take advantage of what one of the county's five newspapers, the Lunenburg *Progress*, referred to as "a boom of splendid proportions" in the fishing industry.

By then, fishing was no longer just a way of making ends meet or even a business in itself to Lunenburgers. It was also a brave, even noble calling.

"There is no body of men in this county who deserve to be held in higher regard than the fishermen," DesBrisay wrote in 1895. "The farmers are a hard-working class, and contribute very largely to the general prosperity. They have, indeed, their days of toil, but they also have their nights of sweet repose. The fishermen must work by day and watch by night, and they have to labor in the midst of difficulties and dangers of which landsmen know only by hearsay."

The men who got together to form W.C. Smith and Company during the fall of 1899 knew, often firsthand, the dangers of the fishing business. But they could also see all around them signs of the industry's growth and its potential rewards.

The prosperity in the fishery had created a boomtown mentality that made itself felt across their entire community. In the fashionable Newtown district on the edge of Lunenburg's original town site, carpenters were busy constructing fussy Victorian homes, complete with widow's walks and Gothic gables, to house the community's newly wealthy, sophisticated and growing merchant class.

That the merchant class was growing was undeniable. During the 1890s, Charles Edwin Kaulbach, the federal MP for the district as well as "the largest ship and real estate owner in the county… and there are few financial enterprises in which he is not more or less financially interested," added to his own not inconsiderable fortune by buying up a whole block of downtown — still known locally as the Kaulbach block — and developing it for more offices and apartments.

Down the street, at the corner of Duke and Lincoln, the four-storey King's Hotel was, after several major expansions and renovations, doing a brisk business renting out its "28 spacious, airy bedrooms supplied with hot and cold water and heated with hot water" to visiting ship owners, fish traders and entrepreneurs from all over the world. After they conducted their business in the hotel's "large and handsomely furnished drawing room," one of its three parlors, its writing room or its private office, they often retired to its "large and commodious dining room where the tables were always bountifully supplied with the delicacies and substantials of the season."

At the nearby barbershop where J. Frank Hall, an ambitious local politician who eventually became mayor of Lunenburg, held court, there was much speculation about the comings and goings of those traders as well as a considerable amount of upbeat gossip about which local entrepreneurs were starting up new businesses, which existing businesses were expanding and endless debate on what their individual and collective prospects might be.

In the late fall of 1899, the regulars at Hall's had plenty to talk about.

James Rafuse, the carriage-maker, was hiring new workers to meet the demand for his carriages. The Lunenburg Iron Co., a local foundry producing stoves and related iron products, had just applied to town council for permission to expand its operations by building on some town-owned land adjacent to its Falkland Street factory. Power Brothers Ltd., the hardware and plumbing supply store that provided the Lunenburg schooner fleet with fog alarms, lanterns and machinery, was rumored to be planning an expansion, as were both the Bank of Montreal and the Royal Bank of Canada.

On the waterfront, two bright young shipwrights named Richard Smith and Alfred Rhuland were busy building a boatyard on Montague Street.[4] There was a new marine railroad to service the fishing and shipping fleet under construction. Two new coastal freighters had recently announced they would be adding Lunenburg to their ports of call and, oh yes, a prominent local fishing captain named William Smith — W.C. as he was known to everyone — had quietly decided to retire from fishing and had bought himself a piece of property on the waterfront where he was now building a wharf and a store. He and his brothers and some other fellows, it was said, were planning to launch a new business there to supply their own and other fishing vessels.

---

4. The yard became justly famous for some of the more than 279 commercial vessels and 107 yachts it built between 1900 and 1976, including both the original *Bluenose* and the *Bluenose II*, a replica of the HMS *Bounty* seen in the MGM film *Mutiny on the Bounty*, a replica of the HMS *Rose*, Admiral Nelson's flagship, and the schooner *Delawana*, which was altered in the yard before being used in *The World in His Arms*, an early 1950s film starring Gregory Peck and Ann Blythe.

4

The Smith Brothers

"WITHOUT the boats, there's no company," William C. Smith told the first meeting of his company's new board of directors in January 1900, adding almost unnecessarily, "The more served, the better."

Although every one of the 11 men in the classroom at the Lunenburg Academy that night knew those things as well and as clearly as they knew how to bait a hook, Smith stated them again for the record because they provided both the rationale for the new company's corporate structure and the intended course of its growth.

W.C. Smith and Company was, first and foremost, a fishing enterprise. That's why the shareholding of the new firm had been skewed to favor its eight fishing-captain shareholders, who held almost 10 times as many shares as its three landlubber-owners.[1] While the three "who don't go to sea," as Smith delicately put it, stayed behind to look after mundane day-to-day office matters, the captains would take care of the real work of selling the company's services to their fellow fishing captains and scouting the waterfront for likely new vessels in which the company could invest, thereby broadening its customer base and expectations for success.

If there was no question that the captains were the company's most important shareholders, there was also no question which one of those captains was in charge.

William C. Smith was a strong-willed, tight-fisted, assertive fisherman-businessman-politician with piercing eyes, a hooked nose and a sharp tongue. Doug

---

1. The shares were divided among the captains as follows: W.C. Smith, 60; G. Abraham Smith, 45; Benjamin C. Smith, 45; James Young, 39; James Smith, 24; Joseph Smith, 18; Isaac Mason, 18; and Martin Mason, 18. Company Secretary H.H. MacIntosh held 15 shares, while accountant George Smith received 12 and bookkeeper Lewis Smith 6.

Pyke, a Lunenburg native who grew up during Smith's heyday and later became a vice president of National Sea Products, says Smith was "a man who would have been a leader in any generation." Although he could be heavy-handed — he once wrote a letter to William Stairs Son & Morrow, one of his company's suppliers, instructing the Halifax firm to donate a new "Union Jack flag about five yards long" for the company store because "you are getting about all our business now" — and was described by a competitor as "just about the toughest bastard on the waterfront," Smith, who served as a local town councillor too, also engendered a good deal of loyalty and not a little love and affection. When he died in 1920, Lunenburg's telephone and telegraph office recorded their heaviest workload ever as friends, colleagues, suppliers and customers paid their respects.

There is nothing on the record to indicate what prompted Smith to retire from fishing in 1899 and start his own business. Although he was already a successful fishing captain in a community where seamen were regarded with respect, Smith was also known to be self-conscious about the fact he had dropped out of school in grade eight in order to go to sea, and he may have seen business success as a way of compensating for this perceived handicap. Whatever the cause, Smith was the only one of the original five sea captains who applied for the company charter not to list his "calling" on the application form as "master mariner." Instead, Smith described himself as a "merchant." The other shareholders included four of Smith's brothers, two nephews, the local school principal and three other Lunenburg skippers.

Benjamin Smith, one of W.C.'s brothers, was one of the Lunenburg fishing fleet's most successful skippers. Although only 36 years old at the time the company was formed, he'd already been a captain of Grand Banks schooners for 10 years and had easily earned his title as a "high liner."[2]

In 1897, he and 15 others had banded together to finance the construction of a new schooner, which Smith named the *Gladys B. Smith* after his first-born child. In its first year at sea, the *Gladys B.* returned to its shareholders $1,099.52, a respectable return of more than 27.5 percent on their initial investment of $5,989.76. The following year, the figure was $4,407.68. Not surprisingly, at the next shareholders' meeting in October 1898, the owners voted unanimously in favor of a motion put by shareholder A.J. Wolff, who was also the

---

2. The title, which would later be adopted as National Sea's brand name, was symbolic of fishing success. Originally coined in the 1850s to describe a crewman who could fill up a bucket of trawl-baited hooks on a longline bucket faster than anyone else, it eventually was broadened to describe the vessel with the best trawl and the one therefore likely to catch the most fish. The captain of this highline vessel, of course, became known as Captain High Liner.

Founders, W.C. Smith and Company Ltd.:

William C. Smith, First President, 1899-1920; G. Abraham Smith, President, 1921-22; Benjamin C. Smith, President, 1922-34; Joseph N. Smith, President, 1934-45; James L. Smith; Lewis H. Smith, Bookkeeper and Assistant Manager, 1899-1915; George N. Smith, Accountant, 1900-1909.

William C. Smith, First President, 1899-1920

G. Abraham Smith, President, 1921-22

Benjamin C. Smith, President, 1922-34

Joseph N. Smith, President, 1934-45

Lewis H. Smith, Bookkeeper and Assistant Manager, 1899-1915

James L. Smith

George N. Smith, Accountant, 1900-1909

town's mayor, "that the sum of one hundred dollars be handed to a committee for to purchase a gold watch for the captain's past services."

As the largest single shareholder in the ship, of course, Smith got more than just a gold watch for his troubles. His profits from the *Gladys B.*, in fact, probably helped him to finance his personal purchase of 45 shares — worth $2,250 — in W.C. Smith and Company a year later.

That was the same number of shares his brother, G. Abraham Smith, also a sea captain, purchased. A pipe-smoking man with hooded eyes, a walrus moustache and a laid-back demeanor, Abraham eventually briefly served as company president in the early twenties after W.C.'s death.

James L. Smith, the oldest of the brothers, held 24 shares. Although he was the only one of the brothers never to hold any executive office in the company, his son, Joseph, also one of the original shareholders, would serve as the company president from 1934 through to the end of World War II.

Joseph, a huge man who was called "Sampson," even by his father, occasionally used his size to good advantage as a sea captain. According to one tale, he once cleared the deck of one of his ships of an unruly group of Newfoundlanders and then "hurled their defiant leader into the harbor."

Joseph's uncle, Lewis H. Smith, was the only one of the brothers not to become a sea captain. Although he'd been both a seaman and a fisherman in his day, the youngest Smith brother's chief claim to fame was that he was a first-rate bookkeeper. After naming him as the new company's bookkeeper and assistant manager that night, W.C. Smith created a minor controversy by announcing that his salary would be $360 a year, considerably more than the president's $200 salary and "damn close to a dollar a day," as Joseph Smith noted with displeasure. Despite those grumblings, W.C.'s decision carried the day as usual.

The other key landlubber-shareholder was also a Smith. George N. Smith, a prim-looking young man with a tidy moustache and an earnest appearance who became the company's accountant, was a nephew of the Smith brothers. His seafaring father had drowned in a boating accident in Lunenburg harbor when George was just a boy. According to company historian Jack Wilcox, "George knew he would stay on dry land and never go to sea, a decision made as he stared at the corpse of his father displayed in a coffin some of the ladies had said was lovely."

Perhaps as a result of his childhood trauma, George also seemed to be the least rooted and least committed of the original shareholders. Within 10 years, in fact, he had resigned his post, left Lunenburg and headed west.

The non-Smith shareholders who completed the list of the company's original owners included three prominent schooner captains — Isaac Mason, Martin

Mason and James Young — whose connections within the fleet would be useful, W.C. believed, to the fledgling enterprise, and the principal of the local school in which they held their first directors' meeting, H.H. MacIntosh, who was, perhaps understandably, given the job of company secretary.

According to MacIntosh's notes of that first directors' meeting, W.C. Smith began by reviewing their current situation.

W.C. Smith and Company Ltd. was to begin its corporate life with paid-up capital of just $15,000. That would be used to buy the waterfront land, building and wharf Smith already owned as well as to purchase stock and provide the initial operating cash for the new company.

The new company's main *raison d'être*, of course, would be to provision fishing vessels with every conceivable supply they would require for a fishing trip — from cooking spices, such as nutmeg and allspice, to fishing lines and bailing buckets.[3] In addition, depending on the company's deal with the particular schooner's owners, W.C. Smith and Company might also arrange to supply the ship's bait requirements as well as handling, on a commission basis, its post-trip fish sales.

In 1900, most of the fish caught by the Lunenburg County fleet was sold as saltfish. Ever since 1386, when a Dutch fisherman named William Buckels discovered that salt would preserve fish so it could be packed for export,[4] saltfish had become a dietary staple in many societies, as well as the basis for much of the world's offshore fishing industry.

John Cabot, for example, returned from his 1497 voyage of discovery to North America with salted cod, which Bristol merchants quickly traded to Spain

---

3. In his manuscript history on the company, Jack Wilcox lists the supplies that might be required by a typical schooner with a crew of 24 as it set out on a three-month fishing trip: "600 lbs. of tobacco, plus that which crew would bring aboard. 16 barrels of flour; 1,100 lbs. of sugar; 60 lbs. of tea; 40 lbs. of coffee; 7 bushels of beans; 1 bushel of dry beans; 60 bushels of potatoes; 5 bushels of turnips; 1 barrel of corned shoulder; 1 barrel of salt pork; 15 gals. of molasses; 50 lbs. rice; 150 lbs. onions; 4 cases eggs; 300 cans of beets, squash, string beans, blueberries, corn, peas, peaches, tomatoes and clams; 24 bottles vanilla extract; 25 lbs. prunes; 48 pkgs. pudding; 24 bottles ketchup; 12 mugs prepared mustard; 25 pkgs. currants; 15 lbs. barley; 25 lbs. evaporated peaches; 100 lbs. fresh meat; 24 lbs. cheese; 100 lbs. salted pollock; 40 bars soap; 24 pkgs. washing powder; 300 lbs. salt spare ribs; 200 lbs. smoked ham; 11 barrels of beef; 75 lbs. of raisins; 100 cans of evaporated apples; 16 cases of milk; 40 lbs. crackers; 40 lbs. baking powder; 15 cans cream of tartar; 15 lbs. calibrates; 2 to 4 lbs. each of nutmeg, pepper, allspice, clove, ginger, cassis and mustard; 20 pkgs. cornstarch; 30 boxes salt; 60 lbs. jam; 30 lbs. lemon pie filling; 20 lbs. mincemeat; 24 bottles lemon extract; 24 pkgs. soap powder; 24 gross of matches; 6 tons coal; 4 bundles kindling; 450 hogsheads of salt; 3 gross wax candles; 20 yds. towelling; 25 yds. torch wicking; 1 doz. torches; 4 coils buoy line; 30 doz. 7-lb. lines; 10 doz. 22-lb. lines; 700 lbs. of lead (for sinkers); 120 gals. of kerosene; 24 dory gaffs; 18 fish forks; 20 pairs of oars; 32 10-lb. anchors; 30 gals. gasoline; 36 pairs of rubber boots; 20 doz. pairs of cotton gloves; 5 doz. pairs of cotton mitts; 150 yds. of cotton cloth for dory sails; 4 doz. suits of oilskins; 1 doz. oiled petticoats; 24 bail buckets; 28 mattresses; 24 water jugs."

4. That discovery was considered so important that Charles V erected a statue in his honor.

and Portugal for wine and oil. In many Spanish-speaking communities, including Spain's New World colonies, salt cod from the North Atlantic became the basis for popular national dishes. By 1900, in fact, five-sixths of Lunenburg's entire salt-cod trade was with Puerto Rico, while the rest was sold to nearby Spanish-speaking Caribbean islands, including Cuba and the British West Indies.

During their sometimes three-month-long fishing trips to the Grand Banks, the crews of the Lunenburg schooners would split their fish — mainly cod — as they caught it and store it aboard ship in a salt-pickle brine. When the vessel returned to port, its owners would sell the catch to middlemen such as W.C. Smith who would negotiate a price for it with one of the major fish-exporting companies, including large Halifax firms such as H.R. Silver Ltd. and A.M. Smith Ltd.

Sometimes, the middlemen would sell the fish as is — salted "green" — but usually they "dried" it first because dried saltfish was worth considerably more in the international marketplace. Although the drying process itself was relatively simple — the greenfish flesh was laid out in the sun and regularly turned until it was dried to the desired hardness — it required constant attention as well as lots of open space, so most of the middlemen, including W.C. Smith and Company, maintained their own networks of local people, known as "makers," who would contract to do the drying on their own properties. The largest single record book in Lewis Smith's office, in fact, quickly became the one called MAKERS.

But the record book the shareholders were primarily interested in was the one in which the company's sales and expenses were tallied. At the end of its first year in operation — with six customer vessels under contract and four shares in a new schooner purchased — "the annual statement of the year's business up to December 31 [1900] was laid on the table [at the company's annual meeting] and, on motion, considered," MacIntosh wrote in his flowing hand. He added without fanfare that "the statement was particularly satisfactory, showing a profit of $5,412.81." At that meeting, the shareholders, who received the first of many dividends — six dollars a share — agreed to a series of measures designed to encourage even more growth in the years ahead. Besides increasing the capital stock in the company by 80 shares at $50 per share,[5] the directors agreed to buy shares in another new schooner then under construction at the Smith and Rhuland boatyard and to build a new store at the busy corner of King and Duke in order to attract new customers as well as to provide the company with more room at the wharf for loading and off-loading ships.

---

5. W.C. Smith bought 18, Abraham Smith 5, Ben Smith 12, James Young and James Smith 6 each, Joseph Smith 4, Isaac Mason 6, H.H. MacIntosh 5, George Smith 4 and Lewis Smith 6.

By the 1905 annual meeting, the company's course of steady but cautious expansion seemed not only well established but obviously justified by the results recorded in Lewis Smith's neat book of accounts and H.H. MacIntosh's understated annual expressions of satisfaction. "Remarks were made by a number of the shareholders on the very satisfactory condition of the company's business," MacIntosh allowed in his report of the 1905 annual meeting, for example.

And well they might. The company had not only made a profit and issued a dividend in each and every year of its operation to date, but it had also steadily increased its assets — which now included another new $3,000 building on Montague Street, $6,000 worth of additional wharf property on the waterfront, an imposingly expensive $525 safe and shares in the ownership of four recently built schooners.

It would have been difficult to blame the directors for feeling a little smug. But the fishing business was not one that allowed much opportunity for smugness.

Although they almost certainly didn't realize that a whole series of profound changes — from the emergence of aggressive new competitors to the development of innovative catching and processing technology — were already beginning to take shape in the larger world outside Lunenburg that would soon have a dramatic impact on their profitable little company, the directors couldn't help but be aware of the unpredictable nature of the fishery itself. Even when they forgot, Mother Nature was quick to remind them.

In March 1904, the schooner *Gladys B.*, which the company owned, was lost off Newfoundland, resulting in the death of one man and the loss of a cargo of frozen herring. Besides the sinking of what a report in the Halifax *Herald* described as "one of the finest and most successful fishing vessels sailing out of Lunenburg Harbor," the tragedy also put a serious crimp in W.C. Smith's spring business.

The herring was supposed to be used as bait by other W.C. Smith-supplied schooners, and the company had to delay their sailings until alternative bait supplies could be found.

5
Can-Do Connor

THEIR paths may have crossed briefly sometime between 1749 and 1753, but it's unlikely James Smith — the British garrison soldier who accompanied the first settlers from Halifax to Lunenburg and then stayed on to become a farmer and help settle the new community — knew John Connor, the British naval officer who came to Halifax in 1749 with Edward Cornwallis aboard the *Merry Jack* and remained to start a family and put down roots in the community.

Even if they'd been the best of friends, neither of them, in their wildest imaginings, could possibly have expected that their descendants would one day put together the building blocks for what would become one of the world's largest fishing companies.

While W.C. Smith and his brothers were cautiously building up their new business in Lunenburg, one of John Connor's progeny, Gary Connor,[1] a gregarious young man with a fortuitous habit of impressing the right people at the right time, was busy making a name for himself as a hustling super-salesman in Halifax, Winnipeg and Montreal.

Connor, who had dropped out of school after grade eight when his mother died and his father's health failed, was still in his teens when he landed what was to become for him a pivotally important job as a warehouseman for Halifax-based Black Brothers Ltd., the largest marine outfitter on the Atlantic coast.[2] One of his major duties was to make sure the saltfish the company sometimes reluctantly accepted in trade from its fishermen-customers was of acceptable quality, and then finding ways to store it to keep it that way until it could be sold.

---

1. Actually, his name wasn't really Gary, but everyone called him that. Born Harold George Connor, he was a voracious reader who was fascinated by biography. As a child, he came upon a copy of *The Life and Times of Garibaldi*. "Dad was so fascinated by the story and he talked so much about it that his friends took to calling him Gary," explains his son Hal.

2. And, coincidentally, the supplier for Ben Smith's schooner, the *Gladys B*.

When Black Brothers became over-extended and was pushed into bankruptcy in 1905, the receivers asked Connor to help them sell the huge store of saltfish then still remaining in the company warehouse. He did such a good job peddling the fish that he came to the attention of Bill Duff, an ambitious Lunenburg schooner owner and would-be politician, who was one of the major players in the Nova Scotia saltfish business.

A Newfoundland-born fisherman who was still called "Captain" by his employees, Duff had come to Nova Scotia in 1895. To further his political ambitions — he eventually became mayor of Lunenburg, a member of the federal parliament and finally a senator — Duff purchased two local newspapers, the Bridgewater *Enterprise* and the Lunenburg *Progress*. To further his financial ambitions, he became the manager of the Atlantic Fish Company and eventually the owner of his own schooner-outfitting company. By the turn of the century, Duff had made his fortune as the owner of a fleet of more than a dozen Lunenburg saltbank schooners.

To find markets for what seemed to be an ever-increasing catch, Duff hired the young man who'd so impressively reduced the Black Brothers saltfish inventory and sent him to Winnipeg to establish a sales office for him there.

The idea was to sell saltfish — easily preserved, convenient to transport, inexpensive and wholesome protein food, as the two men were quick to point out to anyone who would listen — to feed the Chinese laborers then building the railways in the West. Within three months of arriving there, Connor had sold Duff's entire next year's production of saltfish.

Sensing that fish was just one of the many sales opportunities the construction of the railroad offered, Connor soon made a separate deal through one of his farmer-uncles back in the Annapolis Valley to sell Nova Scotia apples in the West too, and then — presumably after living through his first Winnipeg winter — he added hockey gear — sticks and skates from a Montreal sporting-goods store — to his growing number of product lines.

That brought him to the attention of another key businessman, wealthy Montreal investor A.H. Brittain, who owned part of the sporting-goods company that supplied Connor with his hockey gear. Brittain, in turn, introduced him to a well-connected Digby, Nova Scotia, member of Parliament named H.B. Short, and the three of them launched an ambitious scheme to bring fresh, frozen and smoked fish to the major cities of central Canada — Montreal, Toronto, Quebec, Ottawa and Windsor — through a new company they formed called the Maritime Fish Corporation.

Each of them had important and clearly defined roles in the new company. Brittain's job was to convince his friends in the business community to sink enough money into the venture to build two major new cold-storage fish plants in Nova Scotia — one in Digby and one in Canso — that would be capable of supplying the 25 million pounds of fish a year they would need to supply the Quebec and Ontario markets.[3] Connor, with his connections in Nova Scotia and his impressive track record in the fish-peddling business, was to be the firm's chief salesman. Short's job was to use his political influence to remove the one potential fly in their profitable ointment.

At the time, the central-Canadian market was already being supplied with fresh, frozen and smoked fish. It was shipped in by rail from Portland, Maine, which was considerably closer to Montreal than Halifax.

Short was able to use his influence in Ottawa to not only get the federal government to slap a 0.5-percent duty on imported fish, but also to win lower commodity rates for Maritime shippers sending fresh and smoked fish to central Canada by rail.

Once that was accomplished, Connor began bringing other fish companies — including A.N. Whitman & Sons of Canso; Short & Ellis and Howard Anderson, both of Digby; and Brittain's own Montreal-based fish brokerage firm, A.H. Brittain & Company — under the new corporate umbrella.

While that solved an immediate problem by providing the company with land-based facilities, it only served to raise a more troubling one. How were they going to get enough fish to supply such a huge potential market?

The answer, it turned out, was right under their noses.

As part of the purchase of the Whitman fish plant, Connor had also incidentally acquired a coal-burning steam trawler called the *Wren* that the Whitman firm had chartered in England.

In 1910, Brittain went to England to arrange for the continuation of that charter as well as to strike a deal to acquire more surplus North Sea trawlers. As a result, Maritime became the first fish company in Canada to operate its own steam-trawler fleet. The steam trawler, in turn, helped revolutionize the east coast fish-catching sector of the industry.

But not immediately. Or easily. In the beginning, in fact, the introduction of steam trawlers simply touched off another round in what has been a never-ending battle in the fishing industry between the forces of technology and the defenders of tradition.

The early steam trawlers were steam-powered vessels of up to 300 tons, which

---

3. In addition to private financiers, the new company was able to get government assistance to build its cold-storage facilities because of a law then on the books that provided subsidies to anyone building a cold-storage plant and agreeing to operate it as a public utility. Even though, as Connor's son, Hal, pointed out in an interview with Jack Wilcox many years later, their new venture "practically used all" the available space, the fact that it was theoretically available for local fishermen as well meant that it qualified for a subsidy.

were equipped with huge cone-shaped nets. The trawlers dragged the nets along the sea bottom, trapping fish in their "cod ends" and then hauling them back aboard ship using powerful steam-powered winches.[4]

Steam trawling wasn't just controversial because it used a smaller crew to catch more fish in less time than the conventional schooner[5] fishery but also because the use of steam trawlers fundamentally altered the traditional relationship between the fishermen and the fish buyers.

Although some of the early steam trawlers were financed in the traditional way by their captains, crews and local shareholders — the old Lunenburg-64 system — and were therefore able to sell their catch to whichever buyer offered them the best price, the high cost of financing and then maintaining these vessels meant that more and more of them would eventually have to be owned outright by fish-processing companies.

While that might seem to make economic sense to an outsider — by owning the vessels, the companies could ensure themselves a continuous supply of fish so they could make more effective use of their processing facilities, while at the same time establishing a more rational marketing system for their product — it flew in the face of the traditional way things had been done in the fishing industry and so, not surprisingly, many independent fishermen and fish-boat owners lobbied against its introduction.

In the beginning, their efforts were successful. In 1905, for example, when the Halifax Board of Trade called on the federal minister of fisheries to help bring in new trawlers from Scotland to take part in the east coast fishery, the minister curtly dismissed their request. "I do not see that any encouragement could be held out to steamtrawl firms to operate in our waters," he wrote. "You are no doubt aware that to that method of fishing has been attributed the destruction of valuable fisheries off the shores of Great Britain and prohibitory laws have been enforced in inshore areas."

In 1908, in fact, the federal government passed its own order-in-council prohibiting the use of steam trawlers within the three miles of the coast that then constituted Canadian territorial waters.

Despite that, a year later the Nova Scotia government raised alarms about what it called the "imminent peril" to the fishing grounds from rapacious trawlers.

---

4. The fishing aboard steam trawlers was so good, in fact, that Hal Connor, Gary's son, says the early ones carried two extra deckhands just to handle the catch.
5. Trawlers carried a crew of 14 men compared with the schooners, which often required a complement of two dozen. Although the average catch per trip for the new trawlers — 175,000 pounds — wasn't much more than what a schooner could handle, the simple fact was that a steam-trawler trip lasted only about five days, while schooners required up to two weeks to catch that many fish.

A 1911 resolution in the House of Commons darkly described the steam trawlers as "destructive of fish life" and called for an international agreement to ban them.

Although the federal fisheries minister was still claiming, as late as 1912, that "effective steps will be taken" to prevent these insidious vessels from taking over the industry, it was clear that he was fighting — and losing — a rearguard battle against technological progress.

By the beginning of World War I, Maritime Fish boasted five trawlers in its fleet; by the end of the war — thanks to the war-induced market for fish in England — it had 13 vessels.

In less than a decade, Maritime Fish had virtually revolutionized a centuries-old industry. The traditional saltfish industry had been expanded with the introduction of fresh, frozen and smoked products, and the company had replaced conventional schooners with faster and more efficient steam trawlers.

That — and the success the company achieved using these ships — wasn't lost on would-be competitors, including another key fishing entrepreneur named Arthur Boutilier.

6
Buccaneering Boutilier

GARY CONNOR was far from the only east coast entrepreneur willing to gamble on new technology. Arthur Boutilier, whose National Fish Company Ltd. was to become Connor's major rival after World War I, not only followed Connor's lead in chartering steam trawlers to catch his fish, but he also upped the technological ante, first by becoming the first Canadian fish processor to get into the fish-fillet business, and then again a few years later by opening North America's first fish-meal plant.

Boutilier, like both Gary Connor and W.C. Smith, could trace his roots in Nova Scotia back to the 1750s. During the same wave of European immigration that brought the English to Halifax and the Germans and Swiss to Lunenburg, a group of French Protestants — Huguenots — settled in St. Margaret's Bay, a picture-postcard district of productive fishing bays and islands that is located on the southern coast of Nova Scotia between Halifax and Lunenburg. Most of the Huguenots — including the Boutiliers who helped establish a community called French Village in 1752 — became fishermen.

(The Boutiliers were also prolific — so much so, in fact, that Canada's first prime minister, Sir John A. Macdonald, once quipped while reviewing voters' lists: "Ah, yes, the Smiths of Toronto, the MacDonalds of Sydney and now the Boutiliers of St. Margaret's Bay.")

Arthur Boutilier, an ambitious, aggressive young man who moved to Halifax in the early 1900s, set out to make his fortune by combining his family's traditional background in the fishing industry with his own innate entrepreneurial savvy. "He was a real entrepreneur, almost a gambler," one associate later recalled admiringly. "He'd take terrible chances, but everybody liked him and he had an awful lot of get-up-and-go about him. He went bankrupt about four times, but when each bankruptcy was over, he went back and bought everything back and started out again the next day."

After working briefly as a bookkeeper for Halifax-based Albert Fader, one of only two fresh-fish shippers in the province in the early 1900s, Boutilier managed to line up enough investment to launch his own company in 1910. But his North Atlantic Fisheries Ltd., with its major packing plant and cold-storage facility in Port Hawkesbury and head office in Halifax, was too ambitious for the company's resources and it failed a few years later. After a few more false starts and small failures, Boutilier lined up still more investors to back him in a new company called National Fish Company Ltd. in 1917.

Operating this time with chartered trawlers out of rented facilities on the Halifax waterfront, Boutilier quickly became, as one close observer of the fishery put it, "a factor in the business. [National Fish wasn't] as big, nor as old nor as experienced, but [Boutilier was] a real competitor and he made National a really strong competitor of Maritime."

One of the keys to Boutilier's success — and probably his failures as well — was that he was willing to take chances, to move decisively while others were still pondering their next move. In the spring of 1924, for example, National became the first Canadian company to begin using the recently invented fillet knife to prepare its fish for market.

The fillet knife had first been introduced in 1922 by the Bay State Fishing Company, a Boston-based firm that was the largest producer of haddock in the United States. Before then, fish was normally sold whole. Filleting fish involves making it ready for cooking by cutting away the up-to-two-thirds of the fish — including head, tail, bones and innards — that are not suitable for eating.

Filleting before selling not only made fish a more convenient food for consumers to buy and prepare but it also enabled fish companies — for the first time — to establish their own brand identity. While it had been impossible to slap a label on a fresh whole fish, it was as necessary as it was simple to wrap a cellophane, wax-paper or parchment label around the individually wrapped fillets and to identify the company on the cartons in which the fillets were shipped.

Bay State began shipping its first fillets under the brand name "40-Fathom" in 1922. A year later, a brilliant and innovative New York scientist-businessman named Clarence Birdseye[1] began distributing his Birdseye fillets throughout New York State and beyond.

After watching the success of those ventures, Boutilier's National Fish

1. Birdseye was also a key figure in what was to become an enormously significant technological advance in fish marketing. During a trip to Labrador in the 1920s, Birdseye came up with the idea that the freshness of fish could be preserved by quick freezing. At the time, freezing was considered unsuitable as a way of preserving food because the traditional method of slow-freezing it resulted in deterioration and loss of food value. Birdseye, however, noticed that fish caught when the air temperature was less than -40°F immediately froze. When they were later thawed and cooked they appeared and tasted as if they'd been freshly caught.

Company shipped a few 20-pound boxes of fresh fillets to Montreal as an experiment in the spring of 1924. It was such an immediate success that, by the following year, Connor's Maritime Fish Corporation was also quoting prices on fresh fillets of cod, sole and haddock.

Boutilier scored a second and related coup when he introduced German manufacturing equipment known as *Schlotterhaus* to North America. The *Schlotterhaus* equipment took the waste products from filleting — fish flesh and bones — and used cooking and steam-drying techniques to remove the moisture and transform those fish leavings into a powdery, protein-rich fish meal, which could then be sold as feed for animals. Boutilier, who had heard of the German equipment and thought it worth considering for his own operation, "just booked a trip to Germany to look at this thing," remembered an associate with some astonishment, "and he had no idea where he was going to sell the meal."

The Germans took care of that. They not only agreed to sell him the equipment at a reasonable price and send over German technicians to help him install it but they also agreed to buy everything he could produce.

Although Boutilier had to borrow and mortgage to the outer edges of his credit limits in order to purchase the equipment, buy the land and then build a plant to accommodate the sophisticated equipment, the project was an instant success. Boutilier was not only able to use the new plant to squeeze out more profits from fish processing, but he was also able to earn the gratitude of local fishermen by offering to buy some otherwise unmarketable species of fish to use in the plant.

By the time he died just two years later in 1928 of a massive heart attack, much of the rest of the east coast fishing industry was still trying to find a way to follow in his innovative, often daring wake.

Even at cautious and conservative, yet still profitable W.C. Smith and Company in Lunenburg, executives had kept a wary eye on the comings and goings of the Connor and Boutilier interests for more than a decade. Now, with a new and more aggressive generation at the helm, that company too was ready and willing to steer a more adventurous course.

7

W.C. Smith in Transition

WHEN Ben Smith's son, Wallace, returned home to join the family firm after military service in World War I, he was full of new ideas to meet — and beat — the competition from the fresh-fish companies. But his father and his uncles would hear none of it.

"We'd better just wait and see," his father told him cautiously.

As annoying as that conservatism sometimes was to the company's second generation, anxiously awaiting their turn at the helm, it was difficult for them to argue with what that steady-as-she-goes course had accomplished for the firm. As the large "Company Profits" graph on one wall of W.C.'s office so plainly demonstrated, W.C. Smith and Company was doing something right.

In 1911, for example, the chart showed that the company had made a profit of $13,344 — the first time in its short history that it had made more than $10,000 in one year — and declared a dividend of $10 a share. By 1915, the company was reporting profits of $17,716 and the dividend had doubled to $20 a share. By 1918, profits topped $25,435, and the dividend had reached $30 a share.

Although W.C.'s health was becoming so precarious that he asked the board of directors to relieve him of some of his duties as early as 1910, he remained very much in charge of the company's operations — and continued to set its corporate style — during most of its second decade of operation.

Smith was a deal-maker who prided himself on his ability to strike the best bargain in any situation. "Should we decide to purchase all of our marine, excepting copper paints and small paints, from your firm," Smith wrote to one potential paint supplier, "what inducements could you offer that would make worthwhile our decision?"

While W.C. himself may have been a constant throughout the decade, the company he presided over was clearly in transition. Two of the original schooner-captain shareholders, James Young and Isaac Mason, had died, and six other skippers, Lameck Knock, Benjamin Cook, Artemus Schnare, Arthur Ritcey, Abraham Cook and Howard Cook, had joined the firm as shareholders by the end of the decade.

So had both Ben Smith's son, Wallace, an engineer and prominent local athlete, and W.C.'s son, "Billy," who had become hooked on the intricacies of the fish business while growing up in Lunenburg. When they returned from overseas service after the war, the two young men were placed in charge of Lunenburg Coal and Supply, a new company that W.C. had put together from the assets of J.B. Young's Coal, Wood and General Merchandise store, which he had recently bought.

While they were joining the family firm, other Smiths were leaving. George Smith, the accountant whose father had died in that boating accident when he was still a boy, finally decided he'd had enough of the sea and ships, and he resigned and headed west to seek his fortune. Lewis Smith also resigned as bookkeeper, and was replaced by W.C.'s son-in-law, an accountant named M.M. Gardner.

In business, Gardner was regarded as tough-minded, but fair. "In reply to your letter, re: turnips," Gardner wrote to one of the firm's farmer-suppliers, "I would say you may bring them along at once and we will allow you what is right for them." But in politics, Gardner was a zealot. Although he shared the Smith family's large-C conservatism, there was nothing conservative about the ways in which he demonstrated his loyalty to the party. In the Conscription campaign of 1917, for example, he attempted to have the election of Gary Connor's partner, Bill Duff, as the area's new federal MP, thrown out.[1] A few years later, he harangued officials in the provincial Conservative headquarters with complaints about the poor representation being provided by the Liberal MLA J.J. Kinley, and strongly suggested they put up a better-known Tory in the next election so Kinley would be beaten.

Although Gardner was named acting general manager of the firm in 1919, after W.C. Smith's health took a turn for the worse, his preoccupation with politicking almost inevitably meant that much of the company's day-to-day operations would fall to one of its newest employees, a young accountant named Clarence J. Morrow.

Ironically, Morrow, the man who would eventually be credited with putting together and solidifying National Sea Products as a major international fish company, was never a fisherman himself.

---

1. Duff would later return the favor by writing a letter to the local newspaper urging Lunenburgers not to buy the bonds the company was selling to finance construction of its new fish plant.

Born and raised in Nova Scotia's apple-rich Annapolis Valley, Morrow began his business career as a clerk in the Royal Bank of Canada's Annapolis Royal branch, but had to give that up to take over the family grocery business after his father died and his older brother went off to fight in World War I "for better money, part of which he could send home" to help keep the family business afloat.[2]

Running the store, Morrow would recall later, meant he had a place to live in, an apartment above the business, and enough to eat from its inventory, but he says he quickly concluded that the store itself wouldn't be capable of providing a real living for him or anyone else.

Given that, it wasn't surprising that Morrow was ready to "get clear of this grocery business" when an opportunity presented itself. That opportunity came in 1917 in the person of H.A. Porter, a Bradstreet representative who called in Annapolis Royal twice a year to perform credit checks and who knew Morrow from his brief interlude at the Royal Bank there.

"Are you going to make this your future?" he demanded on one visit that year.

"Oh no," Morrow replied quickly. "I'm doing a correspondence course. I'm going to be a chartered accountant."

"Would you be interested in taking a job to do with accounting," Porter wanted to know. "I'm asked quite often if I know of anybody. You know, with the war being on, there are jobs popping up all over."

Within a few weeks, Porter had arranged for Morrow to be interviewed by W.C. Smith. The interview was a mere formality, a chance for Smith to see for himself "the cut of Morrow's jib." Smith had already checked out Morrow's professional credentials with the Lunenburg manager of the Royal Bank who, coincidentally, had been manager in Annapolis Royal during Morrow's time there and was happy to provide a glowing recommendation.

When Smith offered him a job as assistant bookkeeper, Morrow recalled later, "I decided I would make a break and put the business up for sale. The Lunenburg people seemed to like me and the town looked pretty good. I thought it could be a good place to be."

Working from a battered oak desk in the W.C. Smith main office, Morrow moved quickly to modernize the firm's accounting practices. When Gardner moved into the manager's job in 1919, Morrow was promoted to accountant.

---

2. Morrow had been unable to serve in the war himself because of an attack of tuberculosis just as he reached military age. In addition to that bout of illness, which kept him in the sanatorium for a while, and later serious brushes with diphtheria and typhoid and other diseases, Morrow is now in his 90s and in robust health. He only recently stopped driving his car at the urging of his family.

His efforts did not go unnoticed, or unrewarded. At the 1919 annual meeting, for example, the directors complimented him on his new accounting system and then awarded $100 raises to both Morrow and Gardner.

By then young Morrow was himself a shareholder, albeit a minor one, in the Smith firm. When Captain Isaac Mason's shares were put up for sale following his death, Morrow knew they were a good buy. "There was just one fly in the ointment. I had no money." He went to Morris Wilson, a local banker who was then the executor of the estate and later became the president of the Royal Bank of Canada. "I told Mr. Wilson that if the Royal Bank would lend me the money, I would like to buy the shares." The bank agreed to lend him $250 to buy the five shares. "That was my first investment in the company," Morrow recalled later. It was also the beginning of what would be a long and friendly — as well as important — relationship between the company and the bank.

Morrow's abilities were quickly recognized, not only in Lunenburg, where he was elected secretary of the local branch of the Retail Merchants' Association in 1920, but also in the larger world of the fish business. Later that same year, in fact, during the first International Schooner Races[3] in Halifax in October, H.R. Silver, a large Halifax-based fish exporter, tried to lure Morrow away from W.C. Smith and Company. Silver, who was also a shareholder in W.C. Smith and Company, invited Morrow to visit him in his Dartmouth mansion on Silver's Hill overlooking Halifax harbor, where he proposed that Morrow quit his present employment and join his operation. Although he was tempted, Morrow wisely declined.

He was happy in his current job at W.C. Smith but, perhaps more importantly, Morrow also recognized that that firm was in the midst of major changes that might soon mean greater responsibility as well as opportunity for him.

The most significant change came with the death two months later of the company's founder. W.C. Smith had suffered a stroke during the schooner races and he never recovered. "He seems to be making a slight improvement, but very slow," Gardner wrote to a Yarmouth sea captain shortly after the stroke. "I do not think he will ever be active again in business." A few weeks later, in a letter to a Gloucester, Mass., captain, Gardner added: "His left arm, side and leg are practically gone.... He still keeps his bed and I very much fear he will remain there a long time." On December 27, 1920, in an even more ominous tone, Gardner wrote to another Gloucester captain: "His sickness is now very serious. We do not know at what moment the end may come."

---

3. Sponsored by the Halifax *Herald,* the race pitted a Canadian fishing schooner, W.C. Smith's *Delawana,* against an American entry, *Esperanto.* That the American boat won caused great consternation locally and led to the decision to design and build the famous schooner *Bluenose.*

Schooners were a feature of this fisheries fleet from Lunenburg up until the end of World War II. The Theresa E. Connor, *139 feet, was built at Smith and Rhuland, launched in 1938 and made her last trip in 1963.*

It came, in fact, later that same day.

Although Smith's death caused a good deal of sadness and genuine grief, with outpourings of sympathy arriving quickly from friends, colleagues and competitors all over North America, the fact that his death came so slowly gave company directors the opportunity to prepare for a smooth transition of power.

At 2:30 p.m. on December 31, 1920, they held a special meeting of shareholders at which W.C.'s brother Abraham was appointed president. The shareholders also agreed to a six-for-one stock split as a result of surpluses going back to 1916, as well as to divide up $102,500 in a bonus dividend to shareholders and to increase the capitalization of the company to $150,000 from $30,000.

By this time, there were six employees working for the company. Gardner was still the managing director and the main pipeline to the company board, but both Gardner and Morrow, the chief accountant, were paid the same $150 salary a month, a clear indication of how highly the directors regarded young Morrow.

Billy Smith and his cousin Wallace were working for the Lunenburg Coal and

"The biggest load of fish." This photo was taken on the occasion of a record haul arriving in Lunenburg.

Supply operation. Billy, as manager, earned $108 a month, while Wallace, whose engineering background made him the logical one to be in charge of the physical plant, earned $100.

Although Lunenburg Coal had had a successful first year in business, prospects for the rest of the company were not nearly so rosy.

The fish business had been in a period of major transition ever since the introduction of the steam trawler in the early 1900s, and the end of World War I only seemed to accelerate those changes and herald the end of Lunenburg's Golden Age of Sail. In 1914, for example, there were 119 schooners registered in Lunenburg; by 1926 that number had fallen to 92 and, by 1930, to just 64.

Ironically, even as this was happening, W.C. Smith was becoming more active in the fish-brokerage business. By 1920, it owned its own fleet of 20 schooners.

But that was just one of the company's problems, many of which were self-created. While the outfitting side of the company's business was becoming more competitive — there were now five other firms scrambling for the same business — the saltfish business had gone into decline. Despite those very clear and disturbing trends, W.C. Smith and Company's directors decided in 1921 to resurrect a 1908 plan that called for the company to eliminate the middleman by becoming its own exporter of saltfish.

They sent a fact-finding committee to the West Indies and South America, where they established local sales agencies to peddle their product. Back home, Wallace Smith not only rearranged the company's warehouse so it would be able to accommodate huge inventories of saltfish but he also convinced the directors to buy a modern new artificial drying plant[4] so the company could produce the kind of drier saltfish favored by consumers in Cuba, some West Indian islands and South America.

At one level, the changes worked. By 1924, W.C. Smith and Company had become the largest saltfish exporter on the east coast, but ironically, as corporate historian Jack Wilcox pointed out, it was "an increasingly large chunk of a diminishing market."

Although the company presidency had changed hands again by this time — Abraham Smith died and had been replaced by Ben — many of the key plans for the company's future were now being conceived and thrashed out by three of the company's ambitious young Turks during what have later become known cryptically as "the railroad-track meetings."

The three were cousins Wallace and Billy Smith, and C.J. Morrow, who had cemented his own familial connections in the company by marrying Ben Smith's daughter, Jean, in an impressive ceremony at Saint John's Church in Lunenburg in 1925.

Because they all lived in the west end of town and because they all went home for dinner at noon hour, it was only natural that they would walk along the railroad tracks together each day as they made the journey from work to home and back. And it was only natural too that they would talk business as they walked.

"You'd see them heading for the old French cemetery along the track," recalls one Lunenburg elder. "Seemed like they were inseparable companions. One would have his hands behind his back, one would have his hands in his pockets, one would be picking up and throwing stones or fooling around with sticks. In the spring, they'd leap the ties like kids at hopscotch, and in the fall, they'd scuff up leaves. You could set your clock at noon by their appearance."

Although they'd become friends, the three men were quite different in both skills and personality.

Billy Smith, who briefly served as a Conservative member of the legislature, was a tough, no-nonsense administrator. When he hired Doug Pyke, later a

---

4. One company employee described the dryer, which could take a 112-pound lot of fish and reduce it to 100 pounds, as being "like a baseball bat."

W.C. SMITH IN TRANSITION 61

company vice president, as a shipping clerk in the late summer of 1940, Smith told his new employee to report to work first thing Monday morning. "But that's Labor Day," protested Pyke. Retorted Smith: "One thing you have to learn about the fish business is that there are no holidays."

Wallace, "a man of strong frame and large hands who played hockey in Nova Scotia's Senior Hockey League," understood the intricacies of building design, thanks to a degree in engineering, and he had since devoted himself to applying

Celebrating the 25th anniversary of W.C. Smith and Company, a double-page bulletin in the Halifax Herald *on February 3, 1924, included this circle of schooner captains.*

those skills to the special needs of the fish business.

C.J., as he was known to everyone, was the most sophisticated of the three. He not only understood finance, he was a superb negotiator who had the uncanny knack of achieving whatever goals he set for himself.

By the mid-1920s, their shared goal was getting the company into the fresh-fish business before it passed them by. "The company was 13 years late getting into the saltfish business," Morrow recalls. "And we didn't want to wait another 13 years before we got into the fresh-fish business. In through the early twenties," he adds pointedly, the fresh-fish business "was looking awfully good."

During their impromptu meetings along the railroad tracks, adds Wallace, "we threw ideas at each other and some were right crazy ones. We'd discuss them and discard most of them, with no write-ups or minutes or anything like that."

Eventually, however, the trio convinced Ben Smith to lend them his Packard touring car, and two of them — Wallace and C.J. — set off on a fact-finding mission around the province to determine if the company should get into the fresh-fish business. Although most of their visits to local fish plants produced nothing of use, in Yarmouth they learned about a fish freezer owned by someone in Boston that might be for sale. They wrote to the man and "the fellow came down," Wallace remembers. "A result of that conversation was that he had a second-hand plant at Lawrencetown that he wanted to get clear of and we wound up thinking about buying it and having them come down and build [a cold-storage plant in Lunenburg] for us."

Although W.C. Smith's directors approved the idea, they did so with remarkably little enthusiasm. In their reticence, they were merely mirroring the general lack of support for the notion among much of the rest of the business community. Wallace later recalled that he and Ben were in Halifax at the offices of Robin, Jones & Whitman at the time the announcement of the deal was officially made. "I don't think that's a good idea," Handfield Whitman sniffed. "I tried it and it didn't work."

Investors were even less keen to buy the bonds the company issued to finance its new $80,000 cold-storage plant. In the end, most of the bonds were taken up by the Smith family and others associated with the firm in Lunenburg. Perhaps that was why the company had only what Jack Wilcox describes as a "quiet, in-house" ceremony when the new Lunenburg plant was officially opened in 1926.

Despite that show of corporate modesty, the opening of the fish plant was a major turning point in the company's history. First of all, of course, it marked the company's entry, finally, into the fresh-fish business. At the same time, perhaps recognizing the need for a more aggressive approach to this new aspect of their business, the directors also set up a new subsidiary company, Lunenburg Sea Products Ltd., with Billy Smith as its president and Wallace and C.J. as directors, to handle the fresh-fish side of the business. In retrospect, however, perhaps the most important decision the directors made was to name its fresh-fish brand "High Liner," a name that would eventually become as synonymous with National Sea Products as it then was with the Lunenburg fishery.

8
Ralph Pickard Bell

RALPH BELL was 40 years old when he bought his first fish plant in 1927. At the time, as he was the first to admit, "I didn't know anything more about it than you would know about the career of some Scandinavian birds on the other side of Europe."

But that wasn't unusual for Bell, a flamboyant, risk-taking entrepreneur whose approach to the business of business was neatly summed up in a comment he once made to an underling. "You can never be good in business," Bell explained, "until you've been bankrupt a few times."

That, in a sense, was how he got into the fish business in the first place. At the time, Bell was shipping Nova Scotia lumber to England for sale on consignment. One day he received a telegram from his British agents, telling him that the market had collapsed and his lumber had been sold at distress prices. Realizing he had just lost a huge amount of money and desperate to find some way to recoup, Bell remembered a conversation he'd had in the Halifax Club, the exclusive men's club to which most of the city's elite belonged. He'd

Ralph Pickard Bell (KARSH PHOTO)

been playing bridge with Old Man Rainnie of Rainnie Insurance when someone mentioned that there was a bankrupt fish plant in Lockeport, a fishing community south of Lunenburg, that needed a manager.

"Who'd want to get into that stinking business," Bell had snorted as he turned his attention back to his card game.

The answer, suddenly, was that he did. He hurried down to his bank and borrowed the money to buy the Lockeport Cold Storage Company Ltd. before his banker discovered just how much money he'd lost on the lumber in England.

Two years later, when Bell lost almost everything else he owned in the 1929 stock market crash, he packed up his Halifax house and moved his family to Lockeport, where he installed himself as the manager of the fish company and set about rebuilding his business career.

That there is another popular version of that story — one that suggests Bell actually won this first fish plant in a card game at the Halifax Club, a suggestion for which there is no credible evidence — merely serves to emphasize the point that Ralph Pickard Bell was a unique, larger-than-life character whose every action seemed to generate another story.

Bell was born in Halifax in 1887, the son of a prominent Halifax hardware merchant named A.M. Bell. He was precocious even as a child. Gary Connor, who grew up with Bell on Brunswick Street in Halifax's north end, remembers that "Ralph was always in trouble." In 1896, for example, when he was only nine years old, Bell ran away from home after being sent to his room for disobedience. He sneaked aboard a schooner in Halifax harbor, sailed with the ship to the French islands of St. Pierre and Miquelon and then to Newfoundland, where he worked for several months in return for food and a place to stay. He was finally discovered by a family friend who sent him home.

After attending Mount Allison University[1] in Sackville, New Brunswick, Bell joined his father in the hardware business while dabbling in timberland investments in Yarmouth County, in the southwestern part of the province. Following the famous Halifax Explosion in 1917, Bell helped organize and then became the secretary of the Halifax Relief Commission, the agency set up to help rebuild the flattened city.

By that point, Bell was already a prominent, if somewhat eccentric figure in the city who was known as much for his manner as for his business success. There was a suite — Suite 300 — at the Nova Scotian Hotel, a Canadian National Railroad hotel that was then the finest in the city, permanently booked in Bell's name. It was only available for other guests when Bell wasn't using it. The suite,

---
1. Bell later became its chancellor.

which offered a magnificent view of Halifax harbor from its mouth all the way to the Narrows, at the edge of Bedford Basin, was the place where Bell came to plot his strategy and make his deals.

When he bought a company called Leonard Fisheries Ltd. in a surprise move in 1933, for example, Bell retired to his suite to await the inevitable calls from the press. Twenty years later, the suite was also the scene of the climactic discussion between Bell and C.J. Morrow over the future direction of National Sea Products Ltd.

Like many Nova Scotia businessmen, Bell also dabbled in politics. In 1932, he befriended an aspiring Cape Breton Liberal politician named Angus L. Macdonald. To help him out, Bell convinced a dozen other businessmen to put up $1,000 each so Macdonald's political war chest would be well stocked. A year later, after Macdonald became premier of the province, Bell would boast to friends, "We put Angus in the House."

Bell's interest in politics, however, had far more to do with his desire to influence legislation favorable to his business interests — Bell lobbied hard in the late 1940s, for example, against legislation giving fishermen the right to strike — than it did with any particular interest he had in the intricacies of politics itself.

For Bell, the only game that really mattered was business. His activist business philosophy was a paraphrase of the Arthur Brisbane proposition that "the secret of success is the ability to translate thought into action; ideas are of no value unless you do something about them."

Although he did not always succeed — "They're not named after my performance," Bell once said of the peaks and troughs of Bell curves, "but they bloody well could be." — Bell was never one to be deterred by the odds. Or even by his own lack of knowledge.

When he arrived in Lockeport following the stock market crash, for example, Bell plunged into running the fish plant as if he'd been doing it all his life. "He went down to the wharf every morning at five o'clock in his oilskins and he met the skippers," recalls one associate. "He took over that plant and he made it a real competitor for everybody else. And he made a lot of money."

Even before he moved to Lockeport, Bell had begun to turn the money-losing plant around by setting up a fish-meal operation modelled on the one Arthur Boutilier had so successfully introduced a few years before in Halifax.

Although Bell recognized the golden economic opportunity that presented itself when Boutilier died and his estate decided to sell his by-then large and very profitable company, National Fish Company, Bell was still only a minor player in the fishing industry in 1928, and so he was in no position to take advantage of the opportunity.

Neither was W.C. Smith and Company. It was still attempting to digest the huge investment that had got the Lunenburg Sea Products Ltd. division off the ground and was also in the midst of the construction of its first motor-driven trawlers.

That left Maritime Fish Corporation as the most logical buyer of National's assets. Partly, of course, that was because Maritime was large enough to be able to afford to make the deal. But there was another factor that helped make the purchase even more attractive. By this point, Maritime's two principals — Gary Connor and A.H. Brittain — no longer saw eye to eye and were looking for a way to put some physical and psychic distance between each other. The problem, quite simply, was that Connor had begun to feel that he was carrying most of the corporate workload. "Brittain was a good negotiator, and could always appear to solve problems over a number of drinks with friends," explained one associate. "Connor was the guy back at the shop laboring to repair what Brittain would occasionally unravel."

The original plan was for Maritime to buy National and have Connor return to Halifax from Montreal to be its resident manager, thus separating the two men and allowing Connor the autonomy he wanted, but that plan collapsed when Maritime failed to line up financing at four of the country's banks as well as at Royal Trust Company. "They just couldn't get the financing on terms they felt they could operate properly," allows the associate.

In the end, Connor and Brittain struck a deal with the largest fish company in America at the time, Boston-based Atlantic Coast Fisheries Inc., to finance the merger of Maritime and National into one company — twice as large as any other then operating in the Canadian east coast fishing industry — to be known as Maritime National Fish Corporation Ltd.[2]

While that arrangement put together the two key companies who were credited with opening up and developing central- and western-Canadian markets for Nova Scotia fish, the fact that the marriage had been arranged by American fishing interests was bound to make the company an inviting and convenient target for federal government regulators in search of a scapegoat for other problems.

At the time, Ottawa was again under incredible pressure from east coast fishermen to do something about the trawler issue, which had continued to fester since the end of World War I. While the trawler operators and their

---

2. As he'd hoped, Connor was able to return to Halifax as the new company's vice president and general manager. His key assistants in the new venture included both Arthur Boutilier's brother, Walter, and son-in-law, Darryl Laing, a brilliant Rhodes scholar.

supporters in the business community argued that trawlers were not only more efficient but could also provide a guaranteed, continuous supply of fish, the inshore fishermen and schooner operators blamed the trawlers for everything from low fish prices to the destruction of their fishing gear. Besides, they claimed, they could supply all the fish the industry needed themselves, thank you very much.

With W.C. Smith's president, Ben Smith, in declining health —he died in 1934— Lunenburg Sea Products' Billy Smith became the most forceful spokesman for the anti-trawler forces. "There are certain interests in the vicinity of Halifax exploiting the fisheries and the fishermen," he thundered

From the 1900s on, steam trawlers were used in Canadian waters. Their ability to garner large quantities of fish with a net made them an effective and lucrative innovation in the industry.

in one speech to the Lunenburg Board of Trade, citing the case of a group of trawler deckhands who received only $37.73 for one fishing trip but who would have received $148.97 for the same trip made on one of Lunenburg's hook-and-line vessels.

Handfield Whitman, the president of the Nova Scotia Fisheries Development Association, a pro-trawler lobby group, countered with a scathing put-down of his opponents as men who stood in the way of inevitable progress. "One felt sorry for the horse breeders, carriage makers and blacksmiths forced out of business by the automobile," he said, "but the wise carriage maker began to make car bodies, the blacksmith opened a garage and the horse breeder bought a tractor to break up his pasture."

More concrete arguments came from M.B. Archibald, a lawyer representing the key trawler companies, who argued that there were already 80-90 steam trawlers from other countries operating off Canada's east coast, and that eliminating Canadian trawlers from the fleet would hurt Canadian interests without answering the complaints of the anti-trawler forces.[3]

The dispute created some strange alliances. Those opposing the trawlers included not only such former rivals as Smith's M.M. Gardner and federal MP William Duff, the man whose election he had once tried to overturn, but also Moses Coady, a Roman Catholic priest then actively involved in organizing fishermen's co-ops, and even Richard Hamer, the secretary of the United Maritime Fishermen, a group attempting to unionize fishermen. His views were anathema to Ralph Bell, an outspoken opponent of all unions, but also another member of the anti-trawler forces.

The federal government tried to shuffle the whole messy dispute off centre stage in typical political fashion by appointing a royal commission in 1927 to look into the problem, but its report actually turned out to be two conflicting reports — a majority report recommending that the use of trawlers be prohibited, and a minority one prepared by the commission's chairman recommending they be permitted to operate under either self-regulation or with some limited restrictions — and that only served to dump the whole question back in Ottawa's lap.

On April 1, 1930, the federal government responded by issuing an order-in-council that gave aid and comfort to the cause of the inshore fishermen, but reserved its severest blow for American-owned Maritime National. The

---

3. Bell's attacks on the "idiots" supporting the use of trawlers were so strident that the Halifax *Herald* wrote an editorial about him. "There is this to be said for Mr. Bell," allowed the writer, "he is a propagandist — and admits it. He never attempts to disguise the fact. One always knows where he stands, agree with him or not. He does not deal in smokescreens, he comes right out in the open. He does not beat around the bush; nor does he adopt covert tactics. If he is going to hit you, he hits you — and that's all there is about it."

regulations provided that all trawlers operating out of Halifax would have to be licensed, with the actual amount of the license fee to be determined by a tax to be imposed on fish landings. The catch for Maritime National was that there was a difference between the tax charged against trawlers built in Canada — two-thirds-of-a-cent per pound of fish caught — and against those that were foreign-built — one cent per pound.

Considering that the average trawler landed about 5 million pounds of fish per vessel at the time, what that meant in real terms was that Maritime National — with five foreign-built trawlers — would pay roughly $250,000 a year for the privilege of using trawlers to catch its fish, while its chief trawler rival, Leonard Fisheries, with only one Canadian-built vessel, would pay about $33,000, and all the other companies that used schooners or other vessels for fishing would pay no tax at all.

The explanation for all this was simple, according to Gary Connor's son, Hal. "We simply couldn't command the votes that the other side could." With the schooner fleet's traditional saltfish market cut dramatically by the Depression, the schooner owners were anxious to install diesel engines in their vessels so they could go "freshing," as fresh-fish catching was known. Because the schooner industry was labor-intensive and so many small communities depended on it for their survival, "it had great political clout against one trawler-owning company which, at that time, was foreign-owned."

Perhaps not surprisingly, Maritime National refused to pay — F.W. Bryce, the American president of Atlantic Coast Fisheries, even obliquely threatened that the company would pull out if the government went ahead with its plans. The tax, he was quoted as saying, "may keep [Nova Scotia] from taking advantage of her heritage of the sea" — and tossed the ball back in the federal court.

Ottawa countered by suing the company for $21,422 in back taxes, and the case ended up in the Exchequer Court, which ruled in March 1931 that the license fee was beyond the government's power under the Fisheries Act. Ottawa appealed that decision to the Imperial Council of the Privy Council, but before it could make a final determination, the federal government weighed in with a new set of less discriminatory regulations that provided for a flat $500 license fee on each vessel, with trawler licenses to be issued at the minister's discretion.

By that point, however, Ottawa's initial, onerous tax on trawlers and its general support for the anti-trawler forces effectively put a lid on future trawler development during most of the 1930s. The trawler fleet, in fact, fell to just three vessels, while schooner building boomed. Even Maritime National began to charter newly designed year-round Lunenburg power schooners as part of its offshore fleet.

Trawl nets hanging up to dry.

By that point, however, the type of vessel the companies used had become almost irrelevant. Like much of the rest of North American business, the fishing industry was badly battered during the Great Depression of the 1930s. In 1933, for example, Maritime National reported what would be its only annual loss ever and Lunenburg Sea Products' President Billy Smith announced to the press that his company had experienced its worst year on record in 1932.[4]

For Ralph Bell, who had rebuilt Lockeport into a significant player in the fishing industry during the early 1930s, the fishery's economic woes presented what he saw as an opportunity. In 1934, he bought the by-then bankrupt Leonard Fisheries Ltd. of Montreal and in the process scooped up its major assets including "large properties at Montreal, Port Hawkesbury, North Sydney, Ingonish, Halifax, Canso and other points [as well as] a number of fishing vessels, including the steam trawler *Loubyrne*, two diesel motor vessels and the steam tug *Margaret V*."

Bell, the vociferous opponent of trawlers as the ruination of the fishing industry, now owned one himself. But not for long. In 1936, Bell put all of his fishing assets up for sale to the highest bidder.

Bell's explanation for why he wanted out of the fishery at the time seemed logical enough: he was fond of saying that he never stuck with one major investment for more than eight years and, with the Depression ending, he believed the fishery was reaching the peak of its traditional economic cycle. There is some evidence to suggest that Bell was also worried about the growing success of union-organizing efforts among fishermen. There had already been strikes by inshore fishermen in North Sydney in 1930 and 1931, and there was

---

4. Smith didn't tell the press that the company's fortunes had reached such a sorry state that he had reluctantly agreed to allow one of its vessels, the *Geraldine S.*, to become involved in what was euphemistically known as bottle fishing — rum-running. The *Geraldine S.*, named after Smith's daughter, had been launched amid great fanfare in 1928, but the fishing industry had gone bad and management finally had to come to the same decision many other fish companies already had, and balance their fishing losses with some profits from running contraband to the United States. Smith insisted, however, that his daughter's name be removed from the vessel. Known as the *Mahaska*, it had a good year as a rum-runner and helped the company keep its head above water.

By getting into the rum-running trade, in fact, Lunenburg Sea Products was simply following the lead of others in the industry. Wrote Frederick William Wallace in his *Roving Fisherman*, a book about the east coast fishery in the early days of the twentieth century: "Nova Scotia fishing skippers and fishing schooner owners deemed it no crime to quit cod fishing for a spell to load up with cases of alcoholic stimulants at St. Pierre, Bermuda, the Bahamas, or Cuba, and rendezvous at night off the American Atlantic coast with fast motor-boats from the shore — to the captains of which they sold and transferred their cargoes.... Rum-running was deemed no crime by many Canadians since a considerable number of Americans disagreed violently with the prohibition experiment. Vessel owners and skippers in Nova Scotia, men of character and integrity, felt that they were breaking no law if they transported cargoes of liquor to points off the U.S. coast outside of the three-mile limit and delivered the foods to the craft that met or came off to them."

talk that a new provincial trade union act would make it easier for fishermen to organize.

Regardless of his reasons, Bell's decision to offer his fishing interests to both Lunenburg Sea and Maritime National not only touched off a bidding war between the two rivals but also served as the catalyst to restructure Maritime National.

When Lunenburg won,[5] Gary Connor "was awfully mad," recalls his son Hal, who himself later became a National Sea executive. The following year, "Dad screwed up his courage and went to the banks" to try and buy out his American partners. The key to raising the necessary cash, Hal Connor explains today, was winning the support of James McGregor Stewart, a prominent Halifax corporate lawyer and director of the Royal Bank of Canada.

A brilliant scholar who had put himself through Dalhousie Law School by teaching Latin and Greek, Stewart would eventually serve as counsel to the seminal Rowell-Sirois Commission on Dominion-Provincial Relations in the late 1930s and help to transform the small Halifax law firm he joined after graduating from law school into Stewart, MacKeen & Covert, the most powerful corporate law firm east of Montreal. He also — and not incidentally — helped put together the complex 1945 deal that created National Sea Products out of a bunch of small and fiercely independent east coast fish companies.

"Everyone referred to him as God," Connor remembers. "He was the most brilliant lawyer to come out of these parts — one of those people who almost seemed to say nothing, but then when he did say something, you had to listen — and act on what he said."

But Stewart's most important attribute, at least as far as Gary Connor was concerned at the time, was his role as the key link between the already closely connected members of Nova Scotia's business and financial establishment.

Stewart served on the boards of directors of such prominent Maritime companies as Mersey Paper, Nova Scotia Light and Power, Sobeys and Moirs. According to author Harry Bruce, who has chronicled the lives of Roy Jodrey and Frank Sobey, two of the province's most successful industrialists, "Nova Scotian entrepreneurs who wanted financing could not go wrong by consulting Stewart. He had the contacts."

With Stewart's contacts and his legal brilliance, Connor was eventually able to raise enough cash to buy out Atlantic Coast Fisheries. He renamed his new company Maritime National (1937) Ltd. J. McGregor Stewart, not surprisingly, became one of its directors.

---
5. The assets it acquired from Bell included not only Lockeport Company Ltd. but also F.A. Robinson Company of Port Mouton, Leonard Brothers Ltd. of North Sydney, Nickerson Brothers Ltd. of Liverpool and wholesalers D. Hatton and Company and Leonard Fisheries of Montreal.

The result was that Maritime National and the Lunenburg Sea group became the two pre-eminent fishing companies in eastern Canada. And Ralph Bell, after having dramatically shaken up the east coast industry, disappeared from its stage ... but only temporarily.

9

One Company from Many

ON JULY 31, 1945, with the guns of war barely stilled in Europe, Ralph Bell returned, not simply to the fishing industry, but to a new, front-and-centre role as the most important figure in a revitalized east coast fishery.

On that day, Bell purchased options to buy Smith Fisheries Ltd., the holding company for all of the Lunenburg-based companies' assets, and Associated Investors Ltd., which represented the Connor family majority shareholdings in Maritime National. Within a few months, Bell would become the president and major shareholder of National Sea Products Ltd., a new super-company he had helped cobble together during the war years by relentlessly touting the virtues of his strength-in-unity argument to the heads of the region's largest independent fish companies — Lunenburg Sea Products Ltd., W.C. Smith and Company, Maritime National and H.B. Nickerson & Sons Ltd., of North Sydney.

Bell's creation of National Sea Products Ltd. was both a symbol of Canada's post-war optimism and a direct outgrowth of the dramatic transformation that had occurred in the country's business sector during World War II.

When the war began, Canada was still staggering out of the depths of the Great Depression. Six hundred thousand people out of a total population of just 11 million were still looking for work, and the manufacturing sector was moribund, employing altogether only a few thousand more than the total number who were unemployed.

By the end of the war, six years later, Canada had become the "free world's fourth most powerful industrial state." From a standing start in 1939, Canada's war-related industries had grown so quickly that, by 1943, they employed 1.1 million men and women, more even than the peak wartime complement of the armed forces itself, and were largely responsible for the fact that the country's gross national product jumped from $5 billion a year in 1939 to $12 billion in 1945.

What had passed for a pre-war shipbuilding industry, for example — 14 shipyards and 15 boat plants employing 3,400 men, most of them engaged in repair work rather than in the construction of new vessels — had become a dynamic, thriving industry with 80,000 employees in 90 shipyards by war's end, and it had contributed more than 3,000 cargo ships, naval and other specialized vessels to the war effort.

"When you consider that pre-war Canadian industry had never made a tank, a combat airplane or a modern, high-calibre, rapid-fire gun," wrote *Fortune* magazine, "the speed with which industry was organized and production started ranks as an industrial miracle."

"Even the construction of the CPR didn't approach the daring of Canada's undertaking in the summer of 1940," author Bruce Hutchison would write later in *The Incredible Canadian* (Toronto, Longman, 1952), his biography of Canadian prime minister Mackenzie King. "It was less an act of mobilization than an act of faith by a handful of people."

Those "handful" of people were the so-called "dollar-a-year men" — a few hundred of the best and brightest businessmen from across the country whom C.D. Howe, the powerful Liberal minister of the newly formed federal department of munitions and supply, had lured to Ottawa at the beginning of the war to help mastermind the mobilization effort.

The list of those called upon to serve reads like a Who's Who of Canada's post-war establishment: industrialist E.P. Taylor; John Deutsch, later president of the Economic Council of Canada; Donald Gordon, later head of Canadian National Railways; James Coyne, later governor of the Bank of Canada; Maxwell Henderson, later auditor general of Canada; Wallace McCutcheon, later vice president and managing director of Argus Corporation and a senator; and John David Eaton, later president of T. Eaton Co. Ltd.

Indeed, in his book *The Canadian Establishment*, Peter C. Newman says flatly that "it was the network of connections and interconnections between business and government, fathered by Clarence Decatur Howe, that became the Canadian Establishment.... They had come to Ottawa as individuals; they left as an elite.... When the dollar-a-year men fanned out at the close of World War II to run the nation they had helped to create, the attitudes, the working methods and the business ethic they took with them determined the country's economic and political course for the next three decades."

Whatever the merits of Newman's argument in terms of the country as a whole, there is little doubt that the connections forged among a few of those dollar-a-year men in Ottawa during the war years did dramatically alter — and for all time — the direction of the east coast fishing industry.

The key players in that transformation, in fact, Ralph Bell and C.J. Morrow, were both dollar-a-year men.

After he sold off his fishing interests in 1936, Bell had become president of Pickford and Black, the Halifax shipping firm, as well as an active and influential member of the Halifax Board of Trade. Prior to the war, as the head of the board's aviation committee, he had been busily lobbying Ottawa for an airport for Halifax.

Given his dynamic personality, his previous political involvements and the connections he made in Ottawa during that lobbying effort, it probably shouldn't have been surprising that Bell was enlisted as one of Howe's first dollar-a-year men. He became a member of the executive committee of the new department of munitions and supply, a member of the joint defense production committee of the United States and Canada, aircraft comptroller and director general of aircraft production, where he oversaw a budget of $4 billion.

Although Bell clearly revelled in his role — he became friends with C.D. Howe and was decorated by King George V — the fishing industry was never far from his mind, and he would often confide to colleagues that he still regretted getting out of the business.

Bell dreamed of getting back into the fishing business, but on a far grander scale than anything he'd done before. He wanted to bring together all the major Atlantic fishing companies into one big operation that could consolidate the then-fragmented industry and — just as importantly — make it big enough to attract the capital that would be necessary for it to expand.

Bell had lots of opportunities to make his case. A.H. Brittain and Gary Connor from Maritime National and Billy Smith from W.C. Smith and Company were members of the powerful Wartime Fisheries Advisory Board, which often met in Ottawa. From 1942 to 1944, C.J. Morrow also regularly shuttled back and forth between Ottawa and Nova Scotia as the Atlantic Director of Fisheries on Donald Gordon's Wartime Prices and Trade Board, which controlled everything Canadians produced and consumed during the war years.

Whenever any of those fishing-industry people were within earshot, Ralph Bell would press his case. "Now, Con," he would say to Gary Connor whenever he met him, "you go talk to C.J. about this because it's a good idea. Now think about it. When the war is over, this is what we should do." When they were out of range of his voice, he would write letters. "All the time he was there in Ottawa," Hal Connor would recall years later, "he was writing to my father. Dad used to show me the letters. And he was writing to C.J. at the time [too], about the great mistake he'd made getting out of the business, which he described as 'the most fascinating business of all.' He'd say, 'We haven't got the

Plant workers at National Fish and National Sea Products Ltd. in the 1940s.
(BOLLINGER PHOTOS)

capital or enough clout to buy the size of fleet we need, the kind of plants and equipment we need and we haven't got enough clout in the marketplace. We should bring these companies together."

Bell's entreaties got a boost in 1944 when Stewart Bates, who had been asked to look into the industry's problems for the Nova Scotia Royal Commission on Provincial Development and Rehabilitation, issued his *Report on the Atlantic Sea Fishery.* In it, he argued that "under-development in the fishing industry was the legacy of regulations such as the trawler restrictions of the 1930s, and chronically undercapitalized primary and secondary production." Bates suggested that some of the major east coast fishing companies should be merged in order to meet the need for capital.

Although both Morrow and Connor were initially reluctant to give up their independence, Bell's arguments — and the prospects of post-war competition — finally convinced them to join forces in 1945.

By that time, Gary Connor was 60 years old and ready to slow down. During the war years, he had run the plant almost single-handedly. Darryl Laing had spent from 1939 to 1945 overseas while his other key associate, Walter Boutilier, had died in 1942. Connor's son, Hal — a lawyer who joined the firm just before the outbreak of World War II but then left quickly to join the Royal Canadian Navy and spent most of the war overseas — was the most logical successor to his father, but he was considered still too young and inexperienced in the intricacies of the fish business to take over the family business on his own.[1]

Over at Lunenburg Sea Products, the railroad-track triumvirate had broken up. Billy Smith, deciding he wanted a "change of scenery," had sold off all his shares and moved his family to Vancouver during the war. Although both C.J. Morrow, then 50, and Wallace Smith, 49, were still actively involved in the company in 1945, both men were exhausted from the rigors of their wartime activities — C.J., in fact, had continued to work for the company even while serving in Ottawa — and were ready to listen to Bell's suggestions.

They — Bell, Morrow, Smith and Connor — officially joined forces to form National Sea Products Ltd.[2] in September of 1945. Under the terms of the deal, Bell held 51 percent of the common stock in the new company with the previous

---

1. Connor, who ended up spending 44 years in the fish business and eventually became chairman of the board of National Sea Products, says he almost didn't even join the new company Bell put together. "After the war ended, the law firm I'd been with before the war wanted me back and they offered me $2,000 a year to join them. Father said, 'I think we can do a little better than that for you,' and they did. And that's how I came to work for the company." He says he has no regrets. "Over the years I became director of a number of companies — Eastern Canada Savings and Loan, Scotia Square, Central Trust — but the fishing industry was always the one I enjoyed the most. There are so many facets to it — the fleet, the shore plants in out-of-the-way places, the marketing problems — that you can never be bored."

owners holding 40 percent, and the remainder was sold to interested employees. The new company, with assets of $3,195,339.32 — including wharves, buildings, machinery, equipment, vehicles and fleet — instantly became the largest and most important fish company on the east coast.

From the director's point of view, that was to be only the beginning. At an early meeting, the new company's board of directors — Bell, Gary Connor, Hal Connor, H.V.D. Laing, C.J. Morrow, P.J. Smith, R.G. Smith, W.W. Smith and lawyer J. McG. Stewart — set out an ambitious credo. "Your directors have a great and abiding faith in the future of the fishing industry of this province," they declared. "Their aim is to create the highest quality product which experience, care, research and modern facilities can produce; to double the consumption of Atlantic fish in the Canadian market by seeing to it that through better and more efficient methods of distribution the consumer receives a better product at a fair price; to explore and develop other markets throughout the world wherever they may be found; and to establish the company's brands in every market in which fish from this province can profitably be sold."[3]

But even as the directors were setting out those lofty ideals for posterity, there were already the first faint hints in the here-and-now that this might not be a marriage made in corporate heaven.

There were, not surprisingly, serious personality clashes. Unlike his more cautious, deliberative partners, Ralph Bell prided himself on his ability to succeed by operating on gut instinct and making instant, seat-of-the-pants decisions. "Bell was one of those fellows who, if he liked the way you combed your hair, would make you a director,"[4] remembers Charles MacFadden, who joined the firm as an accountant just as National Sea was being formed. "Jeremiah Nickerson must have impressed Bell," adds MacFadden with a laugh, "because that's just what he did in his case." According to company records, Nickerson became a National Sea director on November 22, 1945. He "ceased to be a director January 22, 1946."

Just before National Sea was supposed to begin operations, Bell engineered

---

2. Ironically, in spite of the fact that it was reminiscent of the name of his former chief rival, C.J. Morrow was the person who actually suggested that the company be named National Sea Products Ltd. During a meeting with Bell and Connor in lawyer J. McG. Stewart's office, Morrow remembers, "we went over name after name, and much to the surprise of Ralph and Gary Connor, I said, 'Well, what's wrong with National Sea Products Ltd?'" One early name suggestion — Atlantic Seafoods Ltd. — was rejected, recalls Charles MacFadden, because it "wasn't big enough to reflect their plans."
3. When the company's new directors and management sat down to come up with a new mission statement following restructuring in 1984, the result, ironically, was very similar to this. "What makes it interesting," explains Bill Morrow, "is that I doubt that most of the present management group ever saw this statement."
4. He actually did it on more than one occasion. At one point, he returned from lunch at the Halifax Club to announce that he'd just appointed a former premier, Harold Connolly, to the Board.

yet another deal to purchase the assets of H.B. Nickerson & Sons Ltd.[5] Founded by Jeremiah Nickerson and his father, Harry, in 1935 in Cape Breton, the company had become a modestly successful enterprise by the end of World War II, and Bell believed it would make a nice fit with the rest of the National Sea operation. But the deal was an expensive one. Nickerson demanded $150,000 for his company plus another $10,000 for his fish-meal company and $5,000 for a freighter he owned. In addition, the agreement provided that Bell would appoint Nickerson to the National Sea board and give him an executive job at $7,500 a year.

Bell agreed, but he didn't bargain on the fact that he and Jeremiah Nickerson would soon have a falling out. Although the specific reasons aren't clear, the simple fact is that Nickerson and Bell were probably too much alike to ever work together smoothly.

Nickerson, wrote Jack Wilcox in his unpublished corporate history of National Sea, was "an independent cuss. He was as tough in business as he was when scrapping on the wharf, and developed a reputation on both counts. One time when asked how he managed to keep obstreperous workers in line, in silent answer he raised his arm, flexed his muscles and made a fist."

At any rate, almost as soon as the deed was done, Bell wanted it undone. Despite the combined protests of C.J. Morrow, Darryl Laing, and Gary and Hal Connor, all of whom saw the wisdom in keeping Nickerson under the new corporate umbrella, Bell was intransigent. Jeremiah Nickerson had to go. He was loath, however, to do it himself and so he assigned the task to Stan Lee, his new general manager and director of public relations.

During the war years in Ottawa, C.J. Morrow had met Lee — who'd left his family-owned O'Leary and Lee Ltd. lobster cannery to head up the Nova Scotia branch of the Prices and Trade Board — and the two men quickly became close friends. Morrow was impressed by Lee's abilities as an administrator, a man who had the knack of being able to bring people together no matter how difficult the subject. Even before National Sea was formed, he'd offered Lee a job.

In the beginning, Bell was reluctant to keep him on, but — thanks in no small part to his handling of the Nickerson affair — Bell soon came to depend on Lee to do his dirty work for him. "Stan Lee's job was to undo things," says MacFadden today. "He was a master of diplomacy who got Ralph Bell out of trouble on a regular basis." In this case, says MacFadden, he simply "took Jeremiah down to the hotel and wouldn't let him leave until he quit [as director]. But it hurt Jeremiah. He was proud to be a director."

---

5. Interestingly, Bell didn't buy Nickerson through National Sea but through an affiliated company, Gatehouse, in Montreal. The reason, according to MacFadden, is that that there'd been "mild hollering about this big new company squeezing out the small independents."

Although National Sea, through a Montreal firm called Gatehouse, continued to own Nickerson's for a number of years after that, Nickerson himself dealt with his so-called parent company through accountants. "The public never saw National Sea at Nickerson's. And Nickerson would only come to Halifax occasionally," notes MacFadden. But that made the operation impossible to manage or control. "Staff's attitude was that we had no control over the company. We couldn't trust the figures and we couldn't be responsible for the company we were supposed to own," MacFadden says now. In 1956, National Sea's board of directors agreed to sell the company back to the Nickerson family.

But the Nickersons, like Bell before, would eventually be back.

"It didn't surprise me when they came back," MacFadden says. "I knew that someday, some way, they were going to reach out again." And when they did — again like Bell — they would have a dramatic impact on the company.

INTERLUDE
Cap'n High Liner

WHEN I asked Bill Morrow if he'd ever encountered envy or jealousy from other children while growing up in Lunenburg because he was, after all, the son of the boss of the town's largest and most important employer, he seemed genuinely puzzled by the question.

There was, he recalled, no special cachet in being the boss' son. "The people who had the most respect in a community like Lunenburg were the successful fishing captains," he explained simply. "They always had more respect than the doctors or the ministers or any of the officials in the plant."

That was partly, of course, because everyone in the community — from the lowliest flunkey aboard a schooner to the president of the largest fish company, not to forget all those bankers and shopkeepers and doctors and ministers in between — ultimately depended for their livelihood on the special skills of the local fishing skippers.

The best of them were rewarded with titles that were not only indicators of their position in the community but were, in their way, as prestigious and sought after as a knighthood might be in other times and circumstances.

In Newfoundland, where they do not waste words, the best skippers were known simply as "fish killers." In Lunenburg and other Nova Scotia ports, they were known as "high liners."

The term first came into use almost a century and a half ago to describe a crewman on a fishing vessel who could bait and fill up a bucket of hooks on a longline faster than anyone else. Over time, it came to be used to describe the vessel that caught the most fish each year and every fishing skipper worth his ship wanted to claim the title for himself. In a fishing community, to a be a high liner meant that you were, quite simply, *the* best.

In many ways, the captain of a fishing vessel has always been an all-powerful figure. Traditionally, he picked his own crew, decided when to sail, when to return to port and where to fish. Aboard ship, his word was law. But at the same time, his power has always been very directly circumscribed by other realities. Unlike the captain of a navy ship, for instance, the skipper of a fishing vessel has no coercive powers — he has to earn the respect of his men. Technically, he may have had the power to choose his own crew but, in fact, the crew also ultimately has the power to choose not to sail with any captain who abused his power and authority.

Since the crew were only paid according to the quantity and quality of the fish they caught on a trip — and since it was the captain's job to determine the best fishing grounds — any captain who returned home with his holds empty too often would also have trouble lining up a crew for his next journey.

In many ways, things have changed dramatically in the fishing business over the past 100 years. Today's fishing captains are equipped with wheelhouses full of new and marvellous technological wonders, each one designed to help them find and catch more fish more efficiently than ever before.

At the same time, captains don't always have the final word anymore on where to fish and what species to catch. Their independence is now restricted by everything from the vagaries of the international marketplace to more rules and regulations and quotas than their predecessors could possibly have imagined.

For all of that, however, the captain remains ultimately responsible for the safety of his crew and the success of its voyage.

It takes a special kind of man to be a successful fishing captain. After spending much of his career watching fishing captains close up, Frederick William Wallace, the editor of the *Canadian Fisherman*, concluded that a fishing skipper "had to be a sailor and pilot and vessel handler, and command the respect and cooperation of his crew. He must be a sound judge of weather, knowing his barometer and the signs of change indicated by wind and sky, and he must know the run and set of tides and currents. The nature of the bottoms and the ground which fish frequent at certain seasons of the year is essential knowledge if he is to make good catches. And, above all, he must be a diplomat, using common-sense judgement and possess what is vulgarly known as 'guts.' No timid, nervous hesitating type of man would ever make good as a fishing captain."

That is as true today as it was then, and, as Bill Morrow has known from childhood, the success of those fishing captains is what determines the ultimate success of any fishing company. "We've had some brilliant skippers over the years," Morrow told me. "A lot of them didn't have much formal education, but they knew the sea and fish better than any teacher could ever know his subject. Now you take Tom Pittman, or Frank Tidman, or Morris Nowe ..."

As I began to try to learn more about some of the men who captained the ships and caught the fish, I realized just how right Bill Morrow had been. As totally different in their ways as Tom Pittman and Frank Tidman obviously were — the wild, hard-living Pittman versus the quiet, nattily turned-out Tidman — both men had an encyclopedic knowledge of the sea and an uncanny ability to know where, when and how to find fish.

I also began to realize that their fascinating lives and overlapping careers showed as much about the evolution of the company, from the last days of the saltbank schooner fishery through to the modern era of factory freezer trawlers, as anything that happened in the boardroom during the period.

What follows isn't an exhaustive look at all of the many important and intriguing "Captain High Liners" who have fished for the company over the years, so much as it is a glimpse of a few of the men whose careers seem to illustrate not only their own eras but what has changed — and, as importantly, what has not — in the 90 years since a young Lunenburg highline skipper named Ben Smith got together with some of his family and friends to form a fishing company.

BEN SMITH

Benjamin Conrad Smith grew up as a "wharf rat" playing his childhood games along the Lunenburg waterfront in the shadow of the saltbank schooner fleet. While still a teenager, he apprenticed as a fisherman, and became a captain himself before he was 25.

From the beginning, Smith had an uncanny, inexplicable knack for knowing where fish were to be found as well as for steering a safe course in all sorts of weather.

Smith's success on the fishing banks — his vessels invariably recorded the largest catch each trip — earned him the coveted title of high liner of the fleet. Thanks to his reputation for success, Smith was able to put together a group of local people to help him finance the construction of his own schooner in 1897 when he was still only 33. Smith named his new ship the *Gladys B. Smith* after his first-born daughter, Gladys Beatrice.

The *Gladys B.* was more than just another sailing ship. She was also an object of beauty. Once, when she was in Naples, Italy, delivering a cargo of saltfish she'd caught off Newfoundland, an Italian painter was so taken with her sleek lines, her splendid bowsprit, her clipper bow, her white-winged sails, her precisely architectural lines that he painted her portrait. Copies of it still hang proudly in offices and homes all over Atlantic Canada.[1]

---

1. Ironically, the portrait may not, in fact, really be of the *Gladys B.* Apparently, artists in many European ports would paint pictures of generic schooners that they would then adjust as necessary to match the ship currently in port, and then rush down to dockside to sell their "painting" to the ship's skipper.

Schooners like the *Gladys B.*, of course, weren't just built for beauty. They were fast, efficient 100-ton vessels that were designed to reap the harvest of an unpredictable, treacherous and occasionally deadly North Atlantic Ocean.

What made the *Gladys B.* special, however, was the unique marriage of a finely crafted fishing vessel with the superb skills of her master and hand-picked crew. She was a highline vessel.

Smith's investors in the *Gladys B.* were well and quickly rewarded for their faith in Smith and his ship. By the end of its first season at sea, the *Gladys B.*'s dividend per $93.59 share was already $17.18.

Perhaps not surprisingly, the shareholders unanimously agreed at their 1898 annual meeting to reward Captain Smith with a gold watch to recognize his achievements. Smith likely put part of his growing profits from the vessel's operation into buying shares in W.C. Smith and Company, the ship's chandlering firm he and his brothers and friends established a few years later. Although he continued to operate his own fishing vessels for many years after that, Smith became more and more involved with the business of the family firm and eventually became its president in the early 1920s.

For many in Lunenburg, however, President Ben Smith remained, until his death, "Captain Smith, high liner of the fleet." It was one more indication of just how important a successful fishing captain was regarded in those days.

MARTIN OLESEN

Martin Olesen, a cheerful, hearty Englishman of Danish birth, introduced steam trawling to Canada in the early 1900s as the master of a vessel called the *Rayon d'Or.*

Olesen was the first of a number of key trawler captains lured to Canada in the early twentieth century by Nova Scotia fishing entrepreneur Arthur Boutilier. Boutilier, says former National Sea executive Hal Connor, "had an eye for the possibilities in men. He certainly picked some good ones."

Olesen was a good fisherman, remembers writer Frederick William Wallace, but "he was an entirely different type from the [schooner] skippers I had sailed with previously, being a man of good education, well read and widely travelled." He also enjoyed, even at sea, a good time. In his classic *Roving Fisherman,* Wallace writes about one trip in 1917 in which he shared the captain's cabin: "'Breakfast,' [Olesen] cried. As I donned my clothes, he foraged in a locker, produced two bottles of schnapps and proceeded to fill two small glasses. 'The morning eyeopener,' he said. 'Here's how.'"

Partly because of his personality and partly because of the trawler's then-advanced technology, Olesen ran his ship in a way that left Wallace — who was used to the hands-on approach of Canadian schooner captains — aghast.

"Captain Olesen," Wallace marvelled, "directed operations without emerging out of the snug sea-parlor. He had a first class mate and an experienced crew who went about their work smartly and quietly.... Below in our cabin we could hear the winch heaving in ... the thump of the fish spilling out on the fore-deck. If the catch was light or heavy, the skipper was conscious of it. Without getting up from the sofa, he would hail the Mate in the wheelhouse overhead and tell him in which direction to steer for the next drag."

Olesen eventually returned to Europe — where he was briefly and unsuccessfully engaged in shipbuilding in Denmark — and ended up as marine superintendent for a large fleet of British steam trawlers in Grimsby.

NEWMAN WHARTON

Wharton, who was born at Beach Meadows, Nova Scotia, in 1872, began what was to become a lifetime at sea when he was just 12, working aboard a square-rigged sailing ship operating between Nova Scotia and the West Indies. By the time he was 23, he had his master's ticket.

Newman Wharton

Today, Wharton, who began to fish out of Lunenburg in 1917, is best remembered as the man "who got Lunenburg Sea Products — and Lunenburg — into the fresh-fish business."

While some of the more daring Halifax-based fish companies had been in the lucrative fresh-fish business since 1908, the conservative Lunenburg fleet remained content to stick to their traditional three-trips-a-year saltfishery off the Grand Banks until well into the 1930s.

Despite the size and historical success of the Lunenburg schooner fleet, many others in the fishing industry eventually began to dismiss them as out-of-step with the contemporary world. Author Frederick William Wallace, for example, reports that he was "somewhat mystified in hearing little or no reference to this great Canadian fleet of fine schooners," during a conversation about the North American fishing industry with some Yarmouth skippers in 1912. "'All salt-bankers,' I was told, 'fish only in summertime — March to September — and then lay up for the winter or go freighting to the West Indies. They go to Middle Bank, Quero and Grand, let go the anchor and set the dories out....' If a Lunenburger was ever to go winter haddocking," the skippers told him derisively, "he'd probably lose all his gang, all his dories and all his gear."

Even when W.C. Smith and Company finally brought the Lunenburg-based industry into the twentieth century with the opening of the first fresh-fish processing plant in the community in 1926, many in the local fishery were openly skeptical about its prospects and few of the schooner captains showed any interest in supplying the new plant with fish.

Newman Wharton was the exception. "Wharton helped put Lunenburg in the fresh-fish business almost single-handedly," remembers former Lunenburg fish-plant manager Doug Pyke. "Every Friday, regular as clockwork, Wharton would arrive at the dock with another load of fish."

Wharton's arrival was so predictable, in fact, that even his dog used to show up on the wharf each Friday to greet its master as he brought his schooner, the *Jean and Shirley,* named after his daughters, back into port with another load of fresh fish.

Wharton's regularity allowed Lunenburg Sea Products to survive the industry's initial skepticism — "It didn't take too much fish to keep the plant going in those days," Pyke notes — and begin offering a dependable fresh-fish service to the Montreal market.

"If it wasn't for Wharton, I don't know what might have happened to the company," Pyke says today.

Wharton died in 1955.

HANS HANSEN

Hans Hansen, another Dane recruited by Arthur Boutilier in the early 1920s to help get the fledgling east coast trawling industry on its feet, was "one of the greatest — probably *the* greatest — captains who ever fished here," according to Hal Connor. "I remember one time he brought this steam trawler in and the fish were stacked like cordwood on the deck. He'd caught 418,000 pounds of fish in just one four-day trip. He was an extremely scientific guy who used to take water temperature to help him find fish. He also invented new fish gear and developed a method for extracting cod liver oil from the cod livers."

A huge, powerful man with a guttural accent, he was almost as well remembered below decks for his rages — he used to "fly at the crew, then come down and offer them all a drink of rum," says one man who sailed with him — as he was for his fish-finding ability.

Still, Hansen served as a mentor to a whole generation of Nova Scotia's most successful fishing skippers, including both Frank Tidman and Tom Pittman. "He was a great teacher," explains Connor.

He was also a good investor, and eventually retired to a farm near Kentville, in Nova Scotia's Annapolis Valley.

FRANK & PETER GREEN

"Well, Pete," the old fisherman asked Captain Peter Green as the two men stood on the dock at National Sea's Sea Seald Division in Halifax one day, watching while a trawler was being unloaded, "what's your young fellow going to do?"

Green glanced down at his only son, also named Peter. "He can do anything he likes," Green allowed evenly, "anything *except* fish."

The irony in that is that Peter Green himself was part of a long and honorable tradition in the east coast fishing industry of father-son family fishing.

Peter Green — as well as his father, and his father before him — was born in Greenspond, an island outport community of fewer than 1,500 people in Bonavista Bay in Newfoundland. The community, in fact, was probably named after his forebears, English fishermen who settled the community in the 1690s. Although once a thriving trading port rivalling St. John's, Greenspond's real historical importance was as a fishing centre because of its proximity to Newfoundland's rich inshore cod grounds.

By the 1930s, however, Greenspond was in decline as many of the community's best and most ambitious fishermen — including the Carter brothers, who eventually became important National Sea fishermen too — left their isolated outport homes in search of greater opportunities in St. John's or Canada.

Peter Green's father, Frank, who ranged as far north as Labrador to take part in the annual seal hunt and operated his own schooner with a crew that included two of his sons, Peter and Frank, made the move to St. John's himself in the late 1930s after his schooner was lost at sea.

In St. John's, Green developed such a reputation as a good fisherman and seaman that he and his sons were not only recruited to bring the *Cape Agulhas* — which Maritime National had purchased from Newfoundland's famous Crosbie family — from St. John's to Halifax, where it was to become the newest steel-hulled trawler in Maritime National's fleet, they were also asked to stay on with the ship and form the nucleus of its permanent crew.

Although young Frank joined the navy shortly after the family arrived in

Halifax (he didn't return to fishing, and eventually became chief engineer for Marine Atlantic, based in New Brunswick), both Frank, Sr., and Peter, who became a captain in the late 1940s, quickly established reputations as among the best fishermen in the Maritime National fleet. "They were innovative types," remembers Hal Connor, "not hidebound by the past. They'd try new nets, new types of doors. They'd experiment within reasonable limits."

Peter Green, Captain Frank Green and son Frank outside the wheelhouse of the Cape Agulhas.

According to Frank Green's grandson, Peter, now a prominent Halifax lawyer, his father, uncle and grandfather came to Halifax originally with the specific idea of putting down permanent roots in the new community. "There were a lot of Newfoundland fishermen doing that at the time," he notes.

Later, after his father became established, Peter Green helped other Newfoundlanders to emigrate by hiring them as crew for the fall fishing season that followed each ship's annual refit. "I remember my father phoning Newfoundland to arrange for his crew. 'Tell the fellows to be on the dock,' he'd say. And he'd leave Halifax with just a skeleton crew, pick up the rest in Newfoundland, go fishing and then bring them back to Halifax. That was how a lot of them were able to emigrate in those days. After they got established, they'd send for their families to join them." Peter Green himself was born in St. John's in 1940, the year his father helped bring the *Cape Agulhas* to Halifax. The next year, he and his mother moved to Halifax to join his father.

Young Peter spent seven summers working aboard his father's and grandfather's trawlers. He bought chocolate bars and supplies of a drink called Freshy before each trip, then sold them to the crew while the ship was at sea. Today, he remembers life aboard even the then-modern side trawlers as hard. "When the fish was abundant, they were going 24 hours-a-day — set the trawl, bring it in after an hour. If the fish were running, they were so busy they could never get the deck cleared."

Although the captain wasn't involved in the physical labor of fishing, Green says, the mental exhaustion was at least as severe. "My father would come home from every trip exhausted, and when I was at sea with him, I realized why. He was awake all the time. He never slept. He was up for the set of every trawl. He might catnap for an hour here and there, maybe sleep a little longer if he had a good mate, but most of the time he was working and worrying."

Even at home, Green says, his father could not forget the sea. "He was always watching the weather and he was a compulsive radio listener. If the *Fishermen's Broadcast* came on, we all had to be quiet. And if there was a storm coming, he'd want to get back to sea quickly — partly to get clear of land before the storm hit and partly to be the first one on the fishing banks when it was over. If there was a storm coming, he'd call the mate and tell him to get everybody back to the boat. They were leaving early."

Under such circumstances, Green says today, family life was "too compressed. He was only home for a few days at a time and we had to try to squeeze everything in a few hours. Dad tried — he was at almost all the important events in our lives — but he was always exhausted. We lived in a house with a picture window in the living room and I remember once my oldest sister ran to my father expecting him to catch her. But he was asleep and my sister went straight through the window.

"But give my father credit. There were five kids and he always found a way to be there for us. When I graduated from university — I was the first in the family — it was a big event and my father took the week off from fishing. That was the only way he could arrange it. He did the same thing later when my sisters got married." Although he was usually home for Christmas — his ship would most often arrive in port on Christmas Eve — Green still recalls today with some bitterness the Christmas when "the company announced that they couldn't afford to bring all the ships in at once and that everyone would have to go on with their regular cycles. Dad didn't get home that Christmas."

Both Frank and Peter Green died at sea of heart attacks. Although Peter Green says today that his grandfather was far less obsessed with fishing than his father — he amassed "considerable wealth from some shrewd investments" and retired to a home in Queensland, on the south shore of Nova Scotia near Halifax — he still couldn't resist one last trip to sea. "I was in my senior year of high school and I remember my grandfather arrived at the house one morning to say he was on his way to the wharf to take over a ship for some master who wanted a week off. That was the last I ever saw of him." His father, who died at sea at age 58, didn't even make it to retirement.

Although Peter Green says "I was the first generation in my family who could choose *not* to go to sea," he still remembers with some fondness the bonds that the fishery created. "During those days, most of the fishermen were from Newfoundland, and we all lived in the same neighborhood, the families knew each other and we all went to the same church. There were always people around our house — Newfoundlanders, Portuguese fishermen — it was nothing to have eight or 10 people around the house talking and debating and arguing. And everyone looked out for everyone else. After my father died, a number of the captains used to stop by regularly just to bring us fresh fish. That was just the way it was."

FRANK TIDMAN

Invariably dressed in a shirt and tie and wearing an ever-present fedora, Frank Tidman would — as one associate puts it — "go aboard a steam trawler as if he was about to deliver a sermon."

In fact, he resembled an accountant on his way to the office far more than he did a sea captain heading out for another trip to the fishing grounds. That may have been because Tidman really was an accountant before he became a fishing captain. That accountant's training, with its focus on precision and attention to detail, undoubtedly helped make him a success not only as a skipper but also later as a businessman.

Tidman was born in the British fishing port of Grimsby in 1895, the son of a sea captain who ultimately became the managing director of a company that owned a fleet of fishing trawlers. But his father never encouraged young Frank to follow him into the fishing business. During World War I, in fact, Tidman served with the elite land-based British Grenadiers and returned home to train — according to his father's wishes — as an accountant. In the early 1920s, he decided to emigrate to Canada, ostensibly to take a job in the accounting department at Maritime National Fisheries in Halifax.

Actually, as he would later confide to his son Gordon, now a provincial court judge, he never had any intention of being an accountant. Away from his father's dominating influence, Tidman immediately abandoned accountant's pencils for deckhand's oilskins and began his rapid climb to the wheelhouse.

One of the most scientific of Maritime National's skippers, Tidman once returned home after just three days of fishing with an astonishing 447,000 pounds of fish. How did he manage, Hal Connor once asked him, to almost always catch more fish than anyone else?

"Hal," he replied, "that's a good question, and I don't know what the answer is. If there is an answer, maybe it's patience. I'm a patient man."

Convinced that fish run in the same area at the same time every year, Tidman would keep a very precise log of every fish he caught, and when and how he caught it. If his detailed records told him that there would be fish in a particular area, he would not let even a few disappointing trawls dissuade him. "Patience and persistence," he would explain, "you can't let yourself become discouraged." And almost always Tidman's patience would be rewarded and he would return home with "a good bagful of fish."

It is interesting, if not especially helpful, to remember that Frank Green — another highline skipper from the same era — responded to a disappointing trawl in almost exactly the opposite way. "If he didn't find any fish in one spot," say Hal Connor, "he'd very quickly steam off to next place."

As a skipper, Tidman was also quite different from Green, an outgoing, bluff and hardy Newfoundlander. "Dad was probably an odd skipper as skippers go," admits his son Gordon. "He kept himself aloof from the crew, took his meals in his cabin and always dealt with them through the mate or the bosun. The crew referred to him as 'the old man.' They were loyal, but I think they were also a bit afraid of my father. It was just that he came from a British tradition, and he felt that that was the best way to run a ship."

But away from the sea and the pressures of command, a different Frank Tidman would emerge. Fun-loving, easy-going. He was one of the mainstays of the Elks Club, a private watering hole near the Halifax waterfront that became an important gathering spot for Maritime National skippers. Operated by a couple named Stan and Sophie Kehoe, the apparently nondescript club featured three or four billiard tables, an area in which to play cards and — most importantly — a relaxing atmosphere where the captains could let their hair down after a week of responsibility for the success and safety of their crews.

"Fishing was a terrible life," explains Hal Connor. "The ships weren't very comfortable — pretty damn elementary living conditions — and most of the captains didn't fraternize with their crews at sea, so it was a lonely, frustrating life for them. And they were only back in port for 24 or 36 hours. So when they came to town, they liked to relax, sit down and chew the fat."

When World War II began, the military took many fishing vessels, including Frank Tidman's, to use in the convoys ferrying men and supplies to Europe. As a result, Tidman decided to retire and move with his family to a farm he had purchased near Greenwood in the Annapolis Valley.

As a farmer, Tidman was no less obsessed by detail than he had been as a fisherman. "He raised chickens and grew gladioli," recalls son Gordon, "and he kept very detailed records to the point that he could tell you his profit per gladioli or his profit per hen."

He also kept pigs, which he fed regular doses of cod liver oil in order to — he believed — improve their health and marketability. But he had to abandon that scheme, explains his son with a laugh, "when one wholesale buyer returned a few weeks after the sale to complain that he'd had to give all his customers their money back. "They couldn't tell if they were eating breakfast bacon or smoked fillets."

"Dad gave him half his money back," says Gordon Tidman today. "And I think that was the end of using cod liver oil for feed."

In 1942, Ottawa decided that some of the fishing vessels it had seconded to naval duties should be returned to their original purposes, and Frank Tidman returned to sea.

He finally quit for good in 1954 shortly before he turned 60. Ostensibly, he left because the company said it wouldn't give him a full pension unless he stayed on the job until he was 65 — "If you don't think I'm worth a pension now," he told company officials, "then forget it" — but his son is convinced there were other reasons as well.

"There were new young skippers nipping at his heels out there," Gordon Tidman suggests, "and he still had the highline pride. He didn't want to be beaten at fish catching."

TOM PITTMAN

Tom Pittman was a big man. In every way.

Six feet tall and weighing 325 pounds, he could lift a ship's anchor with his bare hands, and he once ended up in court for slugging a Portuguese deckhand who swore at him after Pittman had ordered him to go to work.

Pittman was no slouch at curse words himself. National Sea officials, in fact, had to take his radio away from him at one point because they couldn't seem to stop him from cursing on it any other way.

Pittman was also, as almost everyone in Lunenburg will tell you, a fishermen's fisherman, a Newfoundlander who taught the Lunenburgers all about the fine art of trawler fishing. Although his widow, Kathleen, allows that "Daddy never had more than a half a day's schooling in his life," his knowledge of the oceans was so encyclopedic and his fishing records so detailed that he developed an almost mythic reputation as a highline captain.

"He was so good he was sometimes lucky," laughs Willoughby Mills, who worked as a cook on Pittman's vessels. "I remember this one time we were down on St. Pierre Bank in October and the weather was bad, so we had to go in to St. Pierre for three, four days in the middle. When we come back out, we only had a little time left to fish but it was still blowing bad, so Tom said, 'I guess we'll have to go back and call this one a "broker."' So we were coming over Middle

Ground when we struck a log or something and bent the propeller a little. Tom said, 'I don't know why, but let's have a try here.' So we shot away and this was in the late afternoon. Half an hour later, we haul back. It was around suppertime and I remember looking out the porthole as the doors came up and there in the net was 35,000 pounds of haddock." He laughs. "Well then, we really started to fish. We only had till the next morning before we had to head back. Well, when we got back, we had 160,000 pounds of haddock."

To make that bit of good luck even better, Mills says, Pittman returned to Lunenburg with every intention of putting his ship in the shipyard for repairs, but since there was no space available at any of the Nova Scotia yards, he decided to make a few more trips to that same fishing spot while he waited for space. "We went out three more times," Mills says, "and came back with 600,000 pounds of haddock. After we went into the yard, one of the other boats tried fishing the same spot and came up empty. The fish had gone somewhere else."

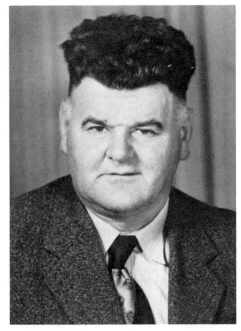

Tom Pittman

Pittman learned his fisherman's skills the hard way. Born in 1899 in Petit Fort, an outport community in Newfoundland's Placentia Bay, young Tom's mother died when he was just six years old, and he began fishing full time when he was only nine "and couldn't see over the side of the dory."

Although he was technically too young to fight, Pittman lied about his age and signed up for service in World War I. At the end of the war, he came to Halifax where he landed a job as a deckhand aboard a Maritime Fish company trawler. He eventually became mate on the *Lemberg*, a Halifax-based trawler captained by Hans Hansen. Partly because there were few opportunities for him to become a captain and partly because the two men got along so well, Pittman remained as Hansen's second-in-command for nearly 20 years until Wallace Smith finally lured him to Lunenburg in 1945 with the opportunity to lead the local industry into the trawler era.

Because Lunenburg's schooner fishermen had made one earlier, unsuccessful effort to get into trawler fishing, Wallace Smith was determined to get an experienced trawlerman aboard when the new National Sea Products Ltd. decided in 1944 to order the *Cape North,* Lunenburg's first trawler since the unsuccessful *Geraldine* was renamed and sent rum-running during Prohibition.

But Smith didn't simply hire Tom Pittman to work aboard the new trawler; he sent him to the Meteghan, Nova Scotia, shipyard where the vessel was being built to make sure that it was properly outfitted for its duties.

After working for six months as mate aboard each of National Sea's first two trawlers — the *Cape LaHave* and the *Cape North*— Pittman was named skipper of the *North* after its original skipper, Nepean Crouse, died in 1946.

For the next five years, Pittman taught a whole generation of top Lunenburg skippers — including Perry Conrad, Elroy Conrad, Matthew Mitchell and Morris Nowe — the ways of the wheelhouse.

Despite that, and despite what Pittman believed was a promise that he would become captain of the newly built *Cape Argus* in 1951, he was passed over for another skipper personally selected by National Sea's then president, Ralph Bell.

Pittman, who'd even given up his almost legendary drinking after getting the *Cape North*'s top job, "wasn't angry" about being passed over, insists his friend Will Mills, "but you could see he didn't care as much after that."

By 1953, Pittman, who had heart problems and had already suffered one small attack, "seemed to have lost his zest for the sea," as one National Sea official put it.

In 1954, the company let him go.

Pittman went to Labrador, where he tried cod trap fishing with his brother but that didn't work out, and he ended up back in Nova Scotia where he spent the next few years working on small fishing boats all over the province. He suffered another heart attack and died in 1960.

Says National Sea chairman Bill Morrow today: "It's always been one of my regrets that we never honored Tom as well as we should have. Because of the way his association with the company ended, he just drifted away and no tribute was ever paid to the accomplishments he had made."

EARL DEMONE

In many ways, Earl Demone is not an untypical son of Lunenburg. He can trace his family roots in the community back to the original Huguenot settlers, and fishing has been both a family business and a family way of life since well before he was born.

When Demone talks about his arrival in this world, in fact, he doesn't talk about being born, he says he "made land on October 11, 1924."

As soon as he legally could, Demone quit school to go fishing himself.

Although he began his seagoing career as a deckhand on one of the last of the famed saltbank schooners in 1940, he soon switched to one of the modern new side trawlers that began operating out of Lunenburg after World War II.

Compared to life aboard a schooner, where fishermen double-bunked in cramped quarters they shared with the galley — "the cook would get up at three or four o'clock every morning to start the fire for breakfast and roast you out of bed, so you were lucky if you ever managed four or five hours sleep in 24" — Demone says now that the trawlers seemed almost luxurious.

Earl Demone, 1951

Almost ... Although crew members got their own bunks in the trawler's forecastle and the galley was in another part of the vessel, space was still at a premium. "There was enough room for a table to play cards and that was about it." Perhaps luckily, there was little time for such diversions. "You worked on the open deck, six hours on, six hours off," Demone remembers. "And if there was fish enough, well, no one got any time off. It wasn't uncommon to work straight through — 36, 48 hours at a stretch." With the exception of Christmas and a month's break in the summer, the routine was almost unvarying. Fishing trips lasted from one to two weeks until the holds were filled with fish, then the trawler returned to port to unload, take on more provisions and head back out to sea.

If the life seems hard to an outsider, Demone says it only seemed normal to him. "People were brought up to that, so it was just the way it was. I was happy as hell, I remember."

After working for a few years for his father, a locally famous captain and independent trawler owner, Demone got a command of his own in 1951 when he became master of the National Sea trawler *Cape Fourchu*, one of the first vessels in the company's fleet with a new, aluminum-lined hold.

Five years later, he decided to build a vessel of his own. "People said I was crazy, but it was just something I always wanted to do," Demone says today. Although he quickly became successful as one of the industry's last major independent owner-operators — he ended up owning two trawlers, the *Cape Roseway* and the *Cape Scotia* — health problems finally forced him to sell his ships to his main customer, National Sea, in 1969. Soon after, National Sea decided to make use of his expertise and invited him to join the company as fleet captain and unofficial chief troubleshooter.

Today, Earl Demone is a National Sea vice president, in charge of a fleet of nearly 60 vessels, including Canada's first factory freezer trawler.

And the fishing business is still a family tradition.

Demone's son, Henry, who began fishing with his father aboard the *Cape Scotia* during his school vacations, is now a vice president (in charge of international and trading) at National Sea too.

"Fish," Earl Demone jokes today, "is in the blood."

CHARLIE CARTER

Another bright, young Newfoundlander from the same outport community as Frank and Peter Green, Charlie Carter joined National in the early 1940s. But his dreams of becoming a captain appeared to founder when he became ill at the end of World War II. "He swallowed this fish bone and developed an infection in his lung," remembers Hal Connor, "and then, shortly after that, he was diagnosed as having TB and sent to the sanatorium." His doctor warned him never to go to sea again because of what he described as "a weakness in his lung."

Assigned to shore-bound duties preparing trawls for company vessels, Carter soon became friends with Hal Connor. "I liked him a lot," Connor remembers, "and it seemed to me he was wasting his life away working in the net loft, so I began to inquire from time to time if he'd be interested in going back to sea again if he could be

Captain Charlie and Mrs. Carter at the christening of the Cape Howe *in 1968.*

shown that it would be okay for his health. He said yes, he'd very much like to get back to sea. So I sent him to see the top-notch lung man in town and he got his files and did a lot of tests and concluded that Charlie was completely healed, that the doctors before had overplayed the dangers."

With Connor's promise that he could be re-examined every quarter to make sure that there were no medical problems, Carter returned to sea as mate for Frank Tidman and eventually became captain of one of the new steam trawlers the company brought over from Britain.

Although he was a successful captain himself, he was not a patient teacher of younger men. "He was hard with the men," agrees Hal Connor, "and for the most part they didn't like him. He was very strict. He fired people he didn't like and I've heard people say that at sea he didn't speak to the men at all except to give orders."

Ironically, when Carter did die at age 60, it was of a heart attack having nothing to do with his lung problems.

PERRY CONRAD

Lunenburg skipper Perry Conrad never considered any job other than fishing. "Back in those days, there was nothing else for young men in these parts to do," he says today. "The fathers were fishing, the place was all fishing, that was just the way it was."

Conrad was only 12 when he joined his father as a deckhand aboard the original *Bluenose* in 1924. Although the sleek schooner had already begun to earn its reputation as the world's fastest schooner, Conrad is quick to add that he "had no part in the racing end of it. I was a flunkey, a 'ketchy' as they called it, on the dory-fishing end of things. I got to blow the horn in the fog and help out whenever I was needed."

In those days, the flunkey, who was usually a boy barely into his teens, didn't earn a wage for his work but he was permitted to cut out and sell the tongues of the fish the vessel caught. "You could make, oh, $75 to $100 for a three-month season," Conrad remembers. "You thought you were rich when you got that." At the time, he says, he also thought that living conditions aboard the schooners were "wonderful, the best they could be. Now, you wouldn't think of living like that."

Conrad's career, in fact, spanned some of the most dramatic changes in the fishery in 400 years, as the traditional saltbank wooden schooners of the early 1900s gave way to the more modern and efficient trawlers of the late 1960s and early 1970s.

By comparison with fresh fishing — a demanding type of fishing that forces

Captain Perry and Mrs. Conrad at the christening of the Cape John.

fishermen to catch lots of fish in short trips in order to land the fish before they spoil — saltfishing was almost leisurely.

Lunenburg saltbankers would make three trips each year to the Grand Banks, spring, summer and fall, as well as a shorter, early-spring voyage to take on herring for bait. During their winters off from fishing many of the schooners operated as trading vessels, carrying cargo to the West Indies and back.

While fishing trips could last up to three months — "When you were salting the fish," Conrad points out, "you could almost stay out forever if you wanted to" — Conrad is quick to add that a good deal of the time was spent not fishing. "There were lots of lay days in those times," he remembers. "Sometimes you'd have to wait for bait, sometimes you'd have to wait for better weather. It was all sail in them days. And nobody fished on Sundays; it was only after we started freshing that we fished Sundays. We didn't do anything at all on Sundays, just rest up for Monday morning. Sometimes, you know, you might be out for three months but you hardly ever came back with your holds filled."

That, of course, isn't to suggest saltbanking was ever an easy life. The fishermen worked from dawn to dusk from small dories that set out their trawls within sight of their mother schooner. "Unless it was thick of fog," Conrad notes, "and then you'd lose sight of the schooner." Conrad, in fact, almost lost his life one time in a fog when a schooner ran over the dory he was fishing from. "There was copper paint on my jacket when I came up," Conrad remembers. That was just one of three times when he ended up overboard while fishing.

During his late teenage years, Conrad would spend his summers fishing — working his way up from flunkey to throater and header (deck jobs that paid wages of between $35 and $40 a trip) and finally into the dory where he got to share in the catch — and then go to school in the winter. Like most boys in the fish business, Conrad says, he would "pass my money over to my father until I was 21. If I needed money, I'd get it from him." Although it was the depths of the Depression, Conrad says it wasn't unusual to come back with $300 for a three-month season in a dory. "We thought we were doing very well at that," he says.

After quitting fishing briefly during prohibition to work in the rum trade, making trips to the Caribbean to pick up up rum that he turned over to buyers at sea — Conrad switched to fresh fishing and signed on as a deckhand aboard the *Isabel F. Spindler*, a vessel operating out of Halifax for Maritime National.

Freshing, says Conrad, was an entirely different way of living as well as fishing. "The trips were only five or six days, but the hours were long. You'd be up at two o'clock [in the morning], have breakfast, bait up your gear and at about 4:30 set out before daylight. We didn't dress no fish during the day, so when the fishing was over — around sundown — you'd sometimes work through to 12 o'clock finishing up. And then be up at 2 o'clock and start again." He pauses. "It was just our way of life then. We didn't know any different."

When their vessel arrived back in port, the fishermen were responsible for unloading it themselves as well as for preparing the ship for its next trip. After that they got paid. "The skipper brought the money down and handed you your share — not in a pay envelope or anything. After they paid you, you had just long enough to go to the telegraph office to get a money order and send the money home. Then you were back to sea again."

Whenever he got a few days off, he and his fellow Lunenburgers would hire a seven-passenger taxi so he could have a brief visit with his wife, Florence, and their two daughters. "On the way home," Conrad jokes today, "we'd be complaining to the driver: 'Is this as fast as this thing goes.' But on the way back, you'd want him to slow down. 'What are you trying to do,' we'd say, 'kill us?'"

Although the fishermen's lifestyle played havoc with family life — "For eight or 10 years, I remember we landed fish on December 24 and we sailed again on Boxing Day, so I never helped trim the Christmas tree," Conrad says. "Mother [his wife Florence] used to say to me, 'You're not married to me, you're married to the boat.' And it was true too, I guess." — Conrad and everyone else accepted it philosophically. "Fishing was my life. When things was good, we accepted that. When things was bad we accepted that too."

Since the men's income depended on how much fish they caught, they vied to get one of the highline skippers such as Nepean Crouse or Leo Corkum. And those captains, of course, chose the top men to serve with them.

In 1945, Conrad signed on as a deckhand aboard the schooner *Fairmorse* ("it was named after the Fairbanks and Morse engine") and then the *Cape North*, where he got the chance to work with two of the Lunenburg fishery's legendary figures — Captain Nepean Crouse and his mate, Tom Pittman. "Tom would show you anything," Conrad remembers. "I learned everything from him — where the best fishing grounds were, how important it was to keep logs. I was only there two years and I became a mate myself."

As mate, you were responsible for mending nets, standing your own watch, taking the wheel and overseeing the work of six of the 12 deckhands. Conrad spent three years as mate aboard the *Cape North* before Wallace Smith approached him to become captain of the *Cape Scatari,* a new Lunenburg-built wooden trawler with aluminum holds.

Conrad, who went on to skipper seven National Sea vessels, including the *Cape Hood*, one of the first Dutch-built trawlers, and the *Cape Nova*, the first stern dragger in the fleet, became the company's senior skipper until he retired in 1968. Today, he works as an examiner, testing would-be local fishermen who want to be certified under the Atlantic Fishermen's Record Book Plan.

MORRIS NOWE

Morris Nowe, who became one of the top highline captains of the 1970s and 1980s, was another of Tom Pittman's disciples.

Born near Lunenburg in 1928, Nowe followed his father into the fishing business in 1948 after spending three years seeing the world from the deck of an Imperial Oil tanker. "I always knew I wanted to go fishing," Nowe says today, "but I wanted to do a little travelling first."

After a short stint on one of the last of the wooden schooners to fish out of Halifax, Nowe signed on as a deckhand aboard the Lunenburg-based *Mahaska,* a one-time wooden trawler, rum-runner and dory vessel that had recently been converted back to trawling. Based on his brief experience with the schooner-based dory fishery, Nowe says he has no regrets about missing that era of "wooden ships and iron men." "Working on a dragger was a lot better than the schooners ever were. [On a schooner], you slept forward in this little hold — maybe 12 guys in a tiny hold with an oil stove that was always flooding and smelling it up, with water in the bilge and one toilet. To go aft to get a meal, you had to get dressed and go out even in bad weather." He laughs. "Nowadays, you can stand watch in your bedroom slippers. I'm not kidding. Some of these guys get up, roll out of their bunk, get a coffee, an apple or an orange and wander out to stand watch without even putting on a pair of shoes."

Even aboard the draggers, however, life was no picnic. "We dressed all the fish on deck," Nowe remembers, "and the ice would freeze right on your back and on your head. I remember lots of times going for a meal and you'd take off your sou'wester and it'd be caked in ice. The work was cold and wet." He pauses

Morris Nowe

again. "Nowadays, everything happens inside."

If the work at sea was hard, there was little respite when the vessel landed. "You'd arrive in port at six a.m. In those days, we had to unload all our own fish. For the first hour, we'd do the haddock roe and the cod livers and then, after the shore workers arrived, we'd start to put out the fish. Lots of times it would take us until seven or eight that night to put out the fish, and nine or ten to clean up. And then you had to be back the next morning by eight a.m. to take on ice blocks and get ready to go out again. After everything was ready, you'd get paid. But then, at one o'clock, it was back to sea again."

Nowe lasted six months aboard the *Mahaska* which, not coincidentally, was as long as the boat itself lasted. "I'd got enough money together to buy my first car — a 1949 Pontiac — and so I decided to take a trip off to learn how to drive it." While Nowe was ashore mastering the intricacies of the automobile, the *Mahaska* was lost at sea during a fishing trip. Although no one died in the accident, everyone's gear, including Nowe's, went down with the vessel. "In those days," says Nowe, "you supplied all your own gear. The only thing the company supplied was the mattress."

His early years at sea convinced Nowe that he wanted to be something more than just a deckhand. "I tried working as a cook for six months aboard the *Cape LaHave* but all that did was convince me that there was more money to be made in the wheelhouse. Our skipper there was a drunk and I figured, 'If he can [be a skipper], why can't I?'"

The quickest, surest route to the wheelhouse was to apprentice with a high-line skipper or mate — "to let them know you're willing to do extra work, to learn what you need to know" — so Nowe switched vessels and joined the *Cape*

Scatari, another wooden trawler with a skipper less familiar with the ways of demon rum. Although he began there as a deckhand, he was soon promoted to bosun, a junior officer who acts as the master's assistant during a watch. "What you did depended on what was going on," Nowe remembers. "When there was plenty of fish, you worked on deck with the deckhands, but when fish was scarce you might go up in the wheelhouse and take over, under direction, while the skipper rested."

Nowe's climb up the ship's ladder was temporarily sidetracked less than a year later when a change of masters left the *Scatari* in the hands of an inexperienced captain. "We had a 'broker' of a trip and we came back with no money," Nowe recalls. "When they asked what went wrong, this fellow said it was the crew's fault, that we wouldn't work with him. Well, the company decided to send one of their key skippers out with us on the next trip to see what was really going on. And, of course, the one that they sent was Tom Pittman. He made the trip with us and within 24 hours we had 80,000 pounds of haddock." After radioing that information to his bosses ashore — "he had to repeat it to them to convince them it was no joke" — Pittman added with a flourish, "I'm telling you, a finer bunch of young men I've never worked with."

On the way back to port, Pittman, who'd been observing Nowe's performance, asked him if he "wanted to be in the wheelhouse."

Four months later, Nowe joined Pittman's *Cape North* as bosun. "It was my big break," he says today. And Tom Pittman? "He was like a father to me. He was one of the real old timers. He'd learned from the bottom up — a deckhand, a bosun, a mate — and he was always willing to help the ones comin' up."

One of the most crucial lessons he learned from Pittman was the importance of keeping detailed notes of his experiences on the fishing grounds. "You learned to keep a record in a writing tablet every day — where you were, longitude and latitude, what you caught and what you knew about what other ones caught — and then keep an index. If you were out on a blind run, you'd go back to your book. The fish tend to have favorite spots where they settle and spawn and you had to know where they was because you were the one who was responsible to make sure it was a good trip."

In 1955, with top jobs on trawlers in short supply and Nowe itching for a command of his own, he and a group of Cape Breton investors teamed up to build a 60-foot vessel he named the *Barbara Kathleen* after his wife and mother. Five years later, the *Barbara Kathleen* caught fire in Newfoundland's Port au Port Bay — a furnace flooded in the freshly painted engine room — and Nowe and his crew had to be rescued by a local fisherman. "I didn't mind until I got off and I was on the dock. Then I got the shakes just thinking how close I came."

When Nowe and his investors couldn't agree on how large a replacement vessel to build, Nowe returned to Lunenburg and soon landed a job as a mate and part-time skipper aboard the *Cape George,* a dragger skippered and partly owned by another legendary Nova Scotia fishing master, Captain Harry Demone. "He was a rough old fellow," Nowe remembers, "but we got along."

Their relationship was helped by the fact that when Nowe made his first trip aboard the vessel as relieving skipper, he returned with the "holds filled with fish and fish on the decks. She was about four or five years old then and that was the first time that had ever happened. I remember he was away and he told me to send him a telegram the day we got in to let him know how we did and he said he would decide then what to do next. So I sent him the telegram and he sent me one back. 'Carry on' was all it said."

Thanks in no small part to Nowe's growing reputation as a fish-finding skipper, National Sea tapped him to become master of one of its new steel side trawlers built in Holland. "It was the rave of the day," Nowe says with a laugh. Nowe was captain of the *Cape Hood* for two years before shifting over to another new National Sea side trawler. For the rest of his career, in fact, Nowe got first choice of new ships in National Sea's expanding fleet — an indication of both his skills as a master and the trust the company had in him to test its new vessels.

Unfortunately, during sea trials for one such new vessel — the *Cape Beaver* — Nowe was involved in a tragic and highly publicized accident that claimed the lives of four fishermen aboard a small wooden scallop dragger.

Nowe was taking the *Beaver* out for its fishing trials on July 31, 1980, when it collided with the *Margaret Jane*, an aging scalloper, in a thick fog near the approaches to Lunenburg harbor. The *Margaret Jane* was heading home to Lunenburg from Georges Bank with a sick crew member when the *Beaver* sliced through the older vessel, cutting it in half, and forcing her 18-man crew to try to abandon the vessel. The *Margaret Jane* sank in less than two minutes. Four of the men didn't make it to safety.

To make this personal tragedy a more public one, the whole event was recorded by an NBC-TV crew from the U.S., which was aboard the *Cape Beaver* preparing a report on a disputed U.S.-Canada fishing treaty. Within seconds of the collision, the crew began recording the dramatic scene as members of the *Margaret Jane*'s crew scrambled off their sinking ship and were pulled aboard the *Beaver*. The footage was shown on newscasts throughout North America.

Testimony at a subsequent federal inquiry into the incident indicated that the *Margaret Jane*, which was not equipped with radar reflectors that would have made it easier to see on radar screens, may not have appeared on one of the two radar screens aboard the *Beaver*.

Although Jeff Weinstock, the NBC cameraman who testified at the inquiry, said that the atmosphere in the wheelhouse prior to the collision was "strictly business — from the time there was a question of something on the radar screen, I don't think anyone relaxed" — the inquiry commissioner, Mr. Justice Gordon Cooper of the Nova Scotia Supreme Court, found that both Morris Nowe and the captain of the *Margaret Jane* had made errors in judgement and committed what were termed wrongful acts.

Specifically, the judge criticized Nowe for pulling the *Beaver* back after his vessel ploughed into the scalloper, arguing that the wooden ship may have stayed afloat longer if the *Beaver* had remained lodged in the side of the *Margaret Jane*. He also suggested that Nowe was not as familiar as he should have been with the radar system aboard his new high-tech vessel and added that he had allowed too many people — that is, the NBC film crew — to be in the wheelhouse and therefore contributed to the ensuing confusion in the moments before the tragedy.

Mr. Justice Cooper suspended Nowe's master's license for six months and fined National Sea $15,000 (the captain of the *Margaret Jane* had his license suspended for three months and his company was fined $7,500).

For National Sea, which had backed Captain Nowe throughout the affair, the sinking of the *Margaret Jane* became the catalyst for a complete re-examination and revamping of the company's training and safety programs. Shortly after the incident, the company hired a retired master mariner, Henry Kohler, to oversee those programs, and today the company boasts one of the most highly qualified and safety-conscious complements of skippers in the fishing business anywhere in the world.

For Morris Nowe, however, the sinking of the *Margaret Jane* was an emotionally scarring and personally traumatizing episode.

"It took me two to three years just to get myself back to normal after that," Nowe says today. "I'll never forget it."

Captain Nowe retired on June 6, 1988. He still lives in Lunenburg.

ALEC GREEN

Alec Green understands all about enterprise allocation and the need to catch the right fish in the right place at the right time for the right market. He even concedes the need for shore-bound company officials to dictate where and when he fishes in a modern market-driven operation.

But sometimes Green can't help himself. He still longs for the good old "dog-eat-dog world of every man for himself and let's beat the other guy. When you wake up in the morning and say to yourself, 'God, What am I going to do to catch more fish than the other guy today?' Now that was fun. That was a challenge."

Green, a beefy 42-year-old Newfoundlander who has skippered the Lunenburg-based wetfish trawler *Cape Fame* for the past eight years, has never been a slouch at meeting that challenge. In 1981 and 1982, in fact, he skippered his ship to first place in the annual Fishing Productivity Award presented at the Nova Scotia Fisheries Reunion and Exhibition to the captain of the Nova Scotia vessel that brings in the highest catch of groundfish during the year. In 1984, he was runner-up. Back in 1970 and 1972, he was mate aboard the winning crews.

Green's nostalgia for the days when a skipper picked his own crew — "the union has more to do with it now" — decided when and where to fish, and was judged solely on how full his holds were is understandable.

Green learned the fishing trade at a time when that was the way the world worked, but since he became a captain himself in 1972, he's been forced to come to terms not only with rapidly changing technology but also with the new demands and new pressures created by a rapidly changing worldwide fishing industry.

"The best thing about being a captain now," Green says, "is when the fish are running and you're catching the ones you're after. The worst thing is the day when you're supposed to be catching redfish and you haul back your first set and it's full of codfish. What do you do?"

Green learned the ins and the outs of the fishing business back in Parsons Harbor, a small Newfoundland outport 50 miles east of Port aux Basques, where Green was born and where his family have been inshore fishermen for generations.

But young Alec himself came of age at just the time when legendary Newfoundland premier Joey Smallwood was attempting to drag his fellow islanders, kicking and screaming if need be, into the twentieth century. Part of his plan was to resettle those in outports such as Parsons Harbor to larger and more modern communities, and to attract new industries to reduce the province's traditional, almost total dependency on the fishery.

Green was just 16 when he abandoned Newfoundland and — like countless other Newfoundland fishermen before him — headed for Nova Scotia to look for work. Ironically, he ended up boarding briefly with Tom Pittman's widow, Kathleen. "He was a fine boy," she remembers today, "but awful shy. He was always afraid to go down and try and talk his way aboard one of the boats."

In August 1963, he landed a job as a deckhand aboard Earl Demone's *Cape Roseway*, an independently owned vessel that sold its catch to National Sea.

Three years later, he joined Morris Nowe's *Cape Royal* as bosun.

For an ambitious young man who wanted to make his way to the wheelhouse, Green says he couldn't have ended up in better situations than sailing with Earl Demone and Morris Nowe. "They were both good teachers, really good," says Green.

And Green was a good student. "You got to be willing, of course, and you got to take some hard knocks, but if you're with guys like Earl and Morris and you show you're interested, they're going to keep pushing you, telling you what to do, so you can learn too.

"When I was on deck, I wanted to make sure I was better than everyone else. If I was mending twine, I had to do it faster than the next guy. If I was splicing wire, I wanted to do it faster."

In spite of new technology and educational programs designed to train modern skippers, Green remains convinced that "the only fisherman to get as a skipper is someone who starts on deck and works his way up the ranks. Schooling is a good thing — no doubt about that — but I still think you got to experience things up close to really be good at them. There's a lot to deal with out there in the North Atlantic — ice conditions and wind and all sorts of conditions — you can't learn how to be a skipper out of a book."

Like many of his predecessors, Alec Green takes pride in having trained yet another generation of young men, including his own brother Jim, what they need to know to become skippers themselves.

Green is the first to admit that fishing is anything but an easy life. Several years ago, he and his crew rescued a boatload of seven fishermen who'd been forced to abandon their vessel in a snow and wind storm off Labrador. "We were just lucky to find them soon enough," Green says with a sigh. "If they'd been out there much longer, they'd have been dead."

Two days later, his brother even more dramatically rescued another ship that had lost its engine and was drifting helplessly into the rocks in shallow water off Cape Race at the tip of the Avalon Peninsula. "It was so bad that the Coast Guard wouldn't go in to try and get a line to them," Alec Green says. "It was a Fisheries Products boat [from Newfoundland] and the captain called in to tell the company what was happening, and I guess the people in the company figured the boat was gone, the men was gone, everything. Half an hour later, they get a call that everything's okay."

Green's brother Jim — ignoring the dangers to himself, his crew (they'd all agreed to try and rescue the crew of the other ship) and his vessel — had maneuvered in close enough to shore to get a line to the drifting vessel and tow it to safety. "They lost the tow twice before they finally got it on," Bill Morrow explains with admiration today, "and I heard later that people on the shore who were watching this happen were convinced that the crews of both vessels were going to go to hell in this one." For his bravery, Green was awarded the Star of Courage from the governor general.

Despite the ever-present danger, and the realities of the anything-but-by-the-clock life he leads — "If we land on a Friday and Thanksgiving's on Monday, we'll have Thanksgiving Friday so we can be back at sea Sunday" — Green admits he wouldn't have it any other way. "I'm too old to quit now," he jokes, adding, "If I told you I didn't enjoy it, I'd be lying." Both of his sons have spent summers aboard ship with him, and "if they decided to go fishing, you know, it wouldn't bother me a bit. It's a good, honest way to make a living."

JOHN KELLY

There were no jobs to apply for in Marystown, Newfoundland, when John Kelly turned 18 in 1955. So he and a few friends decided — like Alec Green — to head for Nova Scotia to try to find a job in the fishing industry there.

His own father had also spent a good deal of his working life in Nova Scotia, working as a saltbank schooner fisherman for Nova Scotia fishing companies most springs and summers and then coming home to Newfoundland for the late fall. "After Christmas, he'd be gone again, back to Nova Scotia to do some fresh fishing. The thing was," Kelly says, "there was more money to be made up there."

Kelly's first job was in National Sea's Louisbourg fish plant, but he quickly decided he would prefer a life at sea catching fish to a life ashore processing them. He moved to Halifax and worked on a steam trawler for a year before arriving in Lunenburg in 1957 because he had decided, as he explains today, "there was more money on the Lunenburg draggers."

For the next seven years Kelly learned the fish business from the decks up while working aboard Earl Demone's *Cape Roseway*. "Captain Earl was quite the guy," Kelly says today. "I learned it all right there aboard the *Roseway*. She was only a hundred-foot and made of wood, but we took her all over the Grand Banks, every-

John Kelly

where. And [Earl's father] Harry and Earl, they was the finest kind. You could ask them any question and they'd tell you the answer. That's where I learned to fish."

By the end of seven years, however, Kelly had done no better than move up to a job as a "fill-in bosun when they didn't have nobody else." The problem was simply that Demone's vessels were so successful and Demone himself was considered such a good teacher there were few openings available in the wheelhouse. As a result, Kelly switched to National Sea's Lunenburg fleet, where he learned even more under skippers of the skills of Perry Conrad and Morris Nowe before he got his own first command in the mid-1960s.

"Wallace Smith and Doug Pyke, they decided to give me this side dragger called the *Seacap*. I had her three years and I was happy too, but then in 1968 I went home to Newfoundland for a holiday and there was this new Atlantic Fish Company opening up in Marystown. So I decided to apply to be captain of one of their boats just to see what happened. And damned if I didn't get one too."

When National Sea decided to open up its own plant in St. John's four years later in 1972, however, the company's recently hired fleet captain — and Kelly's old boss — Earl Demone showed up to invite him to rejoin the National Sea fishing family.

Today, he captains the *Cape Sambro*, a 172-foot stern trawler based out of St. John's, but spends his shore time back in his hometown of Marystown.

Although he's become one of the Newfoundland fleet's most successful skippers, Kelly still occasionally thinks back with awe and wonder at his predecessors. "Now you take the *Cape Roseway*, she never had half the equipment we got today — no fish finders, no Loran Cs, nothing like that — and they couldn't take her fishing to Hamilton Bank and places like that in the winter because she was wooden. But those guys — they knew how to fish."

For himself, Kelly says he has no plans to retire or take a job ashore. "I only worked ashore once and I never made a dollar at it," he says. "Nothin's come to my mind since that I'd want to do on land."

HENRY KOHLER

In a way Henry Kohler doesn't really belong in this gallery of National Sea's most famous and best skippers. Although he hails from Lunenburg and has spent most of his working life at sea, Kohler has never been a fisherman himself and, in fact, has only worked for the company for less than a decade.[2]

But in another way, Kohler, National Sea's corporate fleet captain, is as responsible as anyone for the deserved reputation of National Sea's current gen-

---

2. Others recall that Kohler did "a short stint" as a scalloper, but was unsuccessful at it and gave it up quickly.

eration of skippers as among the best in the business.

He joined the company in August 1981, just a month after a federal inquiry report into the sinking of the scallop dragger *Margaret Jane* by the National Sea trawler *Cape Beaver* criticized both skippers for errors in judgement and wrongful acts.

Although Kohler admits that the timing of the company's decision to hire him may have been partly the result of the *Cape Beaver* incident, he is quick to add that "the company has always been concerned about those issues." Even during the dramatic downturn in the company's fortunes during the early 1980s, he says, "we never felt the effects of the cutbacks in the way other parts of the company did. They never cut back on safety."

Henry Kohler

In fact, the company's decision to hire Kohler in the summer of 1981 probably had at least as much to do with his availability as it did with the *Beaver* tragedy. After a 32-year career in the international merchant marine, during which he had logged more than 2 million nautical miles, Kohler suddenly found himself without a ship to captain in 1981. For the 24 previous years, he'd been skipper of the *R.V. Vema,* a 202-foot research vessel that ranged the world conducting experiments and collecting data for the Lamont-Doherty Observatory at Columbia University. But in 1981, the ship was decommissioned as part of budget cutting at the university.

While he decided what to do next, Kohler returned home to Lunenburg for the summer. "I had actually decided to take a job in Hong Kong, but the day before I was ready to leave, I dropped in at National Sea to see some friends and it just sort of developed from there." The fleet captain's job had been open since 1978 when Earl Demone was promoted to vice president of fleet, but the appointment had gotten lost in the shuffle after the Nickersons became involved in the company.

Kohler was a natural for the job. For one thing, he'd been born and grew up in Lunenburg, and he knew most of the older Lunenburg-based skippers from childhood. For another, as the captain of the *Vema*, he'd recruited many of his seamen-trainees in Nova Scotia and Newfoundland — "I always felt it was a real asset to have grown up where the sea and ships were a way of life," he explains, adding, "It helps to give a good sailor the right attitude and atmosphere, some things you can't learn in a book" — and many of them had eventually returned home to jobs aboard National Sea vessels.

Kohler's own connections to the sea were at least as good as most fishermen's. His father and his mother's father were both foreign-going ship's masters (the equivalent of today's master mariners) and Henry himself took his own first trip to sea aboard his father's vessel with his mother when he was just six months old. Henry's father — a German-born sea captain who deserted a German ship in Buenos Aries in 1918 and signed on as a deckhand aboard a Lunenburg-based trading vessel in port at the time — started in the business even earlier. He was born at sea.

By the time he left school at 16 to sign aboard a tramp ship out of Halifax, Henry knew his future was going to be on the oceans. But he says he never considered becoming a fisherman. "We came from the other side. Between 1850 and 1920, there was a very big foreign trade out of Lunenburg and that was what my family was involved in. It just seemed natural that I would be too."

Kohler's related but different experiences may give him a unique perspective on the qualities needed to make a good fisherman. "To be successful, I think you have to be born with a fisherman's mentality," he says. "We get many engineers through here looking for work, and they may be very competent engineers, but they often don't make good fishermen. They don't have that mentality. A fisherman is a gambler, a hunter, and he's got to be good at what he does or he's not going to make a living. A lot of our fishermen can trace their family history back three or four generations in the fishing business. They know what it's all about. Whether you're talking about the present-day fishermen with all the modern technology or you're talking about fishing in the days of the dorymen, a fisherman has to be competent, he has to be dedicated, to be a hard worker, to be intelligent and then, in addition to all of that, he still has to have that special something, that mentality, that makes him successful. A good fisherman," Kohler adds, "is going to be a good fisherman in any age. I often find myself reminding our young men of this."

It's just one of many things Kohler reminds his young men about. For Kohler isn't just a world-class seaman, he's also a first-class teacher. "After I became a master, I was able to pick my own people," Kohler recalls, "and since I've always had an interest in training young people, I picked people I could use as protégés."

He laughs. "I worked their asses off. It was hard treatment, but I think they came to appreciate it." In fact, many of the current generation of National Sea's most promising young skippers and mates — including Larry Mossman, the skipper of National Sea's factory freezer trawler *Cape North*, and Chris Morrow, his first mate — got their early training while working as crew members aboard the *Vema* in the late 1970s.

After he joined National Sea in 1981, Kohler spent several months going to sea with ships in the National Sea fleet "just to see what the needs were in order to bring things up to what I would consider modern-day standards in the merchant industry." By the beginning of 1982, Kohler had prepared the company's first official set of standing orders to guide the captains in carrying out their responsibilities at sea — "They're very common in merchant shipping but the fishing industry had grown in such a way that those kinds of things weren't written down before" — and had instituted a series of in-house lectures, courses and exercises to make sure all of his crews knew what to do in the event of a fire at sea, a man overboard and so on. He also made arrangements to send many of his most talented and ambitious young fishermen to the Fisheries Training College in Pictou, Nova Scotia, so they could upgrade their skills. "We are preparing a new generation of younger people to come along and take over," Kohler says, adding proudly that "we're way above what the [Canadian Coast Guard] regulations require of our people. The regulations only say that a mate needs to have a Fishing Master Class 3 license, but we demand that they have a Class 2. And in the last three years, we've trained 15 Class 1 masters. That means they can sail any sized vessel anywhere in the world. When I came here, there was only one known Class 1 master in the whole country."

In the past, he says, it may have been possible for a fisherman to get by on experience and intelligence alone, "but today's vessels are extremely sophisticated and the technology is improving all the time. You've got to keep up or you'll be left behind."

For all that, Kohler retains a non-fisherman's sense of wonder and appreciation for the special talents that can mean the difference between failure and success in a fishing captain.

"I don't presume to tell them how to fish," Kohler is quick to point out. "It would be no trouble for me to take out any of our ships, to operate all the gear and everything, but I probably wouldn't catch enough fish to feed myself. That takes a real fisherman."

Part III
The Rise and Fall of National Sea

10
An Era Ends, An Era Begins

Dear RP,
It is nearly midnight and I have four drinks under my belt, but I am so disturbed that I know it is useless for me to go to bed ...

C. J. MORROW put down the fountain pen, took another sip from his rum[1] and stared at the fine, ragged-edged hotel stationery lying on the highly polished walnut writing-desk in the living room of his hotel suite. He knew what he had to do. He had already rung down to Lawrence, the bell captain, for more paper and ink.

It was the night of April 10, 1953.

"Damn it," he complained to the empty room as he took up the pen and began to write again. "Stan has told me of the management committee's decisions on prices and your ideas of inventories ..."

Morrow, in fact, had had conversations last night and through most of the day today with Stan Lee. Ralph Bell had arranged their meeting, theoretically so that Lee could bring C.J. up to date on some decisions that had been taken at a management meeting while Morrow had been out of town. But the more important reason for the meeting was so that Lee could tell Morrow about some decisions Bell had made. Bell was using Lee as his messenger because he knew Morrow would be angry and Bell didn't want to confront him directly.

Morrow was angry, partly at Bell's refusal to deal with him face-to-face, and partly — and more importantly — because he believed the decisions that Bell had taken in his absence were foolhardy.

Neither the pleasant ambience of the surroundings — Morrow and Lee met

---

1. The fact that he had been drinking at all is an indication of how upset he must have been, suggests his son Bill. "He rarely took a drink in those days and I don't think there was ever even so much as a bottle in the house until sometime during the war years."

over drinks in front of a roaring fire in the living room at the Royal Nova Scotia Yacht Squadron's clubhouse overlooking Halifax harbor — nor Stan Lee's inevitable, "smooth flow of precise language, faultlessly delivered" could hide the fact that Bell himself had been responsible for decisions taken in the management committee's name.[2]

Morrow was convinced, as he put it to Lee, that those decisions would "wreck the company, no question." Essentially, Bell had decided to cut the prices the company paid to fishermen, as well as to order the company's plants to reduce their inventory by selling off their current supplies of fish at distress-sale prices and also to begin producing only a fraction of the average quantity of fish they now sold each month.

At first, Morrow tried to argue with Lee. He called Bell's inventory scheme "impracticable and ridiculous.... It will mean either laying up trawlers at an early date or selling frozen fillets on the American market at any price a buyer will pay, for God's sake."

As for the decision to cut prices to fishermen, "we should look at ourselves first, rather than take it out on the fishermen," Morrow suggested. While the Lunenburg side of the company had a reputation within the organization for always standing up for the interests of the fishermen, perhaps partly because it had been founded by schoonermen, Morrow could also cite practical arguments against inflaming the passions of the fishermen now.

"We are surely inviting government intervention, unions and even communism," he argued.

While that was an argument that might have held some water with Bell, a rabid anti-communist who saw unionization as the first step on the road to Marxist hell, Morrow quickly realized that Lee was not Bell, merely Bell's messenger, and that it was therefore useless to try and convince him of the folly of the boss' ways.

But Morrow had by then become convinced of more than just the folly of Bell's ways. He had also come to the conclusion that it would be impossible for him to stay in the company much longer under Bell. He wasn't alone. "We'd all talked about quitting," remembers Hal Connor. "At one point, C.J. and Ron and me and Andy Cunningham got together and said we can't stand it anymore. Either we have to run the company the way it should be run or we have to get out and start our own company."

It had been just one thing after another, Morrow concluded, almost from the first day National Sea had been formed. He realized that many of the problems

---

2. In fact, other members of the management committee had also opposed the decision, including Ron Smith, who fought it "tooth and nail."

were the inevitable aftermath of six years of war. The need to replace and upgrade the fleet, for example, which had been put on the back burner during the conflict, had now suddenly become a pressing matter. At the same time, the company's newly politicized fishermen and plant workers, many of whom had served overseas and whose personal expectations were on the rise during those early post-war years, began demanding a bigger slice of the earnings pie.

But Morrow also knew that far too many of the company's post-war troubles could be traced directly back to the personality and style of one Ralph Pickard Bell.

For all his skills with a dollar, Bell was a lousy manager of people. "He turned out to be the most difficult man to work with that any of us had ever experienced," Hal Connor remembered many years later. "When he was nice, he was so nice you were prostrated with his generosity and his kindness and his thoughtfulness. But when he was bad, he was terrible. He made people cringe, even cry. I have seen women who worked for him burst into tears. He was given to the most awful rages of anybody I've ever known."

And Bell could as easily turn his anger on an associate as a secretary. On one occasion, for example, he humiliated the scholarly Darryl Laing so badly at a meeting of company executives that Laing resigned as corporate secretary-treasurer in spite of Bell's later apology.

As a brigadier during the war, Laing would tell friends later, he had served under Field Marshall Montgomery. "Monty" could be horribly rude, Laing said, and so could many of the others he'd encountered during the war, but Ralph Bell topped them all.

Bell wasn't just rude, he was often downright eccentric. He would sometimes call Hal Connor at three o'clock in the morning, for example, just to ask him a question about some ship down at the dock. He would never announce himself, never apologize for calling at such an unseemly hour. "Hal," he would begin abruptly, then launch into his question without preamble.

He would also call Doug Pyke, the Lunenburg plant manager, after closing time each night to ask about fish prices, the tonnage of the day's catch, the location of various vessels and so on, but would freely admit to Pyke that he was less interested in the information he got than he was in checking "to see if you were on the job."

When he wasn't haranguing his executives by telephone, Bell was busy firing off stinging memos to his underlings, damning them for this or that, and then distributing the so-called "personal and confidential" memos to others in the office. Bell's almost caricature-like performance as the hard-hearted capitalist boss, in fact, may have been one of the reasons why National Sea workers were among those attracted to the tough-talking Communist-led Canadian Fishermen's Union, which had won bargaining rights for fishermen from the Wartime Labor Board in 1944.

In 1947, that union staged a bitter four-month strike against National Sea and other Nova Scotia fish firms. At one level, it was not an untypical labor dispute. Ostensibly, the main issue in the strike was wages. The fishermen wanted a larger share of the lay — catch — and they wanted their share to be paid out *before* rather than after expenses were taken out. While the company said it was prepared to increase the fishermen's share from 50 to 60 percent of the catch, it refused to calculate that on the gross value of the catch and it also refused to go along with other union demands for improved working conditions aboard ship.

But because the dispute coincided with the beginning of the Cold War, there were almost inevitably larger issues beyond wages involved as well. As *Time* magazine was quick to point out, "Lunenburg [Sea Products Ltd.] and the other owners were not so much concerned with the additional money involved. What concerned them was that the union was run by a Red who seemed to be getting too solid a footing in the industry. They had good reason to fear." The magazine described the CFU's leader, Bert Meade, as a "big, flabby 265-pound" labor boss, who had not only organized the "Red-hued" National Maritime Union in the United States but was also on the executive of Canada's communist party, the Labor Progressives.

In a series of inflammatory publications and radio addresses, Bell played on the same theme. The company even financed a series of pamphlets on communism with titles like *Communism v. Free Enterprise in the Fishing Industry* and *Christianity or Communism: Excerpts from Sermons* by the Reverend W.E. Cholerton, who was described as the pastor of the United Baptist Church in rural Berwick, Nova Scotia.

In one province-wide radio address to fishermen made over Halifax station CBH, Bell was at his rhetorical best. "This strike was the stupidest thing in the world, both for you fellows who did the striking and for the vessel owners," Bell told the fishermen, "because neither would ever win. The only fellows who ever stood to win were the men who promoted the strike."

Two weeks later, after the Nova Scotia Supreme Court ruled that the Wartime Labor Board's recognition of the CFU was invalid because fishermen were really co-adventurers who shared in the risks and rewards of each fishing trip instead of actual employees of the company, Bell invited the fishermen to return to their jobs — without their union, of course — and decreed that the captain of the vessel would continue to have the right to choose his own crew and to dictate the sailing schedule.

Although the company had clearly won the strike, it was a costly victory. The strike had cut production by 40 million pounds and reduced sales by $3.5 million. To make matters worse, the fishery recorded its poorest catch of herring in 40 years that season. For most of the next five years after that, in fact, very little seemed to go right for the company.

The company began construction of a new fish plant in Louisbourg but it was plagued by start-up problems and suffered heavy operating losses.

The federal government set the Canadian dollar free to float in the money markets and it increased in value against the U.S. dollar, making Canadian fish difficult to sell profitably there. At the same time, European fish producers, whose currencies were weaker, began grabbing a larger share of a total American fish market that was actually shrinking because meat prices were now so depressed they had become more competitive with fish.

Then in 1951 the annual ice harvest failed because of unusually mild weather and the company was forced to import ice while laying out even more money to finally build its own new ice-making facilities. Bell's response to this series of reverses had been conditioned by his experiences in the 1930s. His credo was to constantly prepare for a new depression by always keeping inventories low. That had become one of many serious points of disagreement between Bell and Morrow, who had replaced Laing as secretary-treasurer of the company. Certain fish species are seasonal, Morrow would attempt to explain to Bell, so you need to have an inventory of those fish available to regulate the market. But Bell wasn't having any of it. Summing up the differences between the two men years later, Bill Morrow would say simply: "Dad was an optimist and Ralph Bell was a pessimist."

But on the night of April 10, it was Morrow who seemed the pessimist. "The way I am feeling right now," Morrow wrote in his letter to Bell, "I would like to sell my shares in NSP at a low price." Morrow's letter produced a quick response. Bell telephoned to arrange for the two of them to meet the next week in Toronto. Although he was friendly enough — "C.J., I genuinely welcome your frank and vigorous letter because I like straight, forthright talk, no matter how critical it may be" — Bell also gave no hint of what he intended to do.

When they finally did get together over a roast-beef dinner in the Victoria Room of Toronto's luxurious King Edward Hotel, Bell began by mildly rebuking Morrow for shirking his responsibility to challenge Bell's excesses. Bell said that he'd seen Morrow as his own logical successor at one point, but because of his disappointment in Morrow's too pliant approach and his failure to become embroiled in what Bell regarded as the requisite infighting, "I continued [as president], perhaps beyond my period of maximum usefulness to the company," Bell explained. "It may well be that a complete reshuffling at this time is just what the company needs most."

But the reshuffling Bell had in mind was not what Morrow expected. Bell, it turned out, was prepared to sell his interest in the company to Morrow and get out of the day-to-day operations entirely. The deal that Bell offered was simple enough. Bell would sell his family's shares to Morrow and give him the option to buy the remaining shares when he died. In return, Bell wanted to keep his salary, car, chauffeur, secretary and office for five years, and then to continue at two-thirds salary for the rest of his life as well as remain a director of the company and an ex-officio member of both the management and the executive committee.

In spite of those demands, Bell pledged not to participate in the active management of the company or to vote against Morrow at the director's level. "I can assure you that while you will always have my frank and vigorous opinion on any question that is up for discussion," Bell explained in a letter the following day confirming the deal, "you can also count on my wholehearted support so long as I remain actively associated with the company."

Bell was quick to point out that the deal he was suggesting was not so much a share sale as a mutually agreed upon "management change. I'll make sure," Bell added quickly, "that the price [of the shares] can be arranged."

But Bell wasn't through being difficult yet. Not only did he later turn down Morrow's seemingly reasonable request for an extra 15 days — until June 15, 1953 — to arrange financing, but he also asked for $18 for each share, a full two dollars more than Morrow believed they were worth. (In the end, after a good deal of discussion, they settled on Morrow's lower figure.[3])

And Bell's promise to help arrange financing didn't pan out either. Bell arranged for Morrow and Stan Lee to meet with officials of the Bank of Nova Scotia in Toronto to arrange a loan. The year before, Bell, miffed at not being named a director of the Royal Bank, moved the company's accounts to the Bank of Nova Scotia, which quickly installed him as a director. Despite that connection, Morrow remembers, "the president raved on about Ralph selling out, how he shouldn't be selling out. Finally, the president asked us how much we needed, and I said, 'Two-point-one million,' and he says, 'Well, suppose we put up a million and you fellows put up a million?' And I said, 'Well, I don't think we can raise a million, but we'll think about it.'"

As he had on many occasions in the past, Morrow turned to his old friends at the Royal Bank. "We got on an airplane that afternoon to Montreal and went

---

3. The company incorporated a holding company, Ocean Fisheries Ltd., to hold the common shares of National Sea during the transfer. In the end, it acquired 133,375 shares from the Bell family, 86,000 from Morrow and 30,000 from the public at a total cost of $4 million.

downtown to see [Bank President] Jimmy Muir. Jimmy said, 'You're going to buy Ralph out. That's great. Just great.' I told him what we needed and he said, 'Morrow, you go home, write your cheque for $2.1 million, and we'll talk about how we'll handle it afterwards.' We weren't there 15 minutes."

Morrow was able to return the favor a short time later when, as the first order of business for the new board, Morrow introduced a motion to return the company's accounts to the Royal Bank.

Ralph Bell's pivotal role in the east coast fishery was finally at an end. Although he later regretted his decision to sell out and even told friends that it was the "only time he cried," Bell kept his word not to interfere in the business. When National Sea opened its huge modern processing plant in Lunenburg in 1964, Bell was invited to the ceremony but didn't attend. Morrow took the occasion to praise him warmly as a "great Canadian," and Bell, in turn, later sent Morrow a personal thank you.

Bell died in 1975.

11
Expansion and Consolidation

THE company that finally emerged from the turmoil of the Ralph Bell years was not the one-big-fish company that Bell had imagined creating back in the 1940s. Instead, it was a collection of small, quasi-independent local fish companies called divisions, each producing its own products under its own label and selling them in its own way through its own distributor to its own customers, and then reporting independently to a head office that was still really more of a corporate clearing house than a head office in the conventionally accepted overall management sense.

Rivalry was evident at every level. Even the company's fishermen, recalls director Hal Connor, saw themselves more as competitors than colleagues. "If a Lunenburg skipper found some fish, he certainly wasn't going to let any of the Halifax ones know about it."

The company's cumbersome corporate structure only seemed to exacerbate the problems. To begin with, there was Ocean Fisheries Ltd., the parent holding company that had been created at the time of the Bell buyout. Its operating arm was National Sea Products Ltd., the company that had originally been set up in 1945 to bring together the Smith and Maritime National interests into one company. National Sea, in turn, controlled eight more subsidiary companies, including its own original Lunenburg Sea Products Ltd., D.H. Hatton and Company and other more recent acquisitions.

During the decade after the Bell buyout, the company bought up a number of other fish companies in Atlantic Canada and the United States, making its intra-corporate relationships even more complicated and unwieldy.

"We were in a real mess of overlapping and duplication," recalls Ian Langlands, now a vice president of the company, who began his career at National Sea in the late 1950s with a consulting firm and worked at several divisions. "At one point," he says with some amazement, "we had five different sizes of five-pound packages."

The result was that by 1960, the company's many and various divisions were selling dozens of different fish products under at least eight different brand names. Lunenburg Sea Products Ltd. for example, sold its under the brand name "High Liner," the Louisbourg Division under "Ten Knot," the Sea Seald Division under "Sea Seald," the Lockeport Company Division under "Seacap," Leonard Brothers under "Isle Royale," the 40-Fathom Division under "40-Fathom" and Eagle Fisheries under "Eagle Brand." Often, that meant that National Sea Products would be marketing essentially the same product under two or three different labels, each one competing with the others for the loyalty of what was by then, no doubt, a thoroughly confused customer.

C.J. Morrow's formidable task as the president of the post-Bell company was to attempt to bring those sometimes warring factions together into one strong, united company at the same time that he expanded the company still further by acquiring even more companies with even more brands in order to meet the constantly changing needs and desires of an ever-evolving and ever-growing marketplace. For the most part, Morrow focused his personal attention on corporate acquisition and expansion — the *sine qua non* of the company's goal to become number one in its field — and left to others the details of how best to meld all of those companies he had acquired into a single homogeneous whole.

Morrow, of course, was only one of several key executives in the reorganized company. The two other most important ones were Wallace Smith, one of Morrow's partners in the original railroad-track triumvirate, and Ronald Smith, the son of an original shareholder, Captain Joseph Smith. Ronald had been lured to W.C. Smith and Company from a job at the Royal Bank in 1928, and had quickly become an important member of its management team. Ultimately, he also became Billy Smith's replacement in the railroad-track triumvirate after Smith retired to the west coast in the early 1940s.[1]

While Ronald oversaw the multifaceted sales side of the operations and Wallace looked after the company's growing fleet of ships and the development of its various physical-plant facilities, Morrow — with his instinctive ability to spot a business opportunity — provided both the financial smarts and the corporate vision that was to spark the company's phenomenal growth in the 1950s and 1960s.

---

1. The other officers of the company included Brigadier H.V.D. Laing, who served as a vice president until his death in 1958, and Andy Cunningham, who became a member of the board of directors and a vice president in charge of by-products. Stan Lee continued as general manager and company secretary until his death in 1961. Hal Connor, who had abandoned a potential career as a lawyer — "The fish business was just so interesting, so different, what with people at sea and plants in out-of-the-way places and the whole aspect of marketing the product all rolled into one operation that I just could never see any other career as possibly being as interesting as the fish business" — came to work with the company as a key director.

"During the decade or so after Bell left, we must have added 30 different companies through mergers, absorptions, buyouts, etc.," recalls Hal Connor. "C.J. was a real acquisitions expert, and it was as a result of all those acquisitions that we really became the largest integrated company."

"Dad got more prominence [than Wallace and Ron Smith]," says Morrow's son, Bill, who joined the company in 1949 and was part of the management team during most of the time his father and the Smiths ran the company, "because he was the one who was more in the public eye and because he was perhaps a little more forward looking than the other two, but they really complemented one another in terms of their management style.

"Dad wasn't interested in plants, but that was Wallace's strong suit," adds Morrow. "Ronald liked sales and he had the kind of strong personality the company needed to do what had to be done there to bring that end of the business under better control. Dad's biggest contribution was in being able to recognize the changes that were taking place inside and outside of the fish business, and figure out how to respond to help the company take advantage of those changes in order to grow."

Those changes, especially outside the fish business, had been rapid and dramatic. During the 1950s North American society had to try to come to terms with the incredible social, economic and technological revolution that followed the end of World War II.

For starters, television arrived on the scene as a new and powerful mass medium. Television made it possible for someone with something to sell to reach millions of potential customers instantly with their advertising message. As a result, television advertising became the most important and effective tool with which to influence the buying and eating habits of an entire generation.

At about the same time, the supermarket emerged suddenly and from nowhere to become one of the most significant retailing phenomena of the twentieth century. Representing far more than simply a change in the way goods were sold, the supermarket became both a symptom and a cause of what was a revolution in the way society organized itself.

The supermarket catered to a more mobile, modern lifestyle, and that encouraged the development of more and larger suburban communities. The always-on-the-go families that were one of the consequences of the suburbanization of North America then created a demand for more convenient foods to suit their lifestyle. And that, in turn, opened up opportunities for companies like National Sea to create and market new frozen convenience foods to satisfy the demand.

Although it's difficult now for most of us to even imagine a world without supermarkets and huge frozen-food sections offering consumers everything from plain vegetables to specialty breads to exotic desserts and even complete gourmet meals, the simple truth is that, for all practical purposes, frozen convenience foods didn't even exist in Canada until the mid-1950s. Neither did the home freezers that made those foods practical for the average consumer.

Clarence Birdseye, an American scientist-businessman whose name pops up regularly in any history of the twentieth-century food industry, was the first to discover the potential of quick-freezing fish during the 1920s. His experiments led the huge General Foods Corporation to begin selling the first commercially prepared frozen foods in the United States in the early 1930s.

One of Birdseye's disciples, William Heeney, became the first person to market frozen foods — raspberries and strawberries — in Canada on an experimental basis in 1933. At first, Heeney recalls, retailers and consumers were skeptical of the process that Birdseye somewhat ominously referred to as "arresting life's processes." In his 1984 history of the frozen-food business in Canada, *Fresher than Fresh,* Heeney recalls that the label on his first frozen-food packages even had to contain a statement declaring that the contents had been packed under the supervision of the federal department of agriculture's Central Experimental Farm. The reason, Heeney explained, was that "there was a strong prejudice against frozen foods because of the fear that they were poisonous."

That prejudice persisted even after World War II. Earl Foster can still vividly remember the lengths to which he had to go to convince retailers and consumers that frozen convenience foods were actually palatable alternatives to fresh or canned products. Foster, who joined National Sea as a salesman in the late 1950s and eventually became its national sales manager, began his career in the late 1940s as a sales rep for a London, Ontario, frozen-food distributor.

One of his duties, he explains now, was to entice reluctant potential customers to simply sample his frozen-food products. He'd mix up a thermos of frozen orange juice to take with him on all his sales calls, he says, and then offer free samples to each grocer he called on. He also regularly visited all of the church groups in his community, offering to provide each of them with a free lunch for their members after their next regular meeting. The lunch, of course, would include frozen orange juice and a dessert of ice cream topped with frozen fruit. It was, he says, "an effective way to get the message out" about frozen foods. But getting the message out was a slow and painful process. And it was made all the slower because of the lack of facilities for storing and displaying frozen foods.

In the days before the emergence of supermarket frozen-food display cases and home freezers, consumers had to rent space in local "locker plants" —

frozen-food warehouses with individual cubicles — in order to store their sides of beef or other frozen products. Because most retailers only had small ice-cream-style freezers in their stores, early frozen-food producers also usually ended up renting their storage space in those local locker plants too. Given that, it only seemed logical to hire the locker-plant operator to distribute them as well.

That's how Earl Foster initially became involved with National Sea and its High Liner brand. Foster, whose employer operated the London locker plant, says selling frozen foods wasn't very sophisticated in those early days. "Each morning we'd load up this half-ton insulated truck with a bunch of different frozen foods — Minute Maid Orange Juice, Aylmer frozen peas, Downeyflake frozen waffles, Swift's frozen pie products — and take them around to all the local grocery stores," he explains. "Each individual store's order would be so small that they would buy their whole order for cash. There was no credit. You'd go in and fill up this little ice-cream-type freezer and then go to the cash register to get your money." In 1955, Foster's employer added High Liner frozen fish sticks to the list of the products he would peddle store-to-store.

Fish sticks, the first frozen convenience seafood, were an instant hit with American consumers when they were introduced there in the early 1950s, partly because they were boneless and easy to prepare, but also — and perhaps more importantly — because they didn't taste like fish. That made them a tasty alternative dish for those who didn't like eating fish on what was then still observed by Roman Catholics and others as "meatless" Fridays.[2]

Quickly recognizing the sales potential of this new product, National Sea officials began producing and marketing its own line of fish sticks in 1953. To help sell them, National Sea also became one of the first major Canadian food companies to put the new mass medium of television to use as a marketing tool. National Sea even sponsored a television program called *Meet the Millers*, which was shown on a Buffalo, New York, channel that Canadian viewers in the critically important southern Ontario market could watch even before the first Canadian stations began broadcasting.

The heirs of W.C. Smith, who had once been so fearful of change that they waited more than a decade before following other companies into the fresh-fish

---

2. The conventional wisdom is that the fishing industry had been artificially propped up for years by the Roman Catholic Church's ban on eating meat on Fridays. "In the old days," agrees Earl Foster, "people ate fish for two reasons: 1) because it was cheap, and 2) because of meatless Fridays. When the Pope pulled the rug out from under us in 1968 [by lifting the ban on eating meat on Fridays], we had to really learn how to sell fish." Although there was a brief fall-off in fish consumption after 1968, which Bill Morrow attributes to the fact that the supermarkets accepted the conventional wisdom that people wouldn't buy fish if they didn't have to and therefore stocked less of it, the company quickly regained its market share by the early 1970s.

business, suddenly became market leaders, setting rather than keeping the pace.

In addition to National Sea's early involvement in television advertising, for example, the company also began experimenting by creating and marketing other prepared frozen-seafood dishes as well. During the 1950s, the company introduced frozen haddock with cheese sauce, a precursor of its current "Light Tonight" entrées, fish fritters, an early version of fish nuggets that turned out to be slightly ahead of its time, and fish and chips, a seafood standby that seemed especially suited to the frozen-convenience-food market.

Fish and chips, which the company began marketing in 1958, not only became popular as a complete dinner-in-a-dish but it also spawned a demand for the company's "hand-dipped" haddock-in-batter, even without the accompanying french fries. Since the battered fish really was hand-dipped and the haddock fresh, it very quickly became another best seller for National Sea after the company decided to market it as a separate product in 1960.

But ironically, the very success of haddock-in-batter led to a crisis for National Sea that eventually pointed up both the company's growing marketing strength and also its fundamental production weakness.

The production weakness was the reality that National Sea was dependent on a sometimes fickle Mother Nature to supply its raw material. Haddock-in-batter's popularity, for example, quickly led to a scarcity of fresh haddock, and that forced the company to switch from haddock, first to cod cut from frozen blocks and then eventually to a newly named species of fish known as Boston Bluefish.

That creation of Boston Bluefish, on the other hand, demonstrated a growing marketing savvy within the company. In reality, Boston Bluefish is just the lowly pollock masquerading under a more attractive — and marketable — name. During the fifties and sixties, pollock was one of the cheapest and most plentiful species of fish available in Canada. Perhaps not surprisingly, its very cheapness and easy availability gave it a reputation as a "poor man's fish dish," and that made it difficult to sell to the middle-class consumers who were the primary buyers of frozen convenience foods.

Recognizing that, National Sea lobbied the Canadian government for a name change to Boston Bluefish, a name the company's marketing specialists believed would seem more attractive to suburban shoppers.[3] They were right. The first test order of 1,800 dozen packages of frozen pollock fillets masquerading as Boston Bluefish — packaged under the Sea Seald label and selling for 29 cents a pound — sold out almost as soon as they arrived on A&P supermarket shelves. By the mid-sixties, Boston Bluefish was being sold successfully in Canadian

---
3. The name was approved for use in Canada, but not in the United States.

supermarkets in everything from fish sticks to battered fish.

But the successful transformation of pollock into Boston Bluefish was only one sign of National Sea's increasingly sophisticated marketing savvy. At about the same time, for instance, the company also introduced brightly color-coded packaging to identify all of its products by fish species. The packaging worked, remembers Earl Foster, who by then had joined the National Sea sales staff. "Frozen food is an impulse buy," Foster notes, "and the packaging just jumped right out at you."

To satisfy the growing consumer demand that his sales team was busy creating, C.J. Morrow launched the company on an aggressive program of growth by strategic acquisition. Morrow was adept at finding companies that would help advance National Sea's ongoing marketing plans or that would provide it with new sales opportunities.

In 1957, for example, Morrow bought the Rockland, Maine, operations of General Foods Ltd. — a filleting plant, ship-repair yard and nine trawlers — and then, two years later, added a new breading line so the company could compete more effectively in the U.S. ready-to-fry market. In the early 1960s, he added a shrimp plant to the company's fish-processing operations after noticing that shrimp consumption was increasing in the U.S. and Canada.

The acquisition of the shrimp plant also showed Morrow at his deal-making best. Salada Foods, the Canadian food conglomerate, had become involved in a Tampa, Florida-based shrimp company known as Shoreline Seafoods. For Salada, the shrimp plant was really only an incidental sideline to its primary Florida interests, which were in orange-juice production. Since Shoreline wasn't doing very well at the time anyway, Salada was more than willing to listen to Morrow's proposal, even though it didn't involve any monetary outlay by National Sea. In a move that was later to prove — coincidentally — pivotal in preventing a takeover of National Sea by a U.S. firm, Morrow acquired Shoreline from Salada for about 10 percent of NatSea's stock instead of for cash.

Even as he pushed boldly into the United States, Morrow was careful to continue to take care of his home turf too. During the late 1950s and early 1960s, National Sea solidified its dominance of the Maritime industry by acquiring a number of small but geographically and strategically important east coast fishing operations.

In 1958, for example, it took over the Louisbourg, Nova Scotia, operations of Gloucester, Massachusetts-based Gorton Pew Fisheries Ltd. Gorton Pew, which boasted a fleet of three trawlers, had previously shared the operation of the Louisbourg processing plant with National Sea. Shortly after it became sole owner of the operation, National Sea announced plans for a major expansion of the facilities there.

EXPANSION AND CONSOLIDATION 131

During that same year, National Sea bought up A.R. Loggie Ltd., which not only operated two New Brunswick plants at Loggieville and Shippegan, but which also owned the only continuous fish fryer in eastern Canada. The acquisition of that fryer — which was much more efficient and predictable than the batch fryers National Sea was then using at its Lunenburg plant — enabled National Sea to begin mass marketing its own line of frozen fish and chips that year.

But Morrow wasn't interested in just buying plants or equipment, he was interested in finding the right people for the right positions to fit his expansion plans for National Sea. One of the other reasons he bought the Loggie operations, for example, was to get the services of Jack Estey, its progressive, dynamic young manager. Morrow's son Jim, who says there was "a charisma" about Estey, remembers that "Dad wanted to make sure Jack Estey was on side so he gave him a good salary and position."

During the final years of his presidency, in fact, Morrow seemed to be very carefully putting into place a new generation of people — besides Estey, there was Ron Smith, sons Bill and Jim, and treasurer Charles MacFadden — ships — between 1957 and 1964, the company launched an average of more than two new trawlers each year — and plants — including the world's most modern fish-processing plant — that would guarantee that the company he had helped transform from a small local ship's chandlering firm into a major international, vertically integrated fishing company would not only survive but prosper for the long term.

"C.J. was a born leader," recalls Hal Connor today. "But he was also very democratic. He had a management that knew the business from the ground up and he was willing to listen to them. If you made your argument carefully enough and logically enough, he was the kind of man who — unlike Ralph Bell — could be persuaded to go along with your suggestion, and even sometimes to change his mind."

*C.J. Morrow, President,
National Sea Products Ltd., 1953-1965*

Although the impact of many of the changes he helped bring about at

National Sea would not really become apparent to outsiders until many years later, there was very little question among those involved in the business, even at the time of his retirement in 1965, that C.J. Morrow would ultimately be regarded as the single most important figure in the development of the modern Atlantic Canadian fishing industry.

By then, National Sea had become an international company with 3,500 employees, 38 of its own trawlers and another six on the drawing board, a new Lunenburg facility that was touted as the world's largest and most modern fish-processing plant, a network of nine other, smaller processing plants all over eastern Canada, Maine and Florida, U.S. marketing offices in Boston and New York, its own wholesale-distribution companies in Montreal and Toronto and, perhaps most important, a recognizable brand name that had become synonymous with high-quality fish and fish products.

Little wonder then that Morrow was able to write with some satisfaction in his final report to shareholders as president in 1964: "Your company is in an excellent position to participate in [the] growing food market and has faith in the potential for increased profits for the immediate and long term future."

It was as much a statement as it was a challenge to the next generation.

12
Transition — 1960-1969

ALTHOUGH Bill and Jim Morrow are brothers, and although they would eventually come to shape and dominate National Sea Products Ltd. as it developed into one of the world's largest international fish companies during the sixties and seventies, their personalities couldn't be more dissimilar.

Bill Morrow is a salesman's salesman who exudes a laid-back charm and sincerity that, according to friends and colleagues alike, is really as sincere as it is charming. Whenever the company has needed to put its best corporate foot forward — such as when Dominion Stores, its largest retail customer, threatened to stop carrying High Liner products because rival Sobeys stores had acquired a large block of National Sea stock — Bill Morrow was everyone's first choice to serve as the corporate front man.

Jim Morrow, on the other hand, is a blunt-talking, no-nonsense engineer who calls them as he sees them, damn the consequences. When the company has needed to get things done in a hurry — such as when it needed to have its Shippegan, New Brunswick, plant rebuilt quickly in the middle of winter after it had been destroyed by fire, and it didn't have time to fiddle over the details of paperwork and the niceties of competitive bidding — it has invariably turned to Jim Morrow as the man to get the job done and done right.

Bill Morrow will tell you today that he never actually had to make a conscious decision to get into the fish business. "I never thought about it until I got close to leaving university, and then I just went into it," he explains simply. "I guess I was just attracted to it naturally."

Jim Morrow, on the other hand, will tell you that he made a conscious, deliberate decision *not* to join the family fish business after earning his engineering degree at Nova Scotia Technical College[1] in 1950. "I didn't really ask about

---
1. Now the Technical University of Nova Scotia.

[joining the company] at the time," he allows, "but I knew that most of the company presidents through the years had come from the marketing side rather than the engineering side, and besides, the company already had an engineer [Uncle Wallace Smith] in its executive ranks at the time, so it didn't look like it would need another one for a while."

About the only obvious traits the Morrow brothers share are an unspoken commitment to the company their father, uncles and grandfather built, and an almost inbred passion for the fishing industry. Even though he didn't join the company immediately, Jim Morrow himself is quick to make the point that "I obviously had an interest in the fishing business because the first job I took after graduation was as engineering consultant to the Fisheries Research Board."

Their interest in the fish business should come as no surprise. "Growing up in Lunenburg," Bill Morrow allows with a laugh, "there wasn't much else to think about." Moreover, Jim, who was born in May 1926, and Bill, born 19 months later, in December 1927, both grew up with what must have sometimes seemed like another "baby" in the family — Lunenburg Sea Products Ltd., the company their father and uncles had conceived and created in 1926. By the time they were teenagers in the 1940s, Lunenburg Sea Products was already the town's largest and most important employer.

Although the boys attended high school at Rothesay Collegiate, a private school in New Brunswick, "because it offered a better sports program than you could get locally," both Bill and Jim spent their summer vacations working in the family fish business.

Bill was just 13 when he landed a summer job in the company's outfitting and retailing store. By the summer of his sixteenth birthday, he was in the saltfish plant, unloading salt steamers as they arrived back from the Grand Banks, scrubbing and drying fish in the plant and then loading up the vessels with the supplies of salt they would need for their next fishing trip.

Although he only worked for a few summers at the production level, Bill Morrow, even as chairman of the board, still retains an unusual affinity for the company's fishermen and plant workers. "Bill Morrow is one of the few executives in high places in this business who really knows the fishermen and plant workers," according to Henry Kohler, National Sea's current corporate fleet captain. "I watch him when he comes down here to Lunenburg. He sees the older fishermen — the young ones too — and he'll stop and talk. He speaks the language. He understands where they come from and what they do."

The only summer job Morrow ever had that was outside the fishing business also involved the sea. In the summer of 1945, he signed on as a steward aboard the *Lady Nelson*, a hospital ship that was bringing home the wounded from

England after World War II. What does he remember? "I remember arriving back in Halifax in August 1945, and seeing this headline in the newspaper announcing the creation of National Sea. When I was walking up from the pier past the Nova Scotian Hotel, I saw my father's car and went inside to find out what was happening."

Four years later, armed with a freshly minted commerce degree from Dalhousie University in Halifax, Morrow finally joined the company on a full-time basis and was immediately dispatched on a modified but nonetheless required version of Ralph Bell's "School of Hard Knocks" introduction to the fish business.

Because he'd already put in his share of hours aboard trawlers and in the plants cutting fish and working in the freezers, young Morrow was sent first to Toronto and Ottawa to work in the company's wholesale operations, and then to Boston, New York and Kansas City, where he spent several months working with the company's largest U.S. wholesale customers. After that bit of on-the-job seasoning, he was brought back to Canada and assigned to become assistant to the sales manager at the company's Sea Seald Division in Halifax. Bell decided on Sea Seald because he didn't believe it was a good idea for Morrow to work in his hometown.

After Bell sold out, however, Morrow was soon in Lunenburg as Doug Pyke's assistant, with special responsibilities for sales and production planning. Recalls Pyke: "It was obvious that Bill had abilities and he was going to play an important part in the company in the future, so C.J. asked me to take him on in Lunenburg and keep an eye on him." He laughs. "The only real advice I gave Bill was when we had a little talk the first day he came in to work. My office was in what's now the Fisheries Museum in Lunenburg, and there was a window looking out toward the breakwater. I told Bill to take a look out that window and see the fishing boats coming into the harbor. I said to him, 'Now, you always remember that it's the fishermen coming in through that breakwater with their fish that puts the ass in your pants. And that's the only piece of advice I gave Bill."

Morrow clearly didn't need much advice. An easy-going, natural salesman who was as good at charming his superiors as he was at winning those who worked beneath him, he became a member of the company's board of directors by 1956, general sales manager by 1960, and vice president of sales by 1963.

In that last job, Morrow says his mandate was clear: he was to make the company's High Liner brand as synonymous with fish as Campbell is with soup.

The first hurdle was to make High Liner *the* company brand. Despite the best efforts of head office, there was still intense rivalry among the company's various divisions, and many managers vociferously fought the notion of ever giving up their individual brands.

Although Morrow used a combination of personal charm, family position and executive power to slowly winnow down the number of labels under the corporate umbrella, his most potent weapon was simply the continuing success of the Lunenburg division's High Liner label in the marketplace.

For that, Morrow could thank his old boss, Doug Pyke. Pyke was, in the words of one associate, "a demon when it came to quality. If the product wasn't up to snuff, you heard about it in no uncertain terms." That meant Lunenburg Division's products were always top quality. And innovative as well.

Thanks to Pyke's willingness to try new things, Lunenburg became the first National Sea division to produce cooked fish products, for example. "At the time," Pyke says with a laugh today, "a lot of people in the company were saying, 'Boy that crazy Pyke. He wants to sell warmed-up fish.'"

Lunenburg Division also was the division to introduce fish sticks in the Canadian market. Fish sticks, however, were clearly a retail product, requiring not only a national marketing and sales force to convince supermarkets to stock them but also consumer advertising and promotional support to convince shoppers to buy them. Pyke willingly agreed to make those kind of down-the-road investments in spite of the fact that, at the time, each National Sea corporate division was regarded as a separate profit centre, and each manager was judged solely on his own division's financial results each year.

"Without Doug Pyke's vision," Bill Morrow says today, "the whole thing just wouldn't have come together. While the other managers were always looking at this month's profits, Doug understood that you had to spend money to make money. Some of the calls he made moneywise, well, I just know that those wouldn't have been the calls some of the other division managers at the time would have made."

For Pyke, there was never any question that High Liner should become *the* National Sea brand. "It had the widest distribution and the best reputation," boasts Pyke, "and we always thought it was the best, so, of course, it should be *the* label."

Not everyone agreed.

Hal Connor, for one, favored Sea Seald, the company's second best-selling brand and a label that had been associated with his father's company, Maritime National. "I could never figure out what the name High Liner would mean to the consumer," Connor says today. "Sea Seald, on the other hand, seemed to me to smack of the sea and of freshness. But I knew that we needed to get it down to one brand and I knew that Bill favored High Liner, so we brought in consultants and I remember one day talking to one of the consultants about the name High Liner and what it meant, and he said: 'Mr. Connor, High Liner means high on the line, top of the line. It doesn't mean fish. You could use it to sell engines or automobiles or anything. All it means is that it's the best.' And that seemed to make very good sense to me." Shortly after that, the board formally agreed to adopt High Liner as its flagship consumer label.

But convincing the company to select High Liner was only the first step in selling the label. Bill Morrow decided the time had come for the company to establish its own sales force to promote High Liner instead of relying so heavily on outside brokers to peddle the company's products to the then-emerging supermarket chains that Morrow realized would be the key to the company's long-term sales success.

In the beginning, Morrow personally directed and led the company's internal sales force in its long and often frustrating assault on the supermarket shelves. "Bill Morrow himself often spent a month or two in Toronto, just calling on grocery stores and selling fish sticks," marvels Earl Foster, then an Ontario-based sales representative. Morrow's personal involvement was critical to the ultimate success of the effort, adds Foster, "because of his very sincere personality and his background as a member of one of the biggest fish families of the east."

Morrow remembers those days now with a mixture of nostalgia and pain. "We detailed every store and every chain in Toronto and we set out to talk to every one of them. But it was a huge job. I'd go home at night after a day of pounding the streets and I could hardly move I was so tired."

In the end, however, it was Don Merchant's broken leg rather than Bill Morrow's sore feet that won the company its first breakthrough spot on a supermarket shelf. Merchant,[2] a hot-shot marketing whiz who had worked for Peak Freen before Doug Pyke lured him to National Sea as national sales manager, had been calling on Power Supermarkets, a major Ontario chain, for close to a year with absolutely no success. But when Merchant arrived one morning to make his regular sales call with his leg in a cast from an accident, Power buyer Harry Guest finally relented. "If anyone wants business that badly," he joked, "we'll give it to them."

But the most important supermarket chain in Canada at the beginning of the 1960s — and the one National Sea needed to gain entry to if it was to achieve its

---

2. Despite Merchant's very real contribution to the development of the company's national-sales operation, Bill Morrow eventually was forced to fire Merchant because, as Morrow puts it today, "Don was too much of a loner. The business became too big for one man, and we had a whole bunch of good young up-and-coming salespeople behind Don, but these trained people were all leaving because they couldn't work with Don any longer. It got to the point where we simply had to do something."

goal of becoming the Campbell Soup of the fish business — was Dominion Stores. There, U.S.-based Booth Fisheries still dominated the fish space in the chain's frozen-food section, with National Sea's sales restricted to just its fish sticks and fish-and-chips products.

But then, in 1960, the supermarket launched a major television promotion called *Domino TV Bingo*. The game was a takeoff on conventional bingo in which grocery-store products instead of numbers were found "under the I." Food producers, of course, paid to have their products included in the game. That not only gave their products national television exposure but it also — and more importantly from the supermarket's point of view — helped cover the cost of the promotion.

Although it cost National Sea $94,000 to take part in the TV Bingo promotion — "In relative terms, the company's investment would represent millions today," allows Ian Langlands. "It was the biggest chunk of change we'd spent up to then [on marketing]." — Morrow and other company executives, including Doug Pyke, decided the potential benefits to be derived from being seen assisting with the Dominion Stores promotion outweighed the economic risks involved. They were right. Their calculated gamble paid off handsomely within a few months when Dominion added eight of National Sea's frozen-fish lines to its supermarket shelves nationally. By 1966, National Sea's High Liner products had almost totally replaced Booth products and took up 90 percent of the space devoted to frozen seafood on Dominion's shelves.

Domino TV Bingo helped convince even some of National Sea's more skeptical executives of the importance of modern marketing as a way of getting its message across to potential customers. That didn't mean, of course, that it was smooth sailing for the marketing side after the success of the television bingo promotion. In 1965, National Sea hired a New York firm, Dixon and Parcels, to redesign the staid High Liner logo to give it a more contemporary image. When the designers came up with a large stylized fish, however, C.J. Morrow dismissed it out of hand. To convince him that the logo would be effective, Bill Morrow and Doug Pyke had half a dozen packages made up with the logo on it and took them into C.J. Recalls Pyke: "We lined them up one on top of the other and said, 'This is the way they'll look in the showcase.' He changed his mind after that."

The company finally introduced the redesigned logo with a splashy saturation advertising campaign that made clear its commitment to modern selling techniques. The campaign not only included a series of "eight-second IDs" on network television but also four-color advertisements in Canadian weekend magazines and even a 50-foot-high sign in full color on top of the White's Fish

Company Division overlooking the Gardiner Expressway in Toronto.

"The company," says Earl Foster, "wasn't afraid to invest in order to develop sales." In 1967, National Sea took a booth at the Expo '67 World's Fair in Montreal, partly as a high-profile way of launching its new line of individually wrapped, boned fillets. Although that effort — which used an impressive high-tech video terminal and display program — paid off directly when the fillets quickly became one of the company's most popular products, the indirect benefits may have been even more important, according to Foster.

Having a booth at the fair, he points out, meant that the company was entitled to tickets to the fair's VIP lounge. "We sent one of those tickets to every buyer in the country," Foster remembers with a laugh. "When that buyer went to Expo with his family and he got tired after tramping around the site all day, he took his family to the VIP lounge for a rest and a drink — on us. When he was there, he was thinking about us." Foster pauses. "I don't know if we ever got our 'bait' back on that one," he says, "but it was worth it in terms of goodwill." So was all the time, effort, money and shoe leather Bill Morrow put into creating a high-profile brand-name identity for High Liner. "That label," says Bill Morrow proudly today, "is worth a hell of a lot. It's not something that actually shows up on your balance sheet but it could mean millions in terms of the real worth of your company."

But Bill Morrow's many selling successes during the late 1950s and the 1960s also had the effect of putting increasing pressure on the company's outdated and cramped Lunenburg processing facilities. Since W.C. Smith and Company was founded at the turn of the century, the company's only major new construction projects were the Louisbourg plant in 1951 and the first Lunenburg Sea Products plant in 1926.

Since then, Wallace Smith, the only company executive with an engineering background, had become an expert at squeezing ever-more useable space out of the Lunenburg operation through infilling and building up. Despite his success at that, the company paid a price in productivity for his inventiveness. The floors of the various plant sections were so uneven, for example, that it was impossible to use a dolly or a forklift to move things around within the plant. "Two men on either end of a 50- or 100-pound box," remembers one executive. "That was how things were moved around in the plant."

By 1958, the jerry-built plant had been infilled and built up to beyond its capacity. The company needed new facilities and C.J. Morrow had begun to talk of what he called his dream — building a modern new facility before he retired. By then, however, Wallace had become set in his ways of doing things and told Ron Smith, the company's vice president, that he was "beating his head against the wall" if he thought anyone could build a new plant that would duplicate on one floor what he'd been able to achieve on several different levels in the current plant. After hearing that, Ron Smith decided that if he was ever going to find an innovative solution to the company's space problems, he would need to bring fresh blood into the company.

Where better to look for fresh blood than within the family?

Smith called Jim Morrow, C.J.'s engineer-son who was working for Kaye Engineering Services in Halifax as a consultant. Ironically, one of his jobs there was helping to build a fish plant for the Newfoundland Fish Development Authority at La Scie.[3] "We'll probably be building a new plant soon too," Smith told him, "and you could be in charge of the project."

Even though he had by then become a senior official with the Kaye firm and could reasonably expect to become its boss someday soon, Morrow jumped at the chance. "It was a once-in-a-lifetime opportunity," he explains. "I ended up-buying the [new] property, arranging for the highway and power access, railways, water access, I was working with the architects, everything, from start to finish. It was my project."

But it was far from a simple one. Besides all the usual problems he had to face, Morrow's job was complicated even more because Wallace initially opposed all of his plans for a new plant, and most other National Sea executives were equally "hellbent" on keeping the plant within the town of Lunenburg.

"I spent two years trying to figure out how to build on the current site," Morrow recalls. "I tried a two-stage approach, but then after working up the cost estimates and the space limitations, I kept coming back to the fact that we'd be a lot better off to go out and find a cow pasture somewhere nearby and then truck the fish to the new plant."

Even as he was sorting through that problem, he was also regularly smacking hard into Wallace's intransigence about building a new plant in any location. One day shortly after he'd joined the company, Wallace visited Morrow in his office in the old Lunenburg Coal and Supply building. "What are you doing?" he demanded.

"I'm designing the new plant," Morrow answered.

"That, in my books, is impossible."

"Uncle Wallace," Morrow said evenly, "I was hired to build a new plant and that's what I'm going to do."

After that confrontation, Morrow recalled, "Wallace became helpful. Within half an hour he sent carpenters over to my office with boards to help me make models. 'Just put a few brads in there and you've got a model,' he said. And he

---

3. The plant was later bought by National Sea Products Ltd.

was right. Within a day, I had a model. A few days later, Wallace comes in, looks at it and says, 'Why not do this? Why not do that?' I said, 'Why don't you build your own model?' And he did. But he never interfered. And his experience and his suggestions," Morrow adds, "were invaluable."

While the company's two engineers were coming to a *modus vivendi*, Morrow continued to grapple with the problem of where to put the new plant. After writing a manual entitled *Criteria for Design of a New Plant*, Morrow hired his former employer, John Kaye, to serve as consultant for the project. At one point, Morrow remembers, he, Kaye and a third engineer named Ken Mitchell walked the entire length of the town's harbor in search of a suitable site. When that failed to produce an answer, they decided to look at the town from another angle, and went over to Battery Point, across the harbor in the county. Ironically, Battery Point was part of the harbor but not part of the town, because Lunenburg's original boundaries were laid out very narrowly to provide for efficient defense against Indian attack.

"We were standing there looking over and talking about the town," Morrow says, "and suddenly I said to Kaye, 'You know, maybe we're standing at the right place right now.' He looked down at the lake [Lohnes Pond] and said, 'Well, we could excavate the lake.'"

Within a week, Morrow had purchased an option on the property for $500 from the farmer who owned it[4] and he and Kaye had begun to test their theory about the land's suitability by drilling holes and taking depth readings in the adjacent waters. Luckily, the level of the bedrock was a full 30 feet below the low-water level, meaning they could dredge the harbor to put in necessary posts and pilings for the plant and its wharves.

With the site decision made, Morrow began to plan the plant itself. Borrowing innovations that had become standard in the other industries and adapting them to the fish business, he created what has been called the largest and most modern fish-processing plant in the world and earned himself an honorary degree from his alma mater in the process.

After visiting ice-making and cold-storage plants all over North America, Morrow designed a system for the new plant in which "you just pressed a button and you had your ice." The ice was made high up in the plant and then dropped down where it was spread by a mechanical raking device and then distributed on a conveyor-belt system throughout the plant and even into the holds of ships at

---

4. The company eventually bought the land from the farmer, "who wanted to make sure that he could get enough to buy a home somewhere else," for $30,000 and began purchasing adjacent land around what would become the plant in order to avoid potential environmental disputes with its neighbors. Today, the company owns about 100 acres of waterfront property around the plant.

the company docks. To replace what Morrow called the "plumber's nightmare" of different piping systems that ran in, around and through the old plant, Morrow placed heavily insulated pipes on the roof outside the plant so they could be easily worked on and, if need be, expanded to meet future needs without becoming too complex or interfering with the esthetics of the plant's interior. Perhaps most importantly, Morrow replaced the old haphazard production line with a modern straight-line system in which the fish entered at one end of the line and proceeded through the cutting, trimming, packing, freezing and cold-storage phases in logical order. At the same time, Morrow designed the plant so that there was a highway-wide strip through the plant to accommodate forklift traffic.

Training people to operate the new equipment wasn't easy, partly because they had difficulty adapting to the new technology and partly because they weren't very sympathetic to it. At one point, recalls Morrow, the five men assigned to learn to use the forklifts weren't doing very well with them. "Finally, I said, 'Let me try.' I didn't tell them, but I'd been practising for months in any spare moment I had. I just took one of those pallets and I dropped it in the middle of these two others in a very tight spot. When I came back a week later, they were doing it themselves for fun. I had no problems after that."

In the end, the plant was completed on time and within budget. Reputed to be the largest groundfish-processing plant in the world, the new $8-million facility, which occupied five-and-three-quarter acres under one roof,[5] was capable of processing 50,000 pounds of fish every hour with a maximum filleting rate of 35,000 to 40,000 pounds an hour and a total annual production capacity of 80 million pounds of raw fish a year.

Although the June 24, 1964, lavish opening ceremonies were staged partly as a celebration of what Jim Morrow and his construction team had accomplished in building the plant and partly as a crowning tribute to the long and successful career of his father, C.J. Morrow, they were also an occasion for Bill Morrow to display his unerring talent for public relations.

Morrow flew 265 of the company's best customers and brokers from all over North America to Lunenburg for a week of lobster dinners, plant tours and cruises on the famous Nova Scotia schooner *Bluenose II*. "Those people not only saw what kind of facilities we had," explains Earl Foster, "but they also got a chance to experience what kind of company we were. The benefits of that kind of promotion are almost beyond calculation."

With the company's facilities finally in place and its share of the marketplace expanding, it was time once again for management of the company to pass to a new generation.

---

5. With expansions since then, the plant now occupies eight acres.

In 1965 C.J. Morrow retired from the presidency and was named chairman of the board. His successor was Ronald Smith, a son of one of W.C. Smith's founders who had joined the firm in 1928 and risen through the ranks to become Lunenburg plant manager, then Halifax-based assistant to the company's general manager and finally general manager himself in the mid-1950s. He was a popular choice for the top job, remembers Bill Morrow, "well liked by the customers and the employees as well as by the fishermen." But he was also already 61 years old at the time of his appointment and everyone, including Smith himself, realized his would inevitably be a transitional presidency.

Despite his ultimately brief tenure in the top job, however, Smith was anything but a mere caretaker president. Bill Morrow describes him as a "strong personality" and credits him with being one of the first to recognize that the company's traditional "management style" needed changing. During his presidency, the company really completed the process of transforming itself from that collection of semi-autonomous units C.J. Morrow had hammered together during the 1950s and early 1960s into a modern, centralized, multinational corporation with control and coordination vested in a head office that was far more than just a president, a secretary and a few bookkeepers.

Despite the incredible growth it had experienced in the preceding decade, National Sea was still structured in 1965 as if it was a small family business. "Ron was the key person in the company, which meant he dealt with everyone," Bill Morrow remembers, "and it seemed that everyone in the company reported to him."

That may help explain why Smith became a leading proponent of the idea of creating a real corporate head office — complete with a layer of vice presidents and corporate managers — in order to enable the company to more effectively deal with the complexities of the modern business world. When he became president, in fact, he decided that preparing National Sea for the future would be one of his own personal projects as president. To accomplish that, he hired a management consultant to help smooth the way for the transition to a more progressive corporate structure in the next generation.

That was far from his only important contribution to the company's evolution. Smith was also the executive most responsible for heading off potentially serious labor strife by voluntarily agreeing to recognize a union as the legitimate bargaining agent for the company's trawler fishermen. And he moved as well to resolve a painful family-business problem by making the difficult decision to fire a member of one of the firm's own founding families.

The union issue had been festering since 1947, when Ralph Bell completely routed the Canadian Fishermen's Union during a bitter four-month strike by trawlermen against the company. Bell, who saw the dispute as a stark battle-to-the-finish between the godless forces of communism, as represented by the CFU, and the righteous armies of capitalism, as represented by National Sea, simply could not allow himself to even entertain the notion during the strike that the fishermen might possibly have some legitimate grievances too.

"He was absolutely adamant," remembers Hal Connor, who says Bell and his managers worked 18 hours a day for the duration of the dispute just to show the fishermen that the company could keep on operating, even without them. The strike finally ended after the Supreme Court of Nova Scotia ruled that fishermen were co-adventurers rather than employees and therefore ineligible to join trade unions. When the fishermen abandoned their picket lines soon after and returned to the boats under the company's terms, Hal Connor recalls today, "Ralph declared victory and said, 'Well, we're not going to have a union in the fleet now for at least 20 years.'"

He was right. But neither Bell's victory nor the court ruling really responded directly to the fishermen's specific complaints. The fishermen's willingness to listen to the CFU's pitch, of course, had had almost nothing to do with its communist leanings and everything to do with their own personal concerns about how much money they were paid for the fish they caught and about safety and working conditions aboard the company's vessels.

Although wages and working conditions did improve somewhat during the 1950s and 1960s, many fishermen continued to chafe at what they regarded as their court-sanctioned status as "co-adventurers."

The Supreme Court's 1947 decision concluded that the fishermen and the company were equal partners in an entrepreneurial adventure.

> Fishermen operating under such an agreement may toil in stormy seas for days and weeks and may catch only enough to pay for the bait, oil and wages of the cook and engineer. The time of the men and the use of any equipment they own is a dead loss; equally so is the use of the vessel with its tackle and the provisions supplied by the owner; equally the captain gets nothing.... But assuming that the owner loses the hire of the vessel and the provisions and the men lose their time and the use of some equipment and that, in this suppositious case, there are no profits to divide, can it be said that the men are employees and the owner an employer? To my mind, the persons in question in the present case were engaged in procuring fish not for the owners or the captain but for the general account of all.... The relationship between the fishermen who share in the proceeds of a fishing voyage under the agreements before us and the owners of the vessel is not

that of employer and employee but of partnership in the limited sense which is sometimes described as a joint adventure.

However logical those arguments may have seemed to the learned judges in the late 1940s, they made very little sense to a lot of Nova Scotia fishermen 20 years later. The problem was that the fishermen saw the partnership as decidedly unequal.

The individual fishermen believed they had little bargaining power when it came to dealing with a huge vertically integrated fishing enterprise such as National Sea. The company owned the boats and it could unilaterally set the conditions under which fishermen worked as well as determine the amount of money they would receive for their catch.

Fishermen could, of course, refuse to work under such company-dictated conditions, but since they were forbidden to act collectively to try to change the company's position, they were powerless to really bargain effectively with the company for better conditions or more money. Such an inequitable situation was a natural rallying point, not only for union organizers attempting to recruit new members to their ranks but also for 1960s-style social activists in search of a cause worthy of their attention.

Even before the failure of the Canadian Fishermen's Union in Nova Scotia in the 1940s, fishermen's unions had taken root in British Columbia. The largest of the west coast unions, the United Fishermen and Allied Workers Union, was formed in the early 1940s as the result of the merger of a number of regional fishermen's associations. It quickly developed a reputation among fish companies there as a controversial, militant union that was often embroiled in long and bitter strikes.

In 1953, it was suspended from the National Trades and Labor Council as a result of a dispute over jurisdiction. In the mid-1960s, the union was fined $25,000 and three of its senior officials sent to jail in British Columbia for contempt of court. One of those officials, Homer Stevens, was a member of the Communist Party of Canada.

According to Silver Donald Cameron in *The Education of Everett Richardson*, his book about the 1970 Nova Scotia fishermen's strike, the UFAWU first became interested in organizing Nova Scotia fishermen in the early 1960s. "When union officials would go to Ottawa to talk about international treaties, hydro projects, unemployment insurance or another of the dozens of other political issues that affect fishermen," Cameron explained, "they would be told, 'You fellows may know the west coast, but what about the Maritimes?'

"In 1952, in the middle of a bitter trawl strike," he added, "the west coast fishing companies pointed to the [unorganized] Maritime situation with approval and the UFAWU worried that the divided and weakened Maritime fishermen would undercut their own contracts." After B.C. herring seiners began coming east to fish in the mid-1960s when the British Columbia herring fishery was closed, the UFAWU decided it was finally time to act.

The first union-organizing committee visited Nova Scotia in 1967 and by the middle of the year reported back to British Columbia that it had established the first UFAWU local in the province at Louisbourg, signed up 70 of 80 fishermen in Mulgrave and formed organizing committees in Canso, Lockeport, Shelburne, Lunenburg, Pubnico and Yarmouth.

In Lunenburg, the fishermen were cautious. They were fed up with what they considered low prices for their fish and many of them believed they needed a union to help them bargain with the company, Lunenburg Fisheries' Eric Nowe says today, but they weren't interested in getting hooked up with a union "that might be out on a six-month strike right away." Instead, Nowe and a group of other trawlermen met with representatives of the Canadian Seafood Workers' Union, a small union that already represented National Sea plant workers, to ask if that union would be interested in representing them too. "They wouldn't do nothing for us," Nowe remembers.

Frustrated but still reluctant to throw in their lot with the British Columbia union, the fishermen decided to tie up the company's boats on their own over Christmas 1967. Although the one-week walkout — which was illegal at the time — did result in a number of face-to-face meetings with company officials and some improvements in fish prices, Nowe says the larger question of the fishermen's right to be represented by a union was never discussed with the company. But it did come up in another conversation that same week between Nowe and a Halifax skipper. The captain had a friend named Charlie Moulton who was a union business agent. Perhaps, he suggested to Nowe, the trawlermen might want to talk to him.

When the Lunenburg fishermen contacted him, Moulton, the business agent for the Canadian Brotherhood of Railway, Transport and General Workers Union, was wary too. While the transportation-oriented union did have a marine component, its members were tugboat crew members rather than fishermen, so the union had very little experience dealing with fisheries issues. To complicate matters, Moulton wasn't sure if his union had the necessary Canadian Labor Congress authorization to organize fishermen. Even if it did, there was still the question of the Nova Scotia Supreme Court ruling. What could the union do if a company simply refused to recognize it?

But in the end, after asking for permission from his union's head office in

Ottawa, Moulton did agree to attend a meeting with the fishermen in Lunenburg. "They had a lot of complaints," Moulton remembers today, "mainly about the price of fish, which was really low. After the meeting, a number of them agreed to sign union cards and we went from there."

When he had what he considered "a large majority of the fishermen" signed up, Moulton decided the only logical course for him to take was to approach the company directly. "I went in to see Ronald Smith and I remember he seemed surprised that we had a majority signed to cards," Moulton chuckles. "He didn't like it too much. That's for sure." But when Smith examined the cards more carefully, he discovered that some of the cards Moulton presented had been signed many months ago. Under the Trade Union Act, unions are required to conduct their organizing campaigns within a specified period of time in order to make sure that those who sign the cards still, in fact, support the union at the time the application for certification is filed.

National Sea's workers weren't covered by the provisions of the Trade Union Act, of course, so the company wasn't really obliged to talk to the union at all, but Ron Smith not only agreed to meet with Moulton, he went one step further. Rather than rejecting the union's request for certification out of hand, Smith said he was turning it down because the union had not got its signatures in accordance with the provisions of the Trade Union Act. That gave Moulton the opening he needed to try again, this time complying with all the provisions of the act in the same way he would have if the fishermen were legally entitled to have a union. A year later, Moulton returned with properly signed cards and Smith responded by voluntarily agreeing to recognize the CBRT as the legitimate bargaining agent for the trawlermen.

Although there were rumors at the time that National Sea's willingness to accept the CBRT was prompted by a fear that the fishermen might otherwise end up with the more radical United Fishermen's union — a conclusion that even Charlie Moulton believes "may have been the case" — Bill Morrow says it simply wasn't so. "We felt that if they wanted a union, they were entitled to one," he says today, adding, "We got hell from our competitors."

Regardless of its motivations, the company's decision turned out to have been exceedingly fortuitous. Less than a year after National Sea agreed to voluntarily recognize the CBRT, more than 200 other Nova Scotia fishermen belonging to the United Fishermen's union went on strike against Boston Deep Sea Fisheries Ltd.'s Acadia Fisheries plants in Mulgrave and Canso, and Booth Fisheries Ltd.'s plant in Petit de Grat. Their chief demand — recognition of their union. By the time the bitter, costly and controversial strike ended 15 months later, everyone involved in the strike had lost. The United Fishermen's union failed to win recognition and retreated to the west coast. Boston Deep Sea announced it was closing both its plants after losing more than $2 million because of the strike. And two years after that, Booth packed its corporate bags and left Petit de Grat as well.

Meanwhile, back in Lunenburg, National Sea and the Canadian Brotherhood of Railway, Transport and General Workers were slowly, cautiously coming to a *modus vivendi*. Although Moulton says that the union's first collective agreement with the company in 1969 "was not a very good contract because we didn't get very far on the the price of fish," the mere fact that the two sides were bargaining at all was a positive step. It was, in fact, the beginning of a process that ultimately created a feeling of mutual respect between the two sides. "I used to negotiate with 26 different companies," says Moulton, who is now retired, "and National Sea was as good as any to deal with. The main person I dealt with was a fellow by the name of J.B. Morrow and the thing I liked about him was that he was always honest. If he said you weren't going to get anymore, well, you knew you weren't going to get anymore. It was just that simple." That relationship may be one reason why there has never been a strike by the trawlermen against the company. "We've come close from time to time," Moulton says, "but we always managed to find a way out before it was too late."

If Ron Smith's decision to hear out Charlie Moulton when he first came calling in 1968 turned out happily for everyone concerned, the same can't be said in the case of Wallace Smith's son, David, whose unwillingness to follow the corporate line not only resulted in his firing but also precipitated a crisis that eventually almost destroyed the company.

Like the Morrow brothers, young David had grown up in Lunenburg in the shadow of a company his father ran. But David went off to the United States to attend a prep school and then Harvard University, where he adapted easily to the faster pace of American life in the 1960s. After post-university stints with Sun Life Investments and General Foods in New York, Smith finally joined the family firm in 1959, but not in its head office or in Lunenburg. Smith was assigned to the company's U.S. sales and marketing division in Boston and soon became its boss.

Almost universally regarded as brilliant, David Smith was also what Bill Morrow describes as a "non-conformist" who found it difficult to operate within the ordinary constraints of a traditional hierarchical business.

"His ideas were innovative, ahead of his time even," says Ian Langlands, "but his ambitions were bigger than the company."

Placed in charge of developing the company's U.S. sales, Smith became so convinced that that market had unlimited potential that he began to demand priority access to the company's fish production in order to develop and service it.

"Because of my training and background, I was used to thinking of being at the head of an octopus that was running things," Smith recalls today, "but that wasn't the situation at National Sea. Historically, the company had gone from a group of independent producers to what was supposed to be one company, but which was really still only a loosely affiliated group of individual plants. The profit centres were at the plant level. And that was a problem for me."

So was the fact the company's basic philosophy had always been to "take care of Canada first, because it's our bread and butter," instead of going after what might seem like a faster but perhaps less dependable U.S. buck. As a result, Smith's pleas for a larger percentage of the company's fish production to develop the U.S. market were almost invariably turned down by the board of directors.

At one level, Smith responded with wit and satire, even publishing a professionally produced take-off on the company's annual report, complete with photos depicting the company's "board of directors" playing pool and showing a photo of Boot Hill cemetery above a caption describing National Sea's employee retirement plan.

More seriously, Smith refused to accept the board's decision to turn down his requests. "David was so adamant that he was right and everyone else was wrong that he began to do things that ran counter to company policy," remembers Jim Morrow. "He had his own printing press and he was turning out his own promotional materials. He began making promises to customers that he simply couldn't fulfill because we couldn't provide the raw materials for him."

"The things he did weren't necessarily unethical," Bill Morrow says now, "but they also weren't the type of things a National Sea executive should be doing. He didn't work within the system and that made life uncomfortable for a lot of his peers."

At the same time, Smith's personal lifestyle alienated other executives. Although National Sea's U.S. head office was located in Boston, Smith himself lived in Scarsdale, New York. "He'd fly in, work three days of 16 to 18 hours a day and then take off for a long weekend in Florida or wherever," remembers Bill Morrow. Adds his brother Jim: "David had a great way of rationalizing his personal lifestyle with his business life."

"I was living a very unusual life," Smith admits today, "but that was because I was an entrepreneurial type, so I wasn't operating on a routine nine-to-five schedule. I was working hard and putting in lots of hours but not in the conventional way. So there was some resentment."

The situation came to a head in 1968 during a U.S. fishing-industry convention when several U.S. fish dealers told Ron Smith they no longer wanted to do business with the company because they didn't want to deal with David Smith any longer. Ron Smith decided he would have to get rid of David, and even spurned offers from both Jim and Bill Morrow to take care of the problem after he retired. "I told him there was no need for him to cause a rift in the family," Jim Morrow recalls, "that Bill and I would solve it, that we didn't deserve to run the company if we couldn't resolve it ourselves. He practically threw me out of the office. He'd decided he was going to take care of it before he retired and that was that."

Smith did attempt to soften the blow by offering David a face-saving out. Instead of firing him outright, he simply closed down Smith's Boston office and consolidated the company's U.S. operations in tiny Rockland, Maine, and offered Smith the chance to relocate there himself or move to Halifax.[6]

After Bill Morrow became president a few months later, Wallace and David approached him with a plan for David to return to the company again, but Morrow wasn't having any of it. Not only did he agree with Ron Smith's earlier decision, Morrow says now, but he also believed it would have been a slap in the face to his predecessor to have reversed the original firing.

The result was bad blood, not only between Ron and Wallace Smith but also between Wallace and the Morrow brothers. "He thought the Morrow boys had let him down," says Jim Morrow.

That simmering family resentment eventually triggered what Bill Morrow says were several attempted takeovers of the company, two of which were "very serious." The second one, in fact, would plunge the company into the worst crisis in its history.

The first serious takeover bid came in the fall of 1968 when Ward Foods — a large U.S. conglomerate that had begun its corporate life as a bakery based in the midwest and which also owned a chain of seafood restaurants there called Zeider Zee — offered to buy the company. Both David Smith and his father, Bill Morrow says today, were prime supporters of the deal.

Ward was one of a host of aggressive, multifaceted companies that had emerged during the mergers' heyday in the mid-1960s, and its own high stock price was based more on the balance sheets of the companies it took over than on any special skills or wisdom of its corporate executives.

At that time, National Sea looked to be a prime candidate for a takeover. Not

---

6. After he left National Sea, David Smith tried his hand at a number of business ventures, including real estate and investments but, says Jim Morrow, "like any Smith or Morrow, his heart is always in the fish business." Smith now lives in Hilton Head, South Carolina.

only did its stock price not reflect the real value of its assets but the company was also clearly entering a period of uncertainty. Ron Smith was about to step down and the new president was not yet in place; some of the major shareholders had recently retired and were anxious to liquidate their assets; and a key stockholder, Wallace Smith, was unhappy with the current direction of the company.

To complicate matters, Ward's president, Chuck Coll, was the kind of guy "who'd come into your office, take off his jacket, roll up his sleeves and settle in," recalls Bill Morrow. "He was a very flamboyant type of guy." And a good salesman. Hal Connor, for example, bought shares in Coll's company even though he opposed the takeover deal itself.[7] Coll's offer — $12 a share, with half in cash and half in a Philippines holding company that Ward controlled — badly divided a previously united National Sea board of directors. Bill Morrow faced the very real possibility of having the company sold out from under him even before he got a chance to become its new president.

The surprisingly simple solution to the Ward threat was first suggested by Charles MacFadden during an airplane trip he and Morrow took to Toronto a few days before the offer was to be considered.

"Why don't you just call Salada," MacFadden suggested, "and buy their ten percent back." National Sea had purchased its Tampa shrimp plant from Salada using stock instead of cash. "If you put the Salada shares together with what you and your supporters now control," MacFadden went on, "that would give you enough shares to stop Ward dead in its tracks."

Morrow was so excited by MacFadden's suggestion that he called T.K. Fingold, the owner of Salada and president of Slater Steel, from a pay phone in the Toronto airport and then headed directly to his home on fashionable Avenue Road.

Although Morrow would marvel later that the den "was as big as most people's houses and there was a desk there that once belonged to Sir Wilfrid Laurier," he didn't waste time that day complimenting Fingold on his taste. After explaining the current situation at National Sea, Morrow came to the point: "Your block is very important to those of us who don't want to sell," he said.

Luckily for Morrow, Fingold allowed how he'd recently been looking at his National Sea stock himself to determine whether he should get into the fish business more deeply by buying more shares and learning more about what makes it tick or whether he should simply sell off his shares and put his money into a business he knew more about.

"Your story," Fingold told Morrow, "convinces me that I should get out. The

---

7. The shares, which he bought for $45, rose to $50 but eventually fell to just $5 a share.

stock is on my books now at $7.65. I'd accept eight dollars for it."

Asking for the weekend to put a deal together, Morrow hurried off to the Royal Bank to arrange a $1-million loan. Before the bank would agree to cover the loan, however, Jack Fortune, the bank's Atlantic regional manager, checked with the bank's three Atlantic-region directors. Ironically, two of them — Frank Covert and C.J. Morrow — were directors of National Sea. The third was legendary Nova Scotia industrialist Jack MacKeen.

With the bank's okay, Morrow flew back to Halifax to try and sell off some of the Salada-owned shares to other, supportive investors. It wasn't a hard sell. In fact, his father, who called from his Florida vacation home to find out what was going on after the bank had called him for his approval, immediately told his son to "put me down for 5,000 shares." By the time Jack MacKeen called to offer to buy 10,000 shares himself "if you need me," Morrow's private-share offering was already oversubscribed.[8]

On Monday morning, Morrow called Fingold and offered him $7.65 a share for his 10 percent.

"But I said eight dollars," Fingold answered.

"Well," Morrow replied carefully, gambling that Fingold would see hard cash in the hand as worth more than stock in the portfolio, "you know how the fish business is, and besides, the people I talked to accepted the deal on the basis of $7.65 a share. I can have the cheque deposited to your account in the Bank of Commerce by 11 o'clock this morning."

Fingold, with some reluctance, agreed.

With those shares now in Morrow's control, the Ward bid was effectively dead. On February 3, 1969, the board of directors' committee considering the deal formally turned it down, citing the company's current depressed prices as the result of an ongoing recession and expressing management's confidence that the company would bounce back soon.

David Smith himself — still a National Sea director — who was one of the members of the committee, unenthusiastically agreed to go along with its decision, but he put on the record his suggestion that the company inform Ward that it would reconsider the U.S. firm's offer if the deal was strictly for cash instead of cash and shares.

Nothing came of the suggestion.

With the Ward threat out of the way, David Smith out of top management, a more modern management structure in place and the union question resolved, Ron Smith could finally retire in good conscience. Although the choice of his

---

8. Ironically, it was during this attempt to prevent a takeover that the Sobey family bought its first major block of shares in National Sea.

successor — Bill Morrow — came as no surprise, the way in which the decision was reached was one more sign that the company had finally made the transition from a traditional family-owned business to a dynamic, modern public enterprise.

During the Christmas break in 1968, Bill Redden, the management consultant Smith had hired to restructure the corporate head office, completed his consulting work by holding a two-day think-in of top corporate executives.[9] Their job was to decide — by consensus — who the next president should be.

There were at least three men in the running for the job — Bill Morrow, Jack Estey and Charles MacFadden. Although both MacFadden and Estey made pitches for the post in their own names, both were ultimately ruled out. MacFadden was regarded as too much a numbers man and not quite presidential enough for the company's top job, and there were concerns about Estey's health. No male member of the Estey family had survived past 50 and Estey had made it clear he himself intended to retire when he reached 50.[10]

While there was some concern that having "another Morrow or Smith" at the helm might send the wrong message to employees, there was also little dispute that Morrow was the logical person for the top job. Morrow, in fact, had almost become *de facto* president already. Ronald Smith's wife had been seriously ill for some time and Smith was spending more and more of his time with her, so a lot of the day-to-day decision-making had begun to fall on Morrow's shoulders anyway. "After a while," Morrow says, "because Ron was so busy with other things, the plant managers began to call me whenever they wanted something."

"Everyone in the room wanted Bill for the job," Charles MacFadden says now. "He had ability and he knew the business. That was important when you had a company that was spread out from head office to trawler. You needed someone with credibility to maintain the employees' loyalty. The Smiths and the Morrows still had great credibility inside and outside the organization. So, in the end, there really wasn't anyone else for the job."

At the time, however, Bill Morrow says now, he wasn't so sure he actually wanted the job. "I was only 39. Hell, there was still lots of time. I was already the highest paid person in the company. I got the highest bonus. And I had enjoyed building up the High Liner brand, a job I didn't feel was finished. I didn't see any reason why I should take it.... But, in the end, Ronald said he was only going to recommend one person for the job and that was me."

In addition to Bill Morrow's selection as president, the 1969 changing of the

---

9. The group included Ron Smith, Bill Morrow, Charles MacFadden, Jack Estey, Hal Connor, Ian Langlands, Jim Morrow and Jim Tupper, the Lunenburg plant manager who was then part of the management team.
10. In fact, he was persuaded to remain until he was 53. Estey is still alive and well today.

corporate guard also involved a number of other shifts in top management — C.J. Morrow retired as chairman of the board and chairman of the executive committee to be replaced by Hal Connor, who assumed the job on a full-time basis. At the same time, the company created a new post of executive vice president, and named Jack Estey to fill the job.

The torch had passed once again, this time to a third generation.

13

The Third Generation

"The Department of National Revenue has indicated that it does not agree with the company's method of computing taxable income for taxation periods ending in 1966 and 1967, and that it proposes to increase taxable income for those periods.... In the opinion of the Company's professional tax advisers, the Company's method conforms with the provisions of the Income Tax Act."
— Notes to Consolidated Financial Statements
1969 Annual Report

BILL MORROW had barely settled into his new president's chair at National Sea when the federal government announced plans to challenge the way the company kept its books. It was the beginning of a troubled decade — played out against the backdrop of ever-increasing foreign domination of the fishery off Canada's east coast — that would see the company and its officers pilloried in public for everything from being "corporate welfare bums" sucking at the public teat to a "bunch of rogues" playing fast and loose with the interests of the company's small shareholders.[1] If there was any consolation to the directors in all of that, it was simply that the company's very growth and success made it a natural target for attack.[2]

Part of that growth and success, however, had come as a direct result of the tax policies that Ottawa was now challenging.

To encourage continued industrial growth and prevent the Canadian ship-

---

[1]. Despite that, the post-Ron Smith National Sea Products became a well-oiled, centralized operation with regular Monday-morning management-committee meetings at which top company officials — Hal Connor, Bill Morrow, Charles MacFadden, Ian Langlands, Jack Estey, Jim Tupper and Jim Morrow — would get together to make sure that each knew what the other was doing and that everyone was working for the larger corporate good.

[2]. Bill Morrow's own obsession with growth was evident from the beginning. Over the objections of some veteran board members, he began to invest in the Newfoundland fishery, first by buying a closed-down St. John's fishing company and then making deals with Premier Joey Smallwood to build vessels in Newfoundland as well. "I could see that the industry's centre of gravity was moving east," Morrow says now, "and we had to be there."

building industry from sinking back into its pre-war doldrums, the federal department of trade and industry had devised a new program after the war that offered accelerated depreciation allowances to ship owners who had new vessels built in Canada. Effectively, it allowed a company building a ship in Canada to write off the capital cost of the vessel for tax purposes over three years instead of the customary 15. If the company subsequently sold the ship, however, it had to repay the federal government, based on the amount of recaptured depreciation — the difference between the amount it paid in taxes under the program and the amount it would have paid if it had taken the ordinary write-off — *unless* it reinvested those funds within a certain period of time to build a new ship. If the company wasn't willing or able to reinvest the money it had saved to build more ships, the program allowed the company to sell off its non-taxable shipbuilding funds to another company that was prepared to invest in building more ships.

Although that may seem like a complicated arrangement, the long and the short of it was that everyone involved — shipbuilders, ship owners, fishing companies, etc. — gained because of it. That may be why the program was widely known among tax experts as "the Angel Deal." But National Sea's sharp-eyed accountants and tax advisors also soon noticed a wrinkle in the plan that allowed the company to gain an even greater advantage from the program.

At the time, National Sea was effectively several companies — there was

Original Cape North

National Sea Products Ltd. and Lunenburg Sea Products Ltd., both operating under the wing of a third company, Ocean Fisheries, the holding company set up to purchase Ralph Bell's shares back in 1953. Since each of the companies was entitled to take a tax write-off on any ship built in Canada, Lunenburg Sea Products, for example, could have a new trawler constructed, operate it for three years while it took advantage of the fast capital-cost write-off and then sell it to National Sea, which, in turn, could earn the same fast write-off again before selling the vessel to another sister company. Lunenburg Sea Products, meanwhile, could reinvest its gain from the sale of the original trawler to construct yet another new built-in-Canada vessel and start the process all over again.

To make that sweet deal even sweeter, National Sea was expanding at a time when much of the rest of the industry was contracting and many independent vessel owners were dropping out of the industry entirely because it had become too capital intensive. Under the terms of the program, National Sea was able to buy up those companies' unused tax credits at up to 70 cents on the dollar, and reinvest them again in building more ships.

Partly because it seemed like such a sweetheart deal — "There's no question that it was a sweetheart deal for everyone involved," Bill Morrow allows today, "but you have to remember what its purpose was and what the people who set it up were attempting to achieve" — Morrow asked National Sea's own tax advisors[3] to vet the company's plan in advance and then also showed it to representatives of the federal department's industry component as well.

"Every one of them," Morrow says today, "told us that what we were doing was proper." From the company's point of view, of course, the scheme also made sound corporate sense. "That's how we built up our fleet," Bill Morrow says flatly.

Not everyone thought the scheme was legal. "There were some young Turks in the revenue department at the time who were looking to make a name for themselves," Bill Morrow says, "and they decided that the whole thing was phony, so they went after us."

The stakes were high. If the company lost, it would have to pay nearly $3 million in back taxes. Perhaps that's why the company hired J.J. Robinette, widely acknowledged as one of the finest lawyers of his generation in the country, to defend its interests.

"He put on quite a show," laughs Bill Morrow. "During the discovery stage, he very effectively demanded to know why — since lots of Canadian companies were doing exactly the same thing as National Sea — the revenue department

---

3. Including Arthur Gilmore, a senior tax advisor with Clarkson Gordon, who had once worked with the department of revenue.

was singling out the east coast, which is the poorest part of the country, and singling out a company that was trying to do something to help make things better in that region of the country as well."

The case ultimately ended with the whimper of a complicated settlement instead of the ringing finality of a court judgement. Just before it was scheduled to go to court, the two sides settled out of court. Although National Sea won its point on the key shipbuilding write-offs, the company did concede in what Bill Morrow says were other, less significant areas. For example, the company did agree to pay taxes on the first few years of operation of its Bermuda-based insurance company, which the revenue department argued was set up not so much to handle insurance business as to channel corporate profits into a tax haven. "We were really okay on that one too, as far as I'm concerned," Morrow says today, "but the accountants and the lawyers thought we should settle."

As Morrow eventually explained it all to shareholders in his 1976 annual report: "The details ... are somewhat complicated, but the net result is that a tax assessment which would have resulted in a tax assessment of five million dollars against previous earnings has been settled for approximately $1.5 million."

Even before that case was finally settled, however, National Sea officials were under fire on another front, and once again hired Robinette to help extricate them from their problems.

In the fall of 1974, the Ontario Securities Commission, which regulates trading at the Toronto Stock Exchange, launched an investigation into a complaint by a small Ontario shareholder that a group of National Sea insiders — Bill Morrow, C.J. Morrow, Charles MacFadden, J.B. Morrow, H.P. Connor and J.B. Estey — had sold a substantial block of National Sea stock just before the company reported significant losses that drove down the value of the company's shares.

Although it did look suspiciously like a case of well-connected insiders using their privileged position to take unfair advantage of unknowing sellers to make a quick and dirty buck, Bill Morrow insists the sale had far more to do with protecting the company's market share — and the long-term position of all shareholders — than it did with taking advantage of fluctuations in the value of the company's shares.

The problem had its genesis in the the early seventies when the Sobey family — operators of Atlantic Canada's largest supermarket chain — began buying significant blocks of National Sea shares. According to documents filed later with the Ontario Securities Commission, Sobeys held about 400,000 shares, or about 28 percent of the company, by early in the spring of 1974.

The potential significance of those purchases on National Sea's own fortunes became startlingly clear when one of the company's Toronto-based sales representatives returned to the office one afternoon in 1974 to report to sales manager Earl Foster that Dominion Stores, then the country's largest supermarket chain, had just decided to "de-list" all of National Sea's products in Ontario. At the time, Dominion was not only National Sea's biggest retail customer but it also represented about one-third of the entire retail market for Canadian fish products.

"I couldn't believe it," Foster remembers, "so I phoned a friend of mine in Dominion and he confirmed it. Dominion took the attitude that Sobeys was really Weston-Loblaw [another major supermarket chain that then held a non-voting 40-percent share in Sobeys Stores] and they weren't going to deal with their competitors. I got on the phone right away and called Bill Morrow."

Morrow flew to Toronto, where he met with Dominion Stores president Thomas Bolton to convince him that the Sobey *family* through Empire Company — rather than Sobeys Stores — was involved in the share purchases, and that the Sobeys were interested in the stock as an investment rather than in connection with any attempt to take control of the company.

"They're not long-term holders," Morrow assured the Dominion executive. "They'll eventually sell." That, Morrow confides today, was one of the reasons why he "wasn't all that upset" three years later when Jerry and Harold Nickerson bought out the Sobey family in the deal that would ultimately dramatically change the face of National Sea.

Even though Morrow was able to temporarily smooth the waters with Dominion, he admits he was far less certain himself about what the Sobeys really wanted. All he knew was that he had to do something to protect the company's retail base. The most logical possibility, he decided, was to find another investor that could act as a counterweight to guard against the Sobeys becoming too powerful within the company.

As luck would have it, the Jodrey family of Hantsport, Nova Scotia, was shopping for a place to invest some surplus cash at the same time. In his book, *The Canadian Establishment,* Peter Newman describes Roy Jodrey, the Jodrey family patriarch, as "one of the most successful investors of his generation." Although he was almost totally wiped out by the 1929 stock market crash, Jodrey rebounded and "eventually became director of 56 companies with [billions] worth of assets stretching from Newfoundland to Venezuela."

In the mid-1970s, the Jodreys — the family empire was by then controlled by son John Jodrey and grandson David Hennigar — were one of the two most important business families in Nova Scotia.

The other, of course, was the Sobey family.

The Jodrey decision to invest in National Sea, however, had nothing to do with any rivalry with the Sobeys, according to David Hennigar. "It was simply that we'd just sold our stock in Fraser Companies [a New Brunswick-based conglomerate] and we were looking for a place to invest it. We wanted to keep the money in the Maritimes, but there weren't that many opportunities available. National Sea was one of them. That's why we went to talk with National Sea management to see if they'd be interested in selling."

Bill Morrow began quietly meeting with David Hennigar in April to discuss the outlines of a possible deal. From Morrow's point of view, the Jodrey people were ideal partners. "They had a reputation for supporting Maritime business and they seldom sold the stock they owned in a company that had Maritime roots, so they would be the kind of investors who would be there for the long haul."

By the end of May, after two more meetings, they concluded an arrangement under which company shareholders sold about 100,000 of their shares — or just under 10 percent of the company — to the Jodrey family. The Jodreys were willing to become significant minority shareholders, Morrow says, but they didn't want to own more than the 10-percent interest in the company that would force them to officially declare themselves "insiders" to the OSC. "We just weren't interested in filling out the bloody forms," as Hennigar explained later.

In order to consummate the deal, Morrow initially expected to acquire the shares Hennigar wanted from Wallace Smith and his family. "The family held about 10 percent of the stock, and since David was no longer involved in the company, the stock would eventually be sold anyway," Morrow reasoned. "Where else were they going to sell a block of that size?" The deal would also have been especially beneficial from Morrow's point of view because it would have gotten rid of what he referred to as the "loose cannon on the deck."

Cape Scatari (GEORGE NAAS PHOTO)

It turned out, however, that Smith

Cape LaHave, *sister ship to the original* Cape North

— still miffed by his son's firing — was only willing to sell a portion of his holdings, so Bill Morrow and other members of the executive committee agreed to make up the difference.

The actual share transfers began early in June following the signing of a formal agreement between the two sides on May 31, 1974. On June 4, 100,000 shares changed hands, followed on June 10 by another 11,400 shares. The final sale came on June 26 at 10:33 a.m., when C.J. Morrow telephoned his broker to order him to sell another 1,000 shares of his company stock.

Although that stock sale was also part of the original agreement with the Jodreys that had been finalized a month earlier, it occurred less than 24 hours after the company's board of directors — of which C.J. Morrow was still honorary chairman — had learned that the company's short-term fortunes were poor. For the first six months of 1974, the company profits would be $1.16 million compared with $2.48 million the year before. And, for the third quarter, the company was actually reporting a $592,000 loss instead of the $1.32 million profit it had achieved a year earlier.

There were all sorts of reasonable explanations for the dramatic change in corporate fortunes. According to Bill Morrow's later testimony to the OSC, the market for fish had been so good in late 1973 "it was a problem of obtaining sufficient supplies." But ice conditions in the spring of 1974 considerably delayed the start of the next year's fishing season. Then, following a brief late-spring rally that convinced Morrow catches might eventually recover, the company's trawlers reported so many "poor landings" in late May and June that he realized the company's third quarter "couldn't bail us out."

At the time he issued his "sell order" on June 26, C.J. Morrow — as he would testify later — thought the company's problems were already a matter of public record. They weren't. Although the directors had authorized management to send a letter to shareholders "informing them of a sharp turnaround in the company's prospects for the remainder of its fiscal year," that letter hadn't officially gone out at the time Morrow sold his shares, nor had the company issued any official public statement on its problems.

The announcement, when it did come, triggered a sharp drop in the value of the company's shares — from the $15.75 a share the Jodreys paid down to eight dollars a share and even as low as three dollars per share during the third quarter.

Again there were logical explanations for the drop, including a two-week strike in Lunenburg in June followed by a 10-week strike in Newfoundland in July, but the collapse of the share price so quickly on the heels of the sales by

Cape Ballard *(Fame Class), 1975* (KNICKLE'S STUDIO PHOTO)

company insiders not surprisingly raised questions among some shareholders about what the directors knew and when they knew it. After one of them formally complained, the OSC launched an investigation that eventually resulted in a December 1975 hearing in Toronto.

Morrow believed the company had been singled out less for its alleged sins and more to send a message to Bay Street generally, and corporate insiders in particular, that "they had to act awfully carefully or look out." For his part, Hal Connor believed everything would turn out fine. The chairman of the OSC at the time was Toronto lawyer Arthur Patillo, a former Maritimer and lifelong friend of Connor. Patillo had even proposed the toast to the bride at the weddings of several of Connor's daughters. Because he was a Maritimer, Connor reasoned, Patillo would ensure that "fair treatment was the order of the day."

Recalls Morrow with a laugh today: "On one of the evenings when we were in Toronto for the hearings, Hal began referring to his 'great friend' Art Patillo. I remember looking at him and saying, 'Hal, if he is your *great* friend, I'd hate to meet one of your enemies.'" Morrow himself was also convinced that the directors had operated reasonably prudently, but he knew that the timing of the sales "made us look like a bunch of rogues and I wasn't too happy to have to talk about it."

The OSC produced a string of witnesses who claimed that the company should have known about the likelihood of a downturn in the industry in 1974, but the company was able to marshal its own evidence to refute those suggestions.

One factor in the company's problems, for example, had been the collapse of the shrimp market, where prices fell by one dollar per pound overnight and resulted in a $1-million loss to the company. That collapse was totally unexpected. In fact, the company's own auditors had been so upbeat about market conditions while they were preparing a prospectus that spring that they had urged the company to increase its profit projections. Morrow resisted because, as he pointed out in his OSC testimony, "I just knew the fish business. I told them I'd be more comfortable with inventory reserves."

The OSC's case against National Sea's executives wasn't helped when the Jodrey family — who, after all, were the main short-term financial losers in the deal — admitted that even though National Sea didn't tell them that the situation was "going to be as bad as it turned out to be," they had no intention "to seek redress" as a result. "The only information [National Sea] disclosed about the financial position of the company," L.D. McCully, the secretary of the Jodrey family's Minas Basin Investments, noted in a letter to the OSC, "was the

Cape Pictou *(Nova Class)*

Cape York *(Argus Class)* (KNICKLE'S STUDIO PHOTO)

Cape Blomidon (COCHRANE PHOTO)

Cape Norman *(Anne Class)*

general comment that the fishing industry generally was in a downtrend and that results would probably not be as good as those of the previous year."

For his part, Morrow told the OSC that it was "embarrassing enough" to realize what had happened after the shares were sold. If he'd known what was actually going to happen before the fact, he insisted, "the sale would never have taken place."

Although the OSC didn't actually issue its decision for several months after the hearings, Morrow says an incident on the last day of the sessions convinced him the company had won. "I went to the National Club [in Toronto] that day to have lunch with some Japanese businessmen we were interested in doing a deal with. The members of the tribunal were there for lunch too and, seeing me alone, they invited me to join them. I said, 'No thanks, I'm meeting a customer.' But right then, I knew we'd won the case."

They did. Although the company did not escape unscathed — "OSC Raps National Sea Knuckles on Insider Trading," declared the headline in the Toronto *Globe and Mail* the day after the June 7, 1976, decision was announced— the OSC ruled that its transgressions were more technical than nefarious. The tribunal decided the company should have made a faster public disclosure that the industry was in trouble, for example, but it was quick to add that "there is not a shred of direct evidence that they [the National Sea directors] positively made use of the information, which they had, for their own benefit or advantage....

Cape Hunter *(Fox Class), 1975*

We were impressed by the veracity and integrity of the respondents."

"We feel completely vindicated," Morrow told the *Globe and Mail.* "There was a rap on the knuckles, but it was a mild one."

National Sea may have won its battle before the OSC, but that was a mere salvo in what was soon to become, in effect, an undeclared war for control of National Sea. Even as the OSC debated the merits of the company's share sale to the Jodreys to counter-balance the Sobey influence, the Sobeys themselves were continuing to gobble up available stocks in the company. On February 3, 1976, for example, the *Globe and Mail* reported that "Empire Company of Stellarton, which is controlled by the Sobey family, has purchased another 6,726 shares of National Sea Products Ltd. of Halifax."

What did the Sobeys want? And why?

14

The Nickerson Return

WHILE National Sea was growing in dramatic leaps and spurts, so — albeit more modestly, but no less dramatically — was H.B. Nickerson & Sons Ltd., another family-owned Nova Scotia fish company, based in North Sydney.

The Nickerson firm had had its beginnings in 1935 when Harry Brooklin Nickerson and his son Jeremiah Belton Nickerson left their native Port L'Hebert on the province's south shore, moved to Cape Breton and bought up a bankrupt cold-storage plant that they transformed into a modestly profitable fish company.

Although the Nickerson firm did briefly become part of National Sea at the time of its founding in 1945, Jeremiah Nickerson, whom Charles MacFadden describes as a "shrewd, self-made man all the way through," was far too independent to ever be comfortable as just another cog in a large corporate wheel. He and his small family business were soon back on their own after buying their company back from National Sea in 1956.

The company remained a self-satisfied, modestly successful Cape Breton-based company — it owned its North Sydney plant, a general store, a few wooden boats and a buying station in Dingwall — until Jeremiah's son, Jerry Edgar Alan Nickerson, joined the firm after graduating from Dalhousie University with his Bachelor of Commerce degree in 1959.

Friends describe Nickerson, a restless, ambitious young man, as "almost eccentric" because of his almost manic energy for business, his penchant for privacy — he rarely grants interviews — and his personal modesty. Even after he became what one writer called "the most powerful entrepreneur in Canada's $2-billion fishing industry," Nickerson continued to live in a modest ranch-style home a mile from the family's North Sydney fish plant, drove a three-year-old car and worked out of a spartan, impersonal office.

Soon after he joined the company, he came into conflict with his father over how the family firm should be developed. "I always felt the industry could have done better from a standpoint of technological developments — new products and marketing," as Nickerson later put it obliquely to journalist Parker Barss Donham in a profile published in *Atlantic Insight*.

Although his father didn't actually retire back to his Liverpool, N.S., roots until 1965, Jerry began putting his own stamp on the family firm — expanding its horizons beyond both the inshore fishery and the province of Nova Scotia — within a few months of his arrival. In 1960 alone, for example, he had two new 60-foot longliners built, snapped up a Newfoundland firm called Bluewater Seafoods, sold it for a profit and then used the money he made from that to have two new deep-sea draggers constructed.

A few years later, in 1965, he was at it again, acquiring fish plants in Dildo and Charleston in Newfoundland, as well as a Riverport, N.S., saltfish company and scallop business operated by his brother-in-law, Ross Ritcey.

The Riverport purchase typified Nickerson's intuitive, decisive approach to doing business. Ritcey was actually planning to sell the plant to someone else and simply called Nickerson out of courtesy to tell him his plans. Nickerson immediately bought the plant over the phone. This became Nickerson's major groundfish- and scallop-processing plant.

"Like all great entrepreneurs, Jerry has an intuitive grasp of business," suggests Peter John Nicholson, a one-time Liberal member of the Nova Scotia legislature who handled Nickerson's relations with government during the late 1970s. "He was always bubbling over with new and fresh ideas, and he was willing to invest all his talent and energy into doing business. That sort of thing inspired terrific confidence in those who work for him. He's a marvellously charismatic individual, as charismatic as anyone I've ever worked for."

In 1969 Nickerson's brother, Harold, a bright, hard-nosed manager with degrees in both law and business administration, returned home after four years as an executive with Domtar Chemicals in Ontario and joined his brother in the family business. Jerry became chairman of the board, Harold the president. The brothers made a formidable team. According to the *Atlantic Insight* article, Harold was "regarded as the nickel-and-dimer who keeps the company's day-to-day operations on track, while Jerry is the visionary planner."

During the next decade the Nickersons' steady corporate growth was fuelled in large measure by government financing. One of the more controversial aspects of their corporate *modus operandi*, in fact, was their penchant for gobbling up bankrupt companies from government creditors at distress prices and on extremely favorable terms. That was how they acquired a large plant and trawler fleet in Georgetown, P.E.I., in 1969, for example, and then picked up Canso Seafoods Ltd. in Canso, N.S., after the Nova Scotia fishermen's strike in 1971.

Joe Zatzman, who was chairman of the Nova Scotia government's Fisheries Loan Board at the time of the Canso deal, says the Nickersons paid the government just "one dollar a year for the use of the boats" at the Canso plant. And Silver Donald Cameron, in his *Education of Everett Richardson,* adds that the Nickersons picked up the nearby Cardinal Proteins plant — in which the government itself had already invested $9 million — for just $100. "That was the base on which Jerry built his empire," says Zatzman.

In 1974 the Nickersons used the same approach again when they bought the Ferguson Industries shipbuilding yard in Pictou, N.S.

While some critics suggested that the brothers used their political connections — Jerry Nickerson is a prominent Liberal — to their business advantage, such suggestions irritate Peter John Nicholson. "Jerry was the kind of guy every DREE [federal department of regional economic expansion] bureaucrat wanted to find more of. He was the guy who was prepared to do things to get a business going, and he would bring forward proposals to them, and then he would succeed with those companies. He did what the programs were designed to do — create jobs, stimulate growth — and he was vilified for it." Nicholson pauses. "You know, it's one of the supreme ironies of all of this that if Jerry had been less successful, he probably would have been more constrained than he was in terms of borrowing and he might not have run into all the problems he did later on... but, of course, that's hindsight."

When the Nickersons weren't buying plants outright, they were buying "into" existing small fish companies, offering them the benefits of both their capital and marketing expertise while leaving the local owners alone to deal with the day-to-day management of fishermen and plant workers.

The Nickerson firm's dramatic corporate expansion during the seventies may ultimately have had less to do with political connections and more to do with the reality that the federal and provincial governments as well as the chartered banks were more than willing to encourage and finance their expansionist dreams.

That probably shouldn't have been surprising. From the governments' point of view, the fishery provided important jobs in rural communities that otherwise had little to offer to attract new industrial development. From the banks' point of view, the fishery very clearly seemed to be a growth industry in the mid-1970s.

The reason was summed up simply in the phrase "200-mile limit." After decades of inaction that had allowed huge foreign fishing fleets to dominate and decimate the east coast fishing grounds, the federal government finally decided to declare a 200-mile economic management zone off its coasts in 1977.

The problem had been brewing since the early 1950s when Captain Harald Salvesen, the chairman of a Scottish general shipping and whaling company, decided that the international whaling industry was on its last legs and resolved to put the lessons his company had learned in operating factory ships for whaling to use in the fishing industry.

Salvesen's company not only pioneered in the use of stern trawlers for fishing and carried out some early experiments with variable-depth trawling but it also became the first to build and operate a factory freezer trawler. The *Fairtry I*, which was launched in Aberdeen in 1954, was a huge vessel for its time — 2,600 gross tons with an overall length of 280 feet — and contained what was considered luxurious accommodation for 80 crew members. But its most significant features were shipboard filleting machines, which had been developed by a German inventor named Rudolf Baader, a fast-freezing plant, which employed multiplate freezers similar to those developed by American frozen-food pioneer Clarence Birdseye, and a fish-meal plant that enabled the *Fairtry* to make productive use — at sea — of all parts of the fish it caught.

The ship's ability to operate at great distances from its home port and to remain at sea for long periods proved attractive to countries, especially in Europe, which had few fish of its own but did need new sources of protein.

The Russians were the first to imitate the *Fairtry*'s design with a vessel called the *Sverdlovsk*, which arrived in St. John's harbor in 1956, along with the U.S.S.R.'s minister of fishing industries, Alexander Ishkov, whose role was to lobby Canadian authorities to grant his country fishing rights in the Grand Banks and other waters off Canada's east coast. Based on Soviet assurances that they were interested mainly in experimental fishing and might indeed even be interested in buying some of Canada's surplus fishing catch, the federal government approved the Soviet request.

Within less than a decade, however, the Soviet fleet in the North Atlantic had grown to 106 factory trawlers, 30 mother ships and 425 conventional trawlers, and it was catching close to 1 million tons of fish each year. But that was only the beginning.

Pulitzer Prize-winning American author William Warner, in his devastating critique of the destruction of the North Atlantic fishery, *Distant Water*,[1] described what he saw on Georges Bank during a fishing trip he took there in 1976: "Ships are all around us, near and far," he writes. "I count some 33, slowly scanning the full circle of the horizon with binoculars. All are foreign fishing

---

1. Much of the information presented here about the history of overfishing in the North Atlantic is drawn from Warner's book.

vessels ... with hard, utilitarian lines that give a grim, or at least businesslike, aspect to the fleet at large. It is a sight to see: a floating metropolis, a city at sea.... One thinks immediately of the fish. How any schools can escape the hidden eyes of this armada, since every ship in the fleet is equipped with multiple underwater electronic fish finders, is difficult to imagine."

Bill Morrow, who says the evidence of the huge Soviet fleets was apparent even in Halifax and St. John's harbors, where Russian vessels taking on supplies became a common sight, remembers one sailing trip he took in the early 1970s. "I'd just bought a boat in Ontario and I was sailing it back from New York. As we were passing through Germain Bank, I remember counting 70-80 Russian trawlers, all fishing for herring."

Initially, the implications of the presence of the foreign fleets in the North Atlantic weren't apparent to most observers, Morrow says, because Canadian fishing vessels' catch rates did not deteriorate that significantly. "But if you looked at the catch in terms of the amount of effort it was costing us to bring it in, you began to realize that we weren't doing nearly as well. We were now building $2-million ships to catch what we used to be able to catch with $250,000 ships. It was only the fact that the technology was improving that allowed us to keep pace."

But not for long. According to Vladil Kirillovich Lysenko, a Russian fishing captain who defected to Sweden in 1975 and later wrote *Crime Against the World*, a book about the way in which the Russian fishing fleet decimated the world's fishing grounds, "the aim of the Soviet government was to catch fish in any quantity and at any price."

Lysenko says that by the mid-1960s, 90 percent of the fishing vessels on Georges Bank were Soviet vessels — "in the main these were large factory freezer trawlers, but in time medium-sized trawlers, herring trawlers and even seiners" — and that huge fleets (the total Russian fishing fleet consisted of an incredible 19,000 vessels by 1976) were simply dispatched to North American waters in flotillas and kept at sea for periods of six months or more.

"One can imagine what happens to the sea bottom when a fleet of between 400 and 500 vessels simultaneously drag their trawls across it," Lysenko writes. "The bottom is scored as though with ploughshares, and rammed down as though with steamrollers. Nothing is left alive for the fish to eat. What is more, this is where the fish breed, and when they lose their breeding grounds, the fish die out without leaving any progeny. But Soviet fishing policy takes none of this into account."

And the Russians, of course, were far from the only foreign fishing fleets virtually vacuuming the North Atlantic sea floor. By the end of the 1960s, West

Germany, East Germany, Poland, Romania, Spain, Portugal and France all had factory freezer fleets of their own in the North Atlantic. Each year, fishing technology became ever more sophisticated, allowing the huge foreign fleets to gobble up even more of what had once seemed to be the inexhaustible harvest of the sea.

It wasn't, of course. Between 1961 — when the Russians first began to seriously fish the area — and 1968, total fish catches for all countries in the North Atlantic increased dramatically from 2.6 million metric tons to 4.6 million tons. But then it began to decline rapidly to the point where scientists were forecasting that several valuable fish species were actually in danger of extinction. Even haddock "was down to an all-time low throughout its Northwest Atlantic range, so low, in fact, that fishery biologists feared the end of a commercially viable fishery, if not species extinction."

The International Commission for Northwest Atlantic Fisheries (ICNAF), set up as part of an international treaty in 1949, was supposed to monitor and control international fishing in the Northwest Atlantic, but it seemed powerless to prevent even its own members from ignoring the gear limitations and quota restrictions it established.

For a time, Canada hoped that the United Nations Law of the Sea Conference might find a way to resolve the problem of overfishing, but its mandate was so large — it was responsible for dealing not just with fisheries issues but also with offshore oil drilling and seabed mining — and the multilateral negotiations so complex that little was actually accomplished in settling the question of who should be allowed to fish in the waters off Canada, how much they should be allowed to catch and under what conditions.

In the end the Canadian government simply decided it couldn't wait for international agreement and announced that it was unilaterally extending its jurisdiction over the waters off its coast from 12 miles to 200 miles, effective January 1, 1977.

While that meant that the government could now restrict the overall fishing effort to allow time for nature to replenish overfished species of fish, it also — and even more importantly from the standpoint of the Canadian industry and the bankers who financed them — meant that the government was in a position to allow Canadian fish companies to get first crack at catching, processing and selling the lion's share of those fish to the world.

That may have been why — even as he was gobbling up smaller fish companies with the assistance and blessing of officials at the Bank of Nova Scotia — Jerry Nickerson began casting a covetous eye at National Sea Products Ltd. as well.

While Jim Morrow says that Nickerson had actually been buying and selling

National Sea stock for many years — "He'd buy when the price was down and everyone was selling, and then he'd sell just before it peaked," Morrow says. "He made money by knowing the cycles" — Nickerson began buying and holding National Sea stock during the mid-1970s, at a time when the company's poor short-term profit picture — it lost $1.3 million in 1974 and stopped issuing dividends in 1975 — combined with growing optimism for the future to make National Sea shares a good buy.

By late 1976, the Nickersons had acquired approximately 10 percent of the outstanding shares of National Sea. But they were, of course, not alone. The Sobey family had also been busily buying shares and by 1977 had acquired an incredible 39 percent of the outstanding stock in the company.

Intriguingly, the Sobeys acquired their largest single block of shares — 65,000 shares — from none other than the family of Wallace Smith. According to a report in the Toronto *Globe and Mail*, in fact, Donald Sobey called the purchase of shares from "the Smith family, one of the originators of the fishing company ... the turning point" in his company's 10-year purchases of National Sea stock.

In the early spring of 1977, the Sobeys — through their investment arm, Empire Co. Ltd. — made a deal with the Nickersons to establish a 21-year voting trust and jointly became the company's largest single shareholder. Shortly after that, the Nickersons triggered a clause in the deal that allowed them to buy out the Sobeys and take effective control of the company.

Many people connected with National Sea are convinced to this day that the Smith sale — the key catalyst for those events — was motivated by lingering resentment over Ronald Smith's firing of David Smith nearly a decade earlier.

"Jerry found the weak link," says Jim Morrow. "Wallace still had a bit of revenge feeling as a result of what had happened earlier and, although he would never admit to this, I think he decided to sell to our arch rival out of spite."

Smith, in fact, did offer his shares to the other main shareholding group — the Morrows, Ronald Smith and Hal Connor — but others are quick to argue that the offer, which was made through Hal Connor, was never serious, or sincere.

"David was completely unreliable," complains Connor today. "I worked awfully hard to get those shares and I thought that we would get them. We had many fervent phone calls about it, but David kept leading me on and later putting me off until, without warning or giving me a chance to stop the sale, he sold. 'I didn't think you fellows were sincere,' he told me, 'so I sold them.' It was a very bitter blow."

One reason for what the *Globe and Mail* would later describe as "the passive way that management seemed to respond to market purchases of large blocks of the company's shares" was Bill Morrow's fear that any protective counter-purchase of shares by the management group might result in yet another round of complaints and hearings by the Ontario Securities Commission.

For their part both the Sobeys and the Nickersons publicly proclaimed that they'd acquired control of National Sea for long-term investment reasons and denied any suggestions that they wanted to run the company itself.

"I just bought the shares," Jerry Nickerson explained almost ingenuously in one interview. Added brother Harold: "As you know, the short-term outlook [for the fishery] is not very good, and we thought that one way we could get by was to tie ourselves in with Sobey so we could cooperate on things of mutual interest."

"The fishing industry is on its heels right now," agreed Donald Sobey in an interview with the *Globe*. "One of the main advantages of a shareholder going into a partnership with Nickerson in the stock is the cooperation we feel we can get with National in the foreign markets. This is where we feel the expansion should come in the fishing industry."

At one point shortly before the Sobeys acquired the Smith block of shares, Hal Connor remembers having a conversation with Frank Sobey aboard a plane as the two men returned to Halifax from a meeting. "Frank said to me, 'Look, why don't you fellows and Jerry Nickerson get together? Wouldn't that be a great alliance?' And I said to him, 'Well, no, Frank, actually I don't think it would. We're not really all that complementary. We compete in all the wrong areas to be of much help to each other. We really need to get involved with someone who can fill in the gaps rather than overlapping with what we already have.'" Connor pauses. "I didn't think anything of it at the time but then, the next thing I know, the thing was done and the Nickersons were partners with the Sobeys and in control of the company."

Despite that, Sobey insisted that Empire had no intention of "taking over the management or anything like that. We have great respect for Bill Morrow's management; we think he's been doing a very good job."

From the beginning the relationship between Bill Morrow and the Nickerson brothers was a curious mixture of mutual admiration and mistrustful wariness. Shortly after the Nickersons formed their voting trust with Sobeys, for example, Jerry Nickerson invited Bill Morrow to a meeting at the Chateau Halifax, a hotel in the same complex as National Sea's head office in Scotia Square in downtown Halifax, and offered to make him a partner in the voting trust. But because Nickerson wouldn't agree to extend the same invitation to other large shareholders — including Harold Connor and Ron Smith — Morrow said no.

A few months later, in June of 1977, Morrow approached Jerry Nickerson to propose a different kind of deal. After pointing out the problems that the Sobey presence as a major shareholder had been causing the company with its major customers, Morrow suggested the Nickersons get together with National Sea's existing management to buy out the Sobeys totally.

"That's an interesting idea," Nickerson allowed, "but it doesn't suit my plans." Recalled Morrow later: "He had a twist in his mouth when he said that."

Morrow, who had his own sources in the Bank of Nova Scotia, knew that the deal between the Nickersons and the Sobeys included a buy-sell clause that allowed one party to buy the other out before October 15, 1977.[2]

That's why he wasn't surprised when, at precisely 8 a.m. on an August morning in 1977, Harold Nickerson arrived unannounced at Bill Morrow's Scotia Square office. Nickerson, whom Morrow would later describe as "Jerry's usual messenger," got right to the point.

"I've come," he explained to Morrow, "to let you know that we've assumed control."

"I already knew that," Morrow answered calmly.

Nickerson couldn't hide his surprise.

"There aren't too many surprises in this business, Harold," Morrow explained, relishing for the moment a psychological triumph he knew to be both minor and hollow. But Nickerson had clearly not come just to tell Morrow what had happened.

"What are your plans, Bill?" he asked solicitously. "Are you happy?"

Morrow decided to play his cards close to his chest. "Oh, I don't know," he said blandly. "I guess I'm going to keep my options open. But," he added pointedly, "I do plan to stay in the fish business."

"We'd like you to stay on here," Harold assured him quickly, adding that he and his brother had no plans to merge National Sea with Nickerson and, in fact, wanted them to continue to compete with each other at sea as well as in the marketplace.

For Morrow, the arrangement was not without its benefits. For one thing, it finally resolved the problem created by the Sobey family's presence as minority shareholders in National Sea. For another, the Nickersons knew the fish business. Given the volatile, cyclical nature of the business, it would be helpful to have owners who also understood the vagaries of the industry. Finally, although they wanted positions on the company's board of directors for themselves, the

---

2. Why did the Sobeys sell? There have been a number of theories advanced, including the argument that the Sobeys themselves had intended to be the ones to buy out the Nickersons and were stunned when the banks helped the Nickersons turn the tables on them. Another — and more plausible theory — is the one advanced by Harry Bruce in his biography of the Sobey empire. He suggests simply that they needed cash to finance their acquisition of Quebec-based Provigo Ltd.

Nickerson brothers appeared to be genuinely committed to operating the two companies separately and to maintaining the existing management in place.

Morrow agreed to stay.

When the deal was publicly announced a short time later, it rocked the province's political and business establishment.

One reason, of course, was that this forced marriage of two of the east coast's largest fishing companies left only about a dozen independent fishing operations, and therefore made the giants even more dominant than they already were in the marketplace. Provincial fisheries minister Daniel Reid, for one, wondered aloud whether the deal would result in the merged company becoming a fish-buying monopoly. At the same time, the federal department of consumer and corporate affairs quietly began looking into whether the deal might violate the spirit of proposed new competition legislation, which had been announced just one day after the Sobey-Nickerson voting trust deal was first made public.

As much as there was concern about what the deal might ultimately mean, however, there was also a good deal of awestruck amazement at the audacity of the virtually unheralded Nickerson brothers. Neither Jerry — "What mattered to Jerry," says Joe Zatzman, "was the fish business. He grew up from the wharf in rubber boots." — nor Harold were listed in *Who's Who in Canada*, for example, and they weren't regarded as real members of the province's exclusive financial elite. Despite that, they had taken over National Sea instead of the other way around.

Nickerson, as commentators were quick to point out, was only one-third as large as the company it was now taking over. National Sea, Canada's largest groundfish company, boasted seven major processing plants with a capacity of 75 million pounds of fish a year, 5,000 employees, a fleet of 30 deep-sea trawlers and worldwide sales of $127 million. Although Nickerson didn't issue sales figures, it employed only about half as many people, had only three major plants and operated only about two-thirds as many deep-sea vessels.

It was, allowed Nova Scotia premier Gerald Regan, "like a horse swallowing an elephant."

What no one could predict at the time was that digesting the elephant would give both the horse and the elephant such a case of indigestion that it would soon threaten to kill them both.

15
Caught in the Nickerson Net

ON THAT morning in the spring of 1977 when Roland Martin boarded an airplane in London for the flight home to Gander, Newfoundland, he considered himself a reasonably satisfied man. He enjoyed his job as Newfoundland's controller and deputy minister of finance, one of his province's top civil service posts, and he liked living in the province where he was born and had grown up. He had no intention, he remembers now, of abandoning either his job or his province.

That was before he met Jerry Nickerson. By chance, Nickerson, who had been in Europe too, was returning home on the same plane as Martin. At the time, Martin was peripherally involved in the fishing industry as the provincial government's appointee on the board of directors of Newfoundland's Fishery Products Ltd. Since Nickerson was in the process of becoming the most important entrepreneur in the east coast fishing industry, it wasn't surprising that when the two men struck up a conversation during the flight, it centred on the subject of the fishery and its apparently bright prospects for the future. Like many others who encountered him, Martin later remembered being extremely impressed by Nickerson's charm and enthusiasm.

Nickerson was clearly impressed as well. Three months later, he called to ask Martin to become the president of InterOcean Ltd., a new company he was in the process of forming to serve as a link between his own company, H.B. Nickerson & Sons Ltd., and another company he'd recently acquired control of, National Sea Products Ltd.

"I had a series of meetings and visits with Jerry and a meeting with Bill Morrow," Martin explains today, "and the chemistry seemed right, the timing seemed right. Jerry and Bill seemed to be heading into an exciting time together. And the 200-mile limit had just come into force, so the future of the whole fishing industry at that time seemed very bright too."

In a March 1978 article in *Canadian Business*, Halifax journalist Harry Flemming used a medical analogy to describe what appeared to be a sudden incredible rebirth of the east coast fishing industry.

"Three years ago, the east coast fishing industry was desperately sick, a terminal case kept breathing only by constant infusions of that ubiquitous miracle drug, federal government money," he wrote. "Low prices and declining catches had raised the industry's need for the stimulant to the point where its physician, Fisheries Minister Romeo LeBlanc, wondered aloud: 'Are we dealing here with a hypochondriac, or an invalid, or an addict?' [But] today," Flemming concluded with a flourish, "the patient is recovering and the prognosis for the industry's future health is dizzyingly optimistic....

"The men who stand to reap more of this potential than any other," Flemming was quick to add, "are Jerry and Harold Nickerson."

Flemming's optimism for the Nickersons and for the industry — which was shared by the federal and provincial governments, banks, investors and officials of the fishing industry itself — was based largely on the expectations of what the new 200-mile management zone would mean for the fishery in the long term.

"With the declaration of the 200-mile limit [on January 1, 1977]," Flemming wrote, "Canada, in effect, became owner and manager of all the fish stocks within 502,000 square miles of Atlantic waters.... As the foreign fleets phase out their operations in Canadian waters and as Canadians gradually move into the void," he suggested, "a new generation of increasingly sophisticated vessels, especially freezer trawlers, will be needed."

That those vessels would cost "up to $15 million each," brought Flemming back to the Nickersons and their new acquisition, National Sea. He quoted "one medium-sized [fishing industry] operator" as suggesting that "'there is no way I can see that we can swing that kind of financing.' [But] Nickersons and National Sea can."

Nickerson and National Sea, Flemming pointed out, were also the only Canadian companies large enough and vertically integrated enough to take advantage of new and lucrative export opportunities that would be created by the increasing Canadian involvement in catching and processing fish off our coasts. Finally, Flemming argued that, in a perverse way, the mere fact the Nickerson companies were already so deeply in debt to fund their earlier expansions meant that governments "will have to jump to Nickersons' tune." According to one provincial official Flemming spoke to, "We're married to Nickersons."

Despite the universal optimism about the future of the fishery and the

Nickersons' part in it, however, the Flemming article does point out that there were many unanswered questions, even then, about what the Nickersons really wanted to do with their acquisition.

Although Jerry Nickerson had insisted in public — and privately to Bill Morrow — that he had no intention of attempting to merge the two companies, "National Sea's future is uncertain," Flemming wrote in his article. "[Although] both companies still operate as fully independent entities, no one really believes this will continue. A knowledgeable source expresses a common view: 'If [Bill] Morrow and the rest of them don't toe the line, they will be replaced.'" Others, including Joe Zatzman, the chairman of the Nova Scotia Resources Development Loan Board, were well aware of the tightrope Bill Morrow walked during those years. "I remember Bill telling me that he had to take a low profile," Zatzman says, "because Jerry was now the chairman and he could just tell him he didn't need him anymore."

Concluded Flemming: "[National Sea] could remain a public corporation under Nickerson control, or Nickerson could turn it into a private company by purchasing the remainder of the outstanding shares."

Noting that Nickerson and National Sea had recently incorporated a new company called InterOcean Ltd., Flemming expressed a commonly held view — both inside and outside the companies — that InterOcean "could become the vehicle through which the destinies of the two companies are determined."

Such speculation did little to make Rollie Martin's job any easier. By the time InterOcean set up its offices in a suite on the 17th floor of the Bank of Montreal office tower, just a few blocks from National Sea's head office in downtown Halifax, its motives were already suspect. Many in National Sea shared Vice President Ian Langlands' concern that InterOcean might eventually "become a holding company [and] National Sea and Nickerson would be just its operating wings."

"There were some suspicions on both sides," Martin admits today. "Part of the problem was that we were defining the job that we were to do even as we were in the process of doing it. We had to take into account that, while we were there to coordinate certain mutually beneficial areas of operation and to work on new investments and joint ventures with the companies together, each company was still doing its separate thing too. That contributed to the fuzziness of trying to define what we were all about," Martin says, but he's quick to add that "there was a lot of goodwill in the beginning too. Everyone felt that we were part of an expanding industry and everyone was anxious to try new things."

In the beginning InterOcean did just that. In addition to being responsible for public relations and for major supply and service purchases — fuel, netting, fish boxes, insurance, etc. — for both companies, InterOcean became a focus for new joint ventures between the two firms. In the late 1970s, which Rollie Martin describes as "halcyon days for both the fishery and the offshore [energy industry]," National Sea and Nickerson formed a jointly owned company — Harbinger Services — to "get a piece of the offshore action" by converting old fishing side trawlers to new offshore safety and supply ships and by leasing containers to oil-exploration companies. In 1980, the two companies, through InterOcean, formed another partnership — Fisheries Resource Development Ltd. — to conduct fisheries-related research and development work.[1]

Bill Morrow, whose years on the marketing side of the fish business had convinced him of the need for a more organized, scientific approach to the whole issue of new product development, was the person most responsible for setting up FRD, which would turn out to be one of the main legacies of the National Sea-Nickerson union.

Morrow's own views on the subject were greatly influenced by his friendship with Paul Jacobs, a visionary former vice president of Gorton's, the huge U.S. fish company. Thanks largely to Jacobs' own efforts, Gorton's had set up its own research and development wing, and Jacobs lobbied for Morrow to do the same at National Sea.

At that time, Ottawa was phasing out its own fisheries-research laboratory in Halifax, and federal officials were putting pressure on both National Sea and Nickerson to fill the void with an additional dose of private-sector spending.

Morrow and the Nickersons agreed that R&D might make a perfect vehicle for collaboration between the two firms. Under the terms of the deal, FRD was to conduct technology-related research for both companies while conducting new-product development work on a proprietary basis for each company separately.

But John Maloney, an MIT-trained food scientist with 15 years' experience in new-product development for major American corporations who was tapped to head up the joint venture, now says that "the only significant product development we did during those years was done for National Sea."

InterOcean did look at a number of overseas joint venture possibilities in Spain and Norway for its parent companies, Rollie Martin says, but nothing came of those.

At the same time that it was supposed to be providing this link between the two companies for joint ventures, however, InterOcean was also often working

---

1. Both Harbinger and Fisheries Resource Development Ltd. were eventually folded into National Sea. Harbinger's activities were wound down when the offshore industry collapsed in the early 1980s, but Fisheries Resource Development Ltd. remains an integral part of National Sea's operations to this day.

as a kind of in-house consultant for each of the companies individually. It assisted National in its purchase of a fish plant at La Scie, Newfoundland, for example, and aided Nickerson when it bought a United States fish-processing company.

To complicate matters even more, Nickerson and National Sea were still operating independently of each other and of InterOcean on many joint ventures and acquisitions. When National Sea became involved in a joint venture in Uruguay, for example, neither InterOcean nor Nickerson was involved at all. And Nickerson itself was continuing on its own dizzying round of acquisitions until, by 1982, it owned almost as many plants as National Sea, although those plants were, for the most part, much smaller than those of National Sea, and many of them operated only seasonally.

Although the sometimes overlapping, sometimes conflicting actions of National Sea, Nickerson and InterOcean created inevitable internal tensions, none of that was immediately apparent to the outside world. The Nickersons' purchase of National Sea, as Parker Barss Donham wrote in *Atlantic Insight*, appeared to be "an enormous gamble [that] paid off like a daily double." By 1979, National Sea's share price had reached a high of $24.75.[2]

The fact that the Nickersons adopted a highly leveraged expansion strategy was in keeping with the way in which the firm had grown so dramatically during the previous decade, but it flew in the face of the Morrow-Smith tradition of frugality and conservatism, and it became clearer and clearer to those inside the firms that the Nickerson-National Sea marriage was anything but a match made in heaven. "Eventually," says Charles MacFadden, "it became like putting two tigers in a cage."

"We never really had the same philosophy as the Nickersons," Jim Morrow explains today. "Jerry didn't just want to be big, he wanted to control all the linkages — the shipbuilding, the transportation, the packing, everything. But that was a physical and financial impossibility. He spread himself too thin."

In retrospect, it's easy to see that Nickerson — as well as most of the rest of the east coast fishing industry — spread itself far too thin. The prospect of future riches following the declaration of the 200-mile limit had fuelled an incredible expansion in catching and processing capacity during the late 1970s. In just two years, the asset base of the big five east coast fish companies doubled from $200 million to $400 million but almost all of that amount was financed by debt.

Although Bill Morrow says it is "unfair to lump National Sea Products in with the others because National Sea had kept its debt-to-equity ratio in an acceptable range," he admits that, given what ultimately transpired, "even National

---

2. By 1982, when the Kirby Task Force was appointed, it was back down to just eight dollars.

Sea should perhaps have increased its level of equity." By the early 1980s, there were 600 fish plants in the Atlantic provinces, three times as many as there had been in the mid-1970s.

One of the few officials to raise alarms about what was going on in the industry at the time was Nova Scotia auditor general Arnold Sarty. "The Nickersons owed the government a lot of money through a lot of different companies," remembers Joe Zatzman, the chairman of the provincial Resources Loan Board, "and the auditor general was concerned. He even thought we should set up a reserve to cover us against possible problems that might arise."

For his own part, Zatzman says he had few qualms about the province's investment at the time. "My argument was that Jerry was creating a lot of employment and I said at the time on a number of occasions that I only wished we had several other Nickersons in the province to develop our natural resources."

It is probably fair to say that the auditor general's concern was not shared by many others inside or outside the industry at that point.

Although the overall amount of fish caught during the period had only increased by one-third, Rollie Martin says the industry's problems were masked by the simple fact that more fish were being caught. "We had a big squid fishery in 1978-79 and a good herring fishery, and that pumped up the figures."

When the industry's fiscal house of cards fell, it did so with a mighty crash. It was almost as if the fishing industry had been mugged in an alley, stumbled into the street where it was hit by a truck and then finally was run over again by the ambulance that was supposed to rescue it. Instead of facing one problem on just one front, the fish companies' difficulties seemed to feed on each other and compound and multiply.

When European currencies began to plummet in relation to the U.S. dollar while Canada's dollar remained relatively stable, European fish exporters were suddenly able to sell their product more cheaply than Canadians in the vital U.S. market. At the same time, the U.S. protein market became more competitive because poultry prices fell — you could get a turkey for 69 cents a pound in an American supermarket in 1981, a broiler for even less — and that depressed fish prices even more.

Moreover, because much of the fish that is eaten in North America is consumed in restaurants rather than at family supper tables, and because people were eating out less often because of the recession, overall U.S. fish consumption fell by as much as 40 percent in some species in 1981.

That decline in consumption resulted in a corresponding increase in the amount of fish being held in storage. Unfortunately for the fishing industry, its inventory problems were compounded because 1981 was not only an unusually good year for catching fish but it was also the year in which interest rates went through the ceiling.

Because fish is expensive to store — industry estimates suggest it costs about three cents per pound per month to keep fish in storage — the fish companies' carrying charges on their storage costs suddenly rocketed up past 20 percent.[3]

But the industry's inventory problems were, in fact, only a symptom of a much larger and seemingly far more intractable problem that was ultimately at the heart of much of the uncertainty in the industry. Because of the way industry-wide quotas worked, fish companies virtually had no choice but to try and catch as much fish as they could as quickly as possible and then keep that fish in cold storage until they could finally sell it.

The large fish companies, led by National Sea and Nickerson, had complained that the system was inefficient and should be replaced by a more realistic plan that would regulate fishing "effort" instead of the number of fish caught. "Even a farmer puts only so many cows in a pasture or so many sheep in a field," explains Bill Morrow, who says the industry wanted the minister to restrict the total number of vessels involved in the fishery. He believed that the inshore fleet had expanded to the point where "the inshore-offshore balance didn't follow the traditional balance." But the big fish companies were not then on good terms with federal policy-makers, and their pleas were ignored.

By 1981 relations between those companies and their Ottawa regulators were at an all-time low. If you had asked anyone in the executive suites of the large east coast fishing companies in the mid- to late seventies to pick their least favorite politician, the name at the top of their lists would almost certainly have been the then federal fisheries minister, Romeo LeBlanc.

Explains National Sea's Hal Connor: "We didn't even operate in the same worlds. We were trying to build a highly productive, capital-intensive company that would last for all time in a very poor province, and he was a powerful, persuasive anti-capitalist who was looking for votes from the inshore fishermen. We simply didn't know how to cope with this guy. Thank God he was eventually overcome."

---

3. And that, of course, was in addition to the money fish companies were paying on the money they'd borrowed to expand in the 1970s. At the time, that borrowing had been encouraged by the banks. "When the fishing industry gets hot," says Roger Stirling, the president of the Seafood Producers Association of Nova Scotia, an industry lobby group to which both National and Nickerson belonged, "we get the usual parade of bankers coming through my office wanting to know more about the industry. In the good times, the banks designate someone to be responsible for getting money to the industry. But when the bloom comes off the rose, the bankers tend to be a lot harder to find. A lot of fish companies came out of that downturn with some not very good feelings about their bankers."

LeBlanc, a former journalist and one-time press secretary to Prime Minister Lester Pearson, was one of the most unlikely — but certainly one of the most interesting — members of Pierre Trudeau's federal cabinet during the 1970s. In order to understand how LeBlanc, who was once described as "a combination of a curé and a social worker," came to be the *bête noire* of Canada's major east coast fishing companies, you need to know something about his background.

One of seven children of a widowed, sometime farmer, LeBlanc grew up in a poor Acadian community near Moncton, New Brunswick. The family was so poor that Romeo, the only member of his family to make it to university, had part of his education financed by the firewood his father gave the local priests in lieu of tuition fees and part by the contributions one of his sisters sent home out of her salary as a maid for a wealthy Massachusetts family. Even so, when he graduated from St. Joseph's College in 1948, he didn't leave with his coveted BA, but with a blank piece of paper instead. The college held on to his degree until all of his outstanding fees were finally paid.

"I know it sounds corny," his former wife told an interviewer in the late seventies, "but if you're going to understand Romeo, you have to understand his background. He's the one person in a thousand from his area who made it and he feels he owes a debt for that. He doesn't want anything more than to help the fishermen and the Acadians. That's what drives him."

The result was a populist politician who was an intriguing and unusual combination of a man who is absolutely driven and yet absolutely ambitionless. He is probably the only backbench MP, for example, to have turned down a chance to be a parliamentary secretary (often a stepping-stone to the cabinet) because the job offered him no opportunity to help improve the lot of his constituents in New Brunswick. When he finally did enter the cabinet in 1974, it was only after receiving personal assurances from the prime minster that he could play the same role for fishermen—articulating their needs and championing their interests—that Eugene Whelan was then playing for Canadian farmers.

In his first speech as minister, LeBlanc bluntly informed a group of Atlantic businessmen of his department's new priorities. "Any entrepreneur or any business that builds either on cheap labor or on very low prices to fishermen, farmers and woodsmen should have correspondingly little claim to the public purse or the public sympathy," he declared.

As minister, LeBlanc insisted on reading every one of the day's blue dockets—requests from the public to which civil servants had prepared replies for the minister's signature — because he was "mortally afraid he might end up signing or saying something that will screw some fishermen in New Brunswick or Newfoundland," as an aide explained it at the time.

One day shortly after he'd become minister, the aide recalled, LeBlanc was absent-mindedly signing the letters when he was startled by an appeal from a Newfoundland fisherman. The man had been too ill to apply for his lobster license before the official cut-off date and was asking that the error be overlooked so that he could continue to earn a living. The bureaucrat's reply turned down the man's plea and said, in effect, that he should try a little harder next year. "That really freaked him," explained the aide.

Despite the relatively small size of his department and the prime minister's own disinterest in the fishery, LeBlanc was said to be a powerful, if quiet voice in the cabinet, principally because the prime minister respected him. Trudeau, it's said, was fascinated by this man who was part of neither his own technocratic new guard nor the Liberal Party's back-slapping, back-room old guard and who demonstrated such a total lack of personal political ambition. In a 1978 cabinet shuffle, LeBlanc even asked to give up part of his portfolio (the department had been called fisheries and environment) because he wanted more time to devote to fisheries. The PM responded by appointing a separate environment minister.

When LeBlanc was first appointed fisheries minister in 1974, the fishing industry was in a state of chaos. That was partly because years of overfishing by efficient foreign fleets had left lesser-equipped Canadian fishermen with an ever-declining share of the catch, and partly because his predecessor, Jack Davis, was intensely disliked by many east coast inshore fishermen. Morale in the federal department was dangerously low. Although Davis had begun the push to create a 200-mile territorial zone off Canada's coast, government policy was still to move cautiously through the political route of the Law of the Sea Conference.

Bill Morrow says the federal government's general attitude toward the fishing industry's need for an expanded territorial limit was best summed up in an earlier meeting between fishing-industry leaders and then external affairs minister Paul Martin. The industry delegation had come to lobby for a 12-mile limit because, under existing regulations designed to help inshore fishermen, Canadian trawlers were forced to stay outside a 12-mile coastal zone, while foreign fleets were allowed to fish within three miles of shore. Says Morrow: "Martin gave this high-powered industry group 20 minutes, of which 10 was taken up with a phone call to sympathize with a friend who had a sickness in the family. Then he dismissed us by saying, 'As long as the U.S. regards the three-mile limit as the international limit, you haven't got a chance for 12 miles. Now go home, boys, and back to your business.'"

By contrast, says Morrow, Jack Davis "took up the cudgel and the Law of the Sea Conference came into being. Most of us believed his influence was important. As a matter of fact, the fishing industry on both coasts helped to finance his last federal election campaign. National Sea Products contributed and arranged for other east coast firms to make a contribution. That's the first — and I suspect only — time the east coast helped a west coast politician."

Unfortunately for Morrow and others in the industry, however, Davis was soon replaced by Romeo LeBlanc. LeBlanc, who carried more clout in cabinet than Davis, did move quickly on the 200-mile-limit issue. His first step was to temporarily close Canadian ports to the Soviet fishing fleet because of its flagrant violations of the agreed quotas. A year later, Canada unilaterally declared control over a 200-mile zone off its coast.

For LeBlanc, however, the 200-mile limit was not so much a means to help the industry as a whole as it was an opportunity to improve the lot of those inshore fishermen to whom he still felt he owed a debt. From the beginning, there was no question LeBlanc wanted to use the limit as a tool to shake up the balance of power within the industry. He often said that if the 200-mile limit did nothing more than increase the profits of the industry giants, then the policy would have been a total failure.

That view was reflected in the Annual Fishing Schedules, the federal fisheries department's allocations of who was to fish for what, where and when. Those schedules awarded what seemed — to the large fish companies at least — to be the lion's share of the benefits of the 200-mile limit to the inshore fishermen, the independent small-boat fishermen who catch fish on a seasonal basis in the waters near shore.

In 1970 the offshore's share of the total annual allowable catch was 47 percent. By 1981, that figure had fallen to 41 percent. Between 1975 and 1981, on the other hand, the number of inshore vessels increased by 82 percent.

To make matters worse from the companies' point of view, LeBlanc, in 1981, turned the offshore's most profitable fishing zone — the Gulf of St. Lawrence — over to the Gulf-based inshore fishermen. To compensate, the federal government suggested the offshore industry catch northern cod off the coast of Labrador, but the companies claimed that, because of the extra fuel costs required to reach those northern cod stocks, the fish would be seven cents a pound more expensive to catch than the Gulf cod they'd previously harvested.

What all of that added up to, so far as the offshore industry was concerned, was blatant discrimination against them by the man who was supposed to be the industry's impartial referee. When they'd been tallying up the potential benefits of the 200-mile limit in 1977, none of the companies had bothered to calculate the impact that the minister's own predisposition to the inshore might ultimately have on their bottom line.

The industry's bottom line — and what awful things had suddenly begun happening to it — was the principal subject for discussion when the Bank of Nova Scotia's board of directors met quietly in St. John's, Newfoundland, in the spring of 1981 to review the bank's suddenly troubled fishery-loan accounts. The Bank of Nova Scotia had not only provided all of the financing the Nickersons needed to wrest control of National Sea in 1977, but it was also the primary banker for most of the large companies involved in the Newfoundland fishing industry. When the industry soured, the bank was holding close to $250 million in curdling loans to various east coast fishing companies. That's why the bank's top management asked recently retired senior vice president George Hitchman to return to work to help straighten out their fisheries loan portfolio.

George Hitchman wasn't the only one trying to figure out how to wipe out those loans. Jerry Nickerson came up with a scheme of his own. In April of 1981, he put his proposal to Bill Morrow as the two men waited for different flights in the airport VIP lounge in Tampa, Florida, where they had been attending the annual meeting of National's Sea's U.S. division. Nickerson told Morrow he was thinking of liquidating H.B. Nickerson & Sons Ltd., and he offered National Sea first crack at the company's assets. Although Nickerson was quick to add that he intended to retain his interest in and control of National Sea, he reassured Morrow that he still didn't have any intention of getting involved in its day-to-day operations; he simply wanted, as Morrow puts it, "to end up with control of one good unit."

Morrow was surprised. "At first I had difficulty believing Jerry was really thinking of getting out of the fish business." He told Nickerson he'd have to think about it and discuss the proposal with others in the company. In the end, National Sea management decided it was only interested in two Nickerson assets — its Riverport plant, which included both a groundfish and scallop fleet, and the Canso Seafoods plant it had acquired from the Nova Scotia government in the early 1970s. "I sensed that those were the best assets Nickerson had," Morrow says today.

Having decided which assets it was interested in acquiring, however, was just the first step in what was to become a complex, lengthy process that would finally shred the illusion of intercorporate harmony between the Nickerson and Morrow interests.

Jerry Nickerson had told Bank of Nova Scotia officials that the assets National Sea wanted to buy were worth $65 million, almost three-quarters of Nickerson's indebtedness to the bank.

"No bloody way," retorted Bill Morrow. National Sea's own estimates of the worth of the assets was a maximum of $30 million "and a large part of that had to be considered 'goodwill.'"

Because the two sides were so far apart in their valuations and because there was the potential for conflict of interest — as the company's majority shareholder, Nickerson, was, in effect, selling his own assets to himself, and if the price paid for those assets was too high, minority shareholders might suffer financially as a result — Merrill Lynch in New York was hired to come up with what is known as "a fairness opinion."

But the first figure Merrill Lynch came up with as realistic — $16.5 million, which included $5 million for what was called "synergistic value" — was far less even than National Sea had been prepared to pay originally. "I told Jerry that if we were on our own in this, we'd pay the $30 million," Morrow recalls, "but that we could be in really serious trouble with the other shareholders if we agreed to pay $30 million after Merrill Lynch said $16.5 million."

Morrow says he came under increasing pressure to agree to a higher price, and not just from Jerry Nickerson. By this point, Nickerson was in such financial difficulty that the Bank of Nova Scotia effectively controlled Nickerson's now 56.5 percent interest in National Sea and had even begun to appoint its own directors to National Sea's board. "I was getting pressure from those directors and from the pro-Nickerson directors on the board," Morrow says. "Jerry's directors were saying, 'You've got to say yes. Otherwise, the bank is going to move in on Jerry.' And some of them were telling me too that if I didn't go along, I'd have to quit or be fired."

George Hitchman increased the pressure in September 1981 when he effectively "fired" Merrill Lynch without waiting for it to submit a final, formal opinion on the worth of the Nickerson assets.

By now Nickerson was sinking deeper and deeper into a financial quagmire. "National Sea stopped paying dividends around this time," Bill Morrow remembers, "and we started to hear rumors that Jerry was slowing down in his payments to the Fisheries Loan Board. That wasn't too serious in itself, but it was an indication." At about the same time, H.B. Nickerson & Sons Ltd. approached the Nova Scotia Resources Development and Loan Board — the provincial government agency through which it had borrowed a good deal of money in the past — to try and negotiate adjustments in loans from the board to several of its subsidiaries in order to transfer cash or collateral to the parent firm. The board turned the request down.

"I was trying to get Nickerson to pay the arrears on its loans, so I was in frequent negotiations with Jerry during this time," Joe Zatzman recalls. "They weren't always pleasant conversations. Jerry felt I was being too tough on them." But Zatzman defends his hard line, noting that "I always looked at the money we lent out as if it were my own money." Besides, he adds, "everyone was having problems, but not everyone was in arrears. We knew National Sea was facing difficulties too, but it was never in arrears to us."

By this point, however, the turndown in the industry's fortunes was also beginning to have an impact on National Sea. In August of 1981, National Sea announced it was temporarily closing down a number of fish plants in eastern Canada, laying up part of its trawler fleet and laying off 1,800 employees. The main factor in the decision, Bill Morrow complained to reporters at the time, was "federal fishing regulations limiting access to fish stocks which can profitably be caught by the trawler fleet."

Fisheries Minister Romeo LeBlanc, for his part, was having none of that. With more adept marketing by the companies themselves, he said, National Sea's problems could have been avoided. "It's a simplistic argument to blame the poor financial situation on the government," he told reporters in Ottawa.

Replies Morrow today: "Romeo never did understand that Canada was competing with Europe, South America and South Africa in the commodity market and with the weak European currencies and the strong U.S. dollar. We were losing $6,000-$7,000 on each load of cod blocks while the Europeans were making a profit selling below our prices."

No matter who or what was to blame, there was no doubt that the problems facing the entire industry were serious. In the late summer of 1981, H. B. Nickerson and the Lake Group in Newfoundland followed National Sea's lead and began closing down plants and laying off workers. By the fall, 4,000 Atlantic Canadians were out of work because of the industry's problems.

As if to emphasize the severity of those problems, Canadian Press reported on October 9, 1981, that National Sea, Nickerson and the Lake Group were discussing consolidating some of their fishing and marketing operations. The announcement had made in a written statement and none of the companies, CP reported, was prepared to say anything more about the discussions at this time.

The discussions, in fact, had come about at the instigation of George Hitchman and the new federal minister of fisheries, Pierre DeBané. Having tried and failed to ease the bank's risk by selling off the Nickerson assets in Nova Scotia, Hitchman had come up with yet another scheme, this time to have National Sea take over management of four Newfoundland companies — Nickerson, the Lake Group, Fishery Products International and Penny — that owed the bank substantial amounts of money.

It probably shouldn't have been surprising that the Bank of Nova Scotia would look to National Sea to help it figure out how best to manage the fish companies it was about to inherit. "At the time, we were still doing significantly better than the rest of the industry," Morrow says, "so Hitchman decided we must be smarter than the rest of the industry."

Without telling him why, Hitchman called Morrow to a meeting at his office in Toronto. When Morrow arrived, he was surprised to be greeted not only by Hitchman but by four senior executives of the Bank of Nova Scotia and several representatives from each of the Newfoundland companies, including, of course, Jerry and Harold Nickerson, who also just happened to be his own majority shareholder.

Morrow was even more surprised when Hitchman made his proposal. Saying that he wanted to find a private-sector solution to the companies' financial problems before the government was forced to step in, Hitchman announced that he wanted to put all of the Newfoundland companies together into one and turn it over to National Sea to manage. At the end of three years, according to Hitchman's timetable, National Sea would end up owning 80 percent of the companies while their original shareholders would be left with 20 percent.

"Mr. Hitchman," Morrow said when he had finished speaking, "could I see you privately for a moment."

Outside the office, Morrow quickly made the point that National Sea was a publicly traded company and that he simply couldn't just agree to throw its assets into a pot. Given that one of the companies involved in the scheme the bank was proposing was National Sea's own majority shareholder, he was also worried about the possibility of conflict of interest. In fact, Morrow added, he wasn't even sure he should be a participant at this meeting. "I'd like to call Bill Mingo and check it out before we go any further," Morrow said.

When he telephoned the company's lawyer in Halifax, however, Mingo told him that he was already acting for Nickerson in connection with some of their other assets and was worried that he too might be in a conflict-of-interest situation. He advised Morrow to call Alec MacIntosh, a well-known Toronto corporate lawyer, to get his advice.

Even though MacIntosh was getting ready to leave for a meeting in Minneapolis in less than two hours, he agreed to see Morrow right away at his office. As soon as he heard what had happened, he told Morrow to get out of the meeting as quickly as possible. Even by staying in the same room, he said, you may be implicating yourself.

But when he went back to the bank to tell Hitchman what he'd been advised, Hitchman brushed his protests aside and led him back into the room. Bill has a little problem, he told the others, so instead of selling him the assets, we're going to lease them....

"Mr. Hitchman," Morrow interrupted, "I can't—"

Finally, Hitchman did get Morrow to agree to have a study team of engineers, businesspeople and bankers study the situation to see if they could come up with a solution that would work.

"We were still working on finding ways to try and put [Nickerson and National Sea] together when all of a sudden, the Bank comes along and says, 'Halt! Now, let's look at putting together a Newfoundland company,'" Rollie Martin remembers.

Like the companies it was supposed to service, Martin's InterOcean had also fallen on hard times. "We'd gone from a group that was expansionist, project-oriented to a group that was almost a task force on survival. We had people working on shutting down plants in Prince Edward Island, we had people working on arrangements to bring together parts of National Sea and Nickerson in Nova Scotia and then, suddenly, we were asked to work on this survival plan for Newfoundland. Essentially, by this stage we were a consulting firm, even though we were still owned by the two companies."

Whatever Jerry Nickerson's real long-range plans for InterOcean might once have been, they no longer mattered. Those employees who'd joined from one of the two companies in the headier days of the late seventies began drifting back to their original firms or finding other jobs during the winter of 1982 and, by the summer of 1983, InterOcean, for all practical purposes, had disappeared too.

So had Hitchman's scheme to have National Sea run the Newfoundland fish companies. Part of the problem was that Hitchman himself wasn't prepared to accept the terms of a deal worked out between National Sea and a Clarkson Gordon consultant the bank had hired. Hitchman essentially fired the consultant after he reported that the only way to make the scheme fly was for the bank to swallow $49 million worth of bad loans first.

Even if Hitchman had okayed that part of the deal, however, it probably wouldn't have worked anyway because the Newfoundland provincial government also balked at a request to provide a $40-million loan guarantee as part of the deal.

The abortive Newfoundland deal was the first public indication of the growing direct involvement of the Bank of Nova Scotia in the east coast fishing industry, and not everyone liked it. Richard Cashin, for one, the president of the powerful Newfoundland Fishermen, Food and Allied Workers Union, told Canadian Press he worried that the industry was in danger of being reshaped "to suit the objectives of the banks." The Bank of Nova Scotia had become more and more directly involved in the day-to-day operations of all the fish companies. On December 22, 1981, it even obtained a power of attorney, allowing it to conduct H.B. Nickerson's business as a part of a deal in which Nickerson put up its 29 offshore vessels as collateral for a second mortgage in order to get desperately needed working capital.

According to Bill Morrow, Hitchman had now begun to despair of being able to resolve the industry's problems by himself. "Hitchman went to DeBané, maybe even Trudeau, and said the bank was going to pull the plug on the industry."

On January 7, 1982, having already agreed to guarantee new loans to help keep the industry afloat in return for a Bank of Nova Scotia undertaking to hold off on calling its old loans, Trudeau appointed his aide, Michael Kirby, to head a high-level task force to figure out what should now be done with the fishing industry.

Initially, the task force wasn't supposed to become involved with the nuts-and-bolts question of the financial restructuring itself. Its job was to look more broadly at the existing situation in the industry — the size of the fleet, the number of processing plants, the marketing system it was using — to determine if, and how, the industry could be made more profitable.

While Kirby's task force began its work on those broad-brush questions, officials at National Sea and Nickerson continued — under pressure from Hitchman and the Bank of Nova Scotia — to try to work out a deal to put at least parts of their two companies together and thereby reduce the level of the bank's exposure.

Early in May 1982, the two sides announced that they had reached an agreement for National Sea to take over the marketing of all Nickerson products made in Canada and sold internationally. At the same time, National Sea agreed to lease two older, medium-sized Nickerson-owned fish plants at Lowell and Westford, Massachusetts.

While Bill Morrow insisted at the time to a reporter from the Toronto *Globe and Mail* that the marketing deal had not been forced on National Sea — "We have talked about doing this as far back as 1973 when we were totally separate companies" — he concedes now that the arrangement left National Sea "with a bad case of indigestion. In theory, it was difficult to argue with the concept," he says, "and if it had been done on a rising market, it would have been a better deal for us. As it was, we were in a sloppy market."

Under the terms of the deal, National Sea had to pay cash up front for Nickerson's fish and it had no say over what or how much Nickerson's fleet was catching. "If we'd controlled production, we could have diverted the Nickerson fleet where it was needed," Morrow says. "Instead, they could catch a lot of ocean perch, for example, which we already had a huge inventory of, and there was nothing we could do about it. I did have a verbal agreement with Harold [Nickerson] that he would slow down production on a pro rata basis if National Sea did, but then I ended up spending all my time arbitrating disputes, and the market downturn meant we never had a chance to work out the refinements in the system."

George Hitchman had no interest in waiting patiently for the refinements to work themselves out. He began telling Morrow how he should run his business. "His favorite phrase became, 'Get rid of it,' Morrow recalls. "It didn't matter that we had 80 percent of the North American holdings of ocean perch in our inventory, something that should have put us in an ideal position to influence the price and the supply. Hitchman just said, 'Get rid of it. Don't worry about the price. Just get rid of it.' Anything that looked surplus to him, he told us to get rid of. 'It's my money,' he'd say."

In December 1982, National Sea took one more step in the process of reducing H.B. Nickerson & Sons Ltd. to a virtual shell of a company when it agreed to buy all of Nickerson's lobster operations in Nova Scotia and New Brunswick — including three processing plants and 11 buying and distribution stations — as well as its 51 percent interest in 11 longliners. The sale came hard on the heels of an admission by Nova Scotia premier John Buchanan that H.B. Nickerson was a full year behind in its loan payments to the province. Although Buchanan attempted to put the best possible face on the situation — "I'm confident Nova Scotia taxpayers will get back every red cent of the $17 million owed to them," he told the Halifax *Chronicle-Herald* — not everyone was nearly so confident.

George Hitchman wasn't. No matter how many of its assets Nickerson sold off, the company's financial situation didn't seem to improve. Finally, Hitchman lost patience. "The whole thing's got to be restructured," he told Morrow one day. According to Morrow, "that's where the nationalization proposal came from."

If Hitchman did suggest to the federal government that it should nationalize the east coast fishing industry, he was only one of literally dozens of people who were making suggestions about what should be done to solve the industry's problems.

As Michael Kirby labored over the final draft of his report, Newfoundland's fisheries minister Jim Morgan, for example, suggested that the task force "will have failed in [its] main task" if it didn't recommend a huge influx of federal money into the fishing industry, while the province's Liberal leader was equally convinced that it "would be cheaper in the long run" to simply allow Nickerson and the other big fishing companies to go broke so that the Newfoundland government could then step in, expropriate them and run them properly.

After the Kirby Task Force filed its report with the government in November 1983, a powerful cabinet committee, chaired by Economic Development Minister Don Johnston and including key east coast cabinet ministers, such as Allan MacEachen and Gerald Regan, was set up to oversee both its implementation and the restructuring of the major fishing companies.

The committee eventually came up with its own proposal to form two huge "super companies" by amalgamating Nickerson with the three Newfoundland fishing companies and leaving National Sea to operate on its own. The rationale for this split, which was actively promoted by the new fisheries minister, Pierre DeBané, was to broaden the Newfoundlanders' traditional cod-fishing base by adding Nickerson's potentially lucrative scallop fleet to its mix and, not coincidentally, to make it more difficult for Brian Peckford's Tory Newfoundland government to sandbag future National Sea corporate decisions that might cost jobs in Newfoundland.

In order to attempt to transform that vision of the fishery of the future into a corporate reality, the cabinet committee naturally turned to Michael Kirby for help. Following completion of his report, Kirby had jumped from federal politics to a job as vice president for corporate affairs at CN, but he was happy to return to the fishing fray once again. In late March he assembled a team made up of some of the best and brightest from his task force and began what amounted to an endless round of shuttle diplomacy as he hurried from Halifax to Toronto to Ottawa to St. John's and back again, talking endlessly with bankers, fish-plant owners and provincial government officials.

INTERLUDE
"Have you ever been to sea, Billy?"

"**R**IGHT then, that was 100,000 of red …" Linda Roxall repeats for the benefit of the unseen person at the other end of the telephone line as she makes a note on the pad in front of her. Eric Nowe has been sitting quietly on the other side of the desk in Roxall's cramped Port Services office in National Sea's Lunenburg headquarters examining the crew list for the fishing trip he is scheduled to begin this morning. Suddenly, he sits up straight.

"Get the coordinates, darlin'," he urges Roxall, "get the coordinates." After more than 25 years of fishing off Canada's east coast, Nowe knows better than most just how critical each seemingly incidental tidbit of fishing intelligence may be in determining whether a trip to sea will be a success or what the fishermen — who are paid for what they catch — appropriately call a "broker."

Since National Sea — the company that hires him to captain one of its vessels — wants Nowe and his crew to catch mainly redfish during the fishing trip he is about to make, the report that another ship caught 100,000 pounds of redfish yesterday is of more than passing interest to Nowe.

The summer of 1988 has not been a good one for catching fish of any kind in Atlantic Canada. As he looks over a daily status report that outlines which National Sea trawlers are landing at what port, when and with how much fish, he notices that one vessel is slated to arrive at the Canso plant later that day with just 115,000 pounds of fish after more than a week of fruitless fishing. "Scandalous, man, just scandalous," he declares to no one in particular. "They'll be lucky to get their $52 a day [minimum wage for a failed trip] for that one."

So Linda Roxall's information that another trawler has hauled in 100,000 pounds in a single day's fishing could be critically important. Was it the result of a few lucky tows? Or is it indicative of a much larger concentration of fish in the same spot, waiting only to be caught? Nowe will try to find out the details later when he contacts the ship's captain by radio-telephone himself to ask for details. For now, he will settle for finding out exactly where the fish were caught. As Linda Roxall repeats the longitude and latitude, Eric Nowe makes a note on a piece of paper.

"Oh and by the way, Eric," Roxall says after she finishes on the phone, "we have some mail we want you to drop off on the *North* on your way —."

"Oh Jeez." Eric Nowe isn't pleased. The *North* is the *Cape North*, National Sea Products Ltd.'s first-ever factory freezer trawler, a floating fish factory that can spend up to two months or more at sea, not merely fishing but freezing and processing its catch too. The *North* is the pride and joy of corporate head office, and the new flagship of the National Sea fishing fleet.

But to Eric Nowe and more than a few other veteran fishermen from the regular fleet, the *North* is little more than a pain in the butt.

For starters, they still worry — despite company assurances to the contrary — that the fish the *North* is catching (500-700 tons of finished product per trip) is fish that should rightfully belong to them and the traditional wetfish boats they fish from. They also fret that they will lose their best young fishermen to the more lucrative guaranteed daily wages now being paid to crew members aboard the *North*. The *North*, moreover, is a nuisance. Other National Sea vessels such as Nowe's trawler, the *Cape Ballard*, often have to steam out of their way to deliver mail to or pick up a parcel from the *North*.

Nowe looks at the status-report sheet in front of him to see exactly where the *Cape North* is currently fishing. "Jesus," he says, again to no one in particular, "that's at least a full day's steam out of our way, more probably."

Linda Roxall, who has heard it all before, ignores his protests. "And Mr. Kimber here," she continues, pointing in my direction, "he's going to be going with you as far as the *North*. He'll be spending a few days there." Nowe says nothing. He simply looks me up and down, trying — without much success — to hide his obvious frustration.

My purpose in making this trip is simply to get a firsthand look at what fishing is really like in the late 1980s. "The boardroom stuff is all very well and interesting," Bill Morrow has told me on more than one occasion, "but it all starts with the fishermen. Without the fishermen, there isn't any National Sea." Because the *Cape North* was scheduled to be fishing within a day's steam of the Nova Scotia coast during this trip, Morrow suggested I travel out to the factory freezer trawler on one of the company's wetfish boats, spend a few days aboard the *North* and then hitch a ride back to port with a returning trawler. "That way you can get to compare the two types of fishing and be back home within a week," he explained. But between the time we agreed to that arrangement and this morning, the *Cape North's* fishing plans — unknown to me — had changed and she was now fishing nearly three days' journey from Nova Scotia, in an area close to 200 miles off the coast of Newfoundland.

Although much has changed in the fishing industry in the nearly 90 years since National Sea began its corporate life as a fishermen's supply operation back in 1900 — the essential and essentially unpredictable reality of fishing has changed little.

It is, in fact, the last major industrial enterprise in the world in which raw material is still hunted instead of raised, grown or produced. On the one hand, of course, the hunters have grown more sophisticated — utilizing everything from ever more efficient nets to high-tech electronic instruments to help them detect and report the presence of fish 1,000 fathoms below the surface of the ocean. On the other hand, the environment in — and the regulations under — which the hunters operate have become increasingly complicated and restrictive.

"We're being pulled in too many different directions," Eric Nowe tells me as we — Nowe, 14 crew members, an official observer representing the federal fisheries department and myself — drive along Nova Scotia back roads in a two-hour, three-taxi convoy from the Lunenburg fleet office to the company's Lockeport fish plant, where the *Ballard* is currently tied up.

Although Lunenburg is ostensibly the vessel's home port, the company — under the terms of its contract with the fishermen's union — is permitted to divert the ship and its cargo of fish to any of the company's Canadian east coast plants for unloading and processing as required by corporate needs to efficiently manage the processing side of its mammoth and complex operations. Under the terms of the agreement, however, the company must transport the men back to their home port and then give them 48 hours free time before requiring them to return to their ship to go back to fishing.

That's how Nowe and the crew members of the *Ballard* got to spend a rare Friday-to-Monday weekend at home. "First time in seven months," Eric Nowe tells me pointedly. The reason such "normal" weekends are rare for fishermen is logical if nonetheless galling to many of them. Because the company's land-based fish-processing plants generally work a five-day week, the company tries to schedule the arrival of its fishing boats from Sundays to Thursdays so it won't have fresh fish sitting in its plant, unprocessed and deteriorating in quality, over a weekend. "It'd be a shame if the plant people couldn't get their weekends off," Nowe says sarcastically, "but the fishermen ... well, who cares about them?"

Despite his unhappiness at having to ferry me to the *Cape North*, Nowe's essentially gregarious nature wins out over his understandable frustration and he proves a friendly enough and a willing, if opinionated guide to the current state of the Canadian fishing industry.

Nowe is not the *Cape Ballard*'s regular skipper. Roy Dagley is, but since Dagley is taking several trips off this summer to tend to a convenience store he owns, Nowe — the ship's mate — is filling in as skipper.

Nowe does not look like a fisherman. A tall, trim man in his mid-50s with greying, close-cropped hair, he wears faded blue jeans, a white golf shirt edged in black, and aviator sun glasses. With a constant stick of chewing gum in his mouth and a strong Lunenburg accent that almost seems overlaid with a Texas drawl, he strikes me as more of a cowboy than a fisherman.

But make no mistake about him. He is a fisherman. His father was a fisherman before him. And his older brother, Morris, under whom he learned the essentials of the business, was one of National Sea's top skippers until his retirement earlier this year. Nowe's own oldest son — he has four children, two boys and two girls — has just taken up scalloping after spending two years studying forestry. "He came back a little while ago and announced he wasn't going back to forestry — he wants to go fishing," Nowe tells me with a smile. "'If you're going to do it,' I told him, 'you work your ass off for three or four years on deck and then you set your sights on the wheelhouse. The wheelhouse, that's the only place you want to be.'" He shrugs. "I told his mother, 'Don't argue, he's got to make up his own mind.' What else are you going to do?"

Nowe's wife's parental concern about her son's decision to abandon his university training for the fishing business has to be tempered, at least slightly, by the realization that fishing has long been a family business for the Nowes. "At one point," Nowe boasts, "there were seven of us from our family all working for National Sea at the same time." His wife, who comes from a Lunenburg fishing family too, has worked in the plant herself. And today, their son-in-law, Terry Hayward, is one of the rising stars of National Sea's fishing fraternity and a mate aboard the *Cape North*.

Despite that, and despite his own 30 years on the sea, Nowe tells me firmly that he plans to retire in five years or so when he is 60. And, he insists, he no longer believes fishing is a proper business for a young man to get into. "You can't make any money any more," he tells me. "There's too many rules and not enough fish."

Not that many years ago — Eric Nowe can remember the time — wetfish trawlers like the *Cape Ballard* would steam four or five hours out of Lunenburg harbor, "shoot away and haul back" for a few days until the holds were full to bursting with whatever was running — cod, haddock, pollock — and return to port to sell it to the company, no questions asked.

Today, there are a thousand different rules and regulations — international treaties, national quotas, company policies — that restrict where you fish, which species of fish you harvest in which zones and even how many bruises of what size there can be on each fish.

"The last trip I frigged it up myself because I was trying to do what the company wanted," Nowe complains. "The company wanted us to bring back so much pollock and so much cod." In their first few days off Lunenburg, they hauled back 100,000 pounds of pollock. "But the company wanted the pollock last so it would be freshest, so I figured, okay, let's go down off Georges [Bank, the rich fishing ground southeast of Nova Scotia] and get some cod and then we'll come back up here and get the rest of the pollock. So we went down to Georges, not much there, so a few days later we came back. And nothing — they were gone. Not one bloody pollock anywhere."

Nowe does not dispute the company's need to catch the kinds of fish the marketplace is demanding rather than settling, as in the old days, for whatever the fishermen can catch. "We're market driven now," he says matter-of-factly. And he doesn't even quibble with the company's need to get its fish in a particular order so the most in-demand and most valuable species arrives at the dock freshest. He simply points out that all of it makes the job of the fishermen —"the guy at the end of the line" — that much more difficult.

The fisherman's job has never been an easy one.

By the time the first of the companies that ultimately became National Sea got their start at the turn of the century, Lunenburg was already famous for its "iron-men-and-wooden-ships" fishermen. Three times a year — spring, summer and fall — they would sail out of Lunenburg harbor in their esthetically beautiful but workman-like schooners and head for the Grand Banks off Newfoundland.

The living conditions aboard those vessels — where the fishermen might spend as long as three months at a stretch — could quite rightly be considered Dickensian. Consider, for example, this description by American writer and fisherman George Matteson: "The crew sleep in the forecastle (fo'c'sle), the cramped, poorly ventilated space below deck in the very point of the bow. All cooking is done on an oil-fired stove in the same tiny space. When the stove is off, the forecastle is often cold and damp, smelling of mildew, sweat and fish. When the stove is on, it is terribly warm and smells of rough food and hot oil. Overall, it is like living in a defective incinerator."

Frederick William Wallace, a Canadian writer who spent a good deal of time aboard the Canadian fishing fleet in the early years of this century, was no less downbeat about conditions in the living and sleeping quarters. "The stove glowed red-hot," he wrote of one trip, "[and] the rank odor of disturbed bilge-water mingled with tobacco reek, tarred lines, oil-skins and fish."

While a fishing boat is still no luxury liner, living conditions have improved dramatically. Aboard the *Ballard*, for example, the ship's officers each have a private cabin, and the fishermen bunk two to a cabin. There are showers and flush toilets, a separate galley, even TVs and VCRs.

But living conditions aboard those fishing vessels at the turn of the century were less of a concern among the fishermen themselves than you might expect. That's partly because the fishermen simply didn't expect better, and partly because, when they were catching fish, the fishermen rarely slept for more than a few hours at a time anyway. When they did, they were likely so exhausted from their day's labors that their sleep was undisturbed by the lack of space or the smells or even the extremes of heat and cold.

During the era of the saltbank fishery, the fishermen worked from dawn to dusk, trawling by hand from small dories that were set out from the mother ship, and then often spent their evenings preparing their trawls for the next morning or finishing dressing the fish they'd caught for storage. All of that work was done on deck, often in rough weather — "Rough weather is so much a part of the deep-sea fishermen's life that he doesn't think anything of it," Wallace reported — or driving rain — "Wetness means nothing to fishermen [either]. It's a wet business anyway. If it isn't rain, it is spray or handling dripping lines and gear, or standing in pens of wet, slimy fish."

Even after the day's work was done and the fishermen settled down for an hour or so of card-playing or talking before turning in for a few hour's sleep, they could still be required back on deck. In his *Roving Fisherman*, for example, William Frederick Wallace recalled an incident that occurred one night after a long day's fishing. He was discussing politics with some fishermen in the fo'c'sle when the captain suddenly called out: "'All out! Git the jib in an' stick a reef in your mains'l....' It was dark and the gallant schooner was driving through it with the sprays flying. The wind was cold and strong and the men staggered on the wet, sloping decks. In the murk far astern, Seal Island light flashed. 'Haul in your sheet.' Twenty of us, strung along the weather gangway, pulled in unison, pausing only to regain our balance as the schooner rolled down in the gusts. The Skipper eased the helm down and the long heavy boom was draggered amidships and the tackles hooked in and made fast. The sail was quickly lowered and the wind knocked out of it. Standing on the taffrail, two of the younger men leaped up on the boom and clambered out on the footropes of the spar — projecting some 15 feet over the water astern. The reef-tackle was hooked into the earring; the reefband hauled flat along the boom; the earring lashed.... In a very short time, the job was completed, the sail hoisted again and the vessel swung off on her course." And the men went back to arguing politics as if nothing unusual had happened.

If anything, working conditions became even worse when the industry switched from a traditional salt fishery to fresh fishing during the early years of the twentieth century.

The saltbank fleet not only used what we would regard today as inefficient fish-catching technology, but it also had to depend on wind power to move it to, from and around the fishing grounds. That meant there were plenty of what the fishermen referred to as 'lay days' in which they didn't fish because they were waiting for a breeze to take their vessel to a better fishing spot. The fact that it usually took most of three months to fill their holds with fish, coupled with the fact that the ships could remain at sea almost indefinitely anyway because the catch was salted, took some of the pressure to be fishing all the time off the schooner skippers. They could quite logically decide to stop fishing each day at sundown or not to fish at all on Sunday. After all, what was another day here or there over a three-month period?

Fresh fishing was different. It was a race against time in which fishermen had to work round-the-clock if necessary to catch as much fish as quickly as possible to fill the hold, so the ship could return to port before the first-caught fresh fish rotted and couldn't be sold. That not only made sea days busier but it also increased the level of personal danger associated with fishing. "The work of a trawler is fraught with danger to life and limb," Wallace wrote. "In those ships, the price of safety is eternal vigilance.... A moment of forgetfulness or carelessness and an arm or a leg can be torn off, a foot or a hand mashed to a pulp."

Even today, fishing is still an extremely difficult, dangerous job. "A coal miner faces the greatest risk of any land-based worker in America," George Matteson wrote in *Draggermen*, his 1979 study of the U.S. east coast fishing industry, then added: "But every day a fisherman works, he is two-and-one-half times more likely to be killed.

"Setting and retrieving the net requires very careful teamwork and absolute concentration. The men repeat the same tasks dozens of times a week, hundreds of times a year, and thousand of times in a lifetime at sea. One mistake over that time will mean a man badly hurt, perhaps dead. Every step of setting and recovering the net is done in exactly the same way each time. Each man performs the same tasks down to the last detail. By establishing this sort of routine, it is more likely that there will be no confusion, no steps left out and less chance of an accident."

Still, accidents do happen. Nowe tells me about the time a few years ago when he watched from the wheelhouse as one of the warps — the steel cables used to control the trawl doors that keep the net open underwater — went slack on deck as if the door had caught on an embankment on the bottom of the ocean. "Suddenly, it snapped back up and this fellow happened to be standing by it when the warp came up like this," he indicates the area between his right arm and his side, "and took the man's whole arm right off. Just like that. The fellow looks down and he looks around and all he says is, 'Boys, I think my arm's gone."

On the *Ballard*'s last trip, a deckhand suffered a broken arm while he attempted to jump from one section of the vessel to another just as the ship was being buffeted by a sudden wave. "Even though he couldn't do no more work, he stayed out for three more days so we could finish fishing," Nowe says admiringly. "These guys, they're pretty tough."

They are. Fishing, in fact, remains one of the few industries left in which a person can be hired with virtually no education and no skills, save a good strong back and a willingness to work, and eventually earn his way to the top in the wheelhouse. That's not to suggest for a moment that fishermen aren't bright, simply that the skills required to become a top fisherman are not taught in any school but must be learned at sea by hard experience. It is a point of pride with the fishermen I talk to that there isn't a single skipper in National Sea's fleet today who didn't start out as a lowly deckhand.

The captain of the *Cape North*, Larry Mossman, dropped out of school when he was only 17 to become a deckhand. He not only worked his way into the wheelhouse but all the way to the master's job on the biggest and most important ship in the entire National Sea fleet before he was even 30, Nowe tells me pointedly. "And they couldn't have found a better man in the company for the job."

"Most fishermen are school dropouts," Nowe adds matter-of-factly. "I am. And I'd wager so is everyone else aboard. Just look around you."

We're standing in the wheelhouse of the *Cape Ballard* as the crew members quietly, efficiently go about the business of making ready to sail.

They are, in fact, probably a not untypical group of fishermen. There are 14 of them. The usual crew for the trawler is 15 plus the skipper but one of the regulars broke his collarbone last night, and Eric Nowe has turned down Linda Roxall's offer of two available greenhorns as replacements. "We don't need no bodies just taking up space," he explained. "This is a good group and we can handle what needs to be done." It also, and not coincidentally, means there will be one less person who will be entitled to share in the proceeds of their catch.

The crew members range from 18-year-olds in Van Halen T-shirts to men in their mid-50s with wives and grown families. "If a man's going to be a successful fisherman and have a family," Eric Nowe says, "he's got to have an understanding woman at home, someone who understands you're going to be at sea most of the time and not be around for your family and not make a lot of money. If a wife wants to see more of her husband or she wants to have more money to spend, well, that's it then. We lose a lot of good young fishermen these days because of family stuff."

Although Manuel, the bosun on this trip, is Portuguese, most of the other crew members are from in and around the ship's home port of Lunenburg, one of Canada's most famous fishing communities.

Their individual and collective connection with the fishery dates back generations. Take the chief engineer, for example. He started fishing with his own father 25 years ago, and that's the way his father started before him. "Dad started when he was nine," he tells me one evening. "On the saltbankers. I remember he came back from one trip — three months it was — with all of $16 to show for all his time. He died at sea. In an accident aboard the *Cape Scotia*. He was 64."

Accidents are far from the only occupational hazards fishermen face. At least two of the crew on the *Ballard* have had problems with alcohol. That shouldn't come as any surprise, Nowe explains, because of the lifestyle fishermen lead. Fishermen spend anywhere from 10 to 12 intense days at sea away from family, friends and the comforts of ordinary life. When they arrive back in port, many feel the need to let off steam and celebrate their fishing success or drown their sorrows if the trip was a broker. Because there is so little time ashore — usually only two days before their ship sails again — a fisherman will sometimes try to pack too much shore life into too short a time. What that can spawn is a vicious cycle of fishing and partying and fishing and partying that ultimately leads to a serious alcohol-dependency problem.

"Some guys party for 48 hours," the chief engineer tells me, "and then they end up back aboard. 'What'd you do?' I ask them. 'Oh, I had a great time,' they say, but they can't even remember what they did."

Gary, one of the trawlermen, was like that, Nowe tells me, but a few years ago, he decided to straighten himself out. "First he went to the Rehabilitation Centre up in Dartmouth, but there were too many weird types there for his liking, so he decided he would just do it all by himself. And he has," Nowe adds with almost fatherly pride. "Today, he spends his time off with his 36-foot Cape [Island] boat he bought. He keeps it polished up like a car. And now, instead of spending his money on booze, he buys all kinds of candy and pop to take with him every trip. Don't you, Gary?" Gary obligingly opens his duffel bag. It is filled to the brim with all manner of candy and chocolate bars. He grins.

Another trawlerman — an older man who has spent time in the hospital as a result of medical problems related to his alcohol abuse — has not been so successful. After a weekend of partying, he arrived back aboard this morning reeking of alcohol. Soon after we clear port, Nowe confronts him. "You know, —, I almost wasn't going to take you with us this time," he tells him in a tone that is part father-confessor, part angry schoolmaster. "You can't keep doing this to yourself and you can't keep showing up here smelling of the stuff. You're on your last legs around here, old man, you know, so think about it. You're the only one who can do anything about it." The trawlerman looks down at the floor, then finally shuffles silently off to his cabin for a few hours of sleep to help put the weekend behind him and prepare him for the long trip ahead.

Perhaps not surprisingly, there are rules forbidding crew members from bringing alcohol or drugs aboard ship without the express permission of the captain. The only time there's alcohol aboard the *Ballard*, a crew member says, "is when we're heading for home from the last trip before Christmas. Then the captain breaks out a bottle and we have a little party."

"So Stephen," Eric Nowe says expansively when we return to the wheelhouse, "you own a yacht? This here is yachting weather." It is. We are finally at sea. It is a clear, cool, sunny summer day with just a light breeze. The only thing you can see in any direction for eight to 10 miles is blue water and blue sky. "On a day like this," Nowe says, "I can't think of any place I'd rather be."

But there are other times, Nowe adds, when the fishing grounds are so "t'ick o' fog" you can't even see the bow of your own vessel from the wheelhouse. Days, sometimes weeks, on end of fog. "That's depressing." And in the North Atlantic, of course, there is also the ever-present danger that a sudden storm that will appear from nowhere and play havoc with a vessel and its crew.

Back in the early 1900s, Wallace described the onset of one such storm that began on an apparently calm evening while the crew were down below listening to favorite phonograph records. Wrote Wallace: "'Put that one on again,' the skipper began. 'That's a catchy —' He never finished, for at that moment the *Morrisey* took a terrible lurch to port. The man who was holding the phonograph took a header into the lee bunk and every fellow to windward was hurled across the cabin to sprawl down into the lee lockers and into the lee bunks.... There was a frightful creaking of the vessel's hull and she could be felt twisting like a basket under pressure. A great crashing and roaring sounded on deck; the daylight was blacked out, and down the skylight and gangway poured the frigid Atlantic — filling the cabin a foot deep and almost choking us with the steam and ashes which blew out from the blazing hot stove."

Storms at sea, of course, can be far more than an inconvenience. They can be killers. "We were right around here," Nowe tells me a day later as the *Ballard* slips past Cape Race on the eastern coast of Newfoundland, "the night the [oil rig] Ocean Ranger went down. We were riding out the same storm." Although Nowe heard the Mayday, there was nothing he — or anyone else — could do. All 84 men aboard the oil-drilling rig were lost, a reminder of just how alone and isolated and helpless you can really be in the middle of the North Atlantic.

The *Ballard*'s crew had their own reminder less than a year ago when an electrical fire in the ship's galleys forced the crew to issue their own Mayday signal. Luckily, they managed to get the fire out themselves and proceeded to shore under their own power. "But it makes you think," admits Nowe.

Today, there is plenty of time to think. The *Ballard* is making straight for the *Cape North*, and Captain Nowe says he sees no point in beginning to fish until after they've gotten rid of their cargo. The reason is that the fishermen deliver their catch to the dock fresh and must return to port within a certain number of days after they take their first fish in order to prevent the fish from becoming rotten and inedible.

So today, two full days after they steamed out of Lockeport, the *Ballard*'s crew is still doing busy work — repairing nets, replacing markers on the warp so that both trawl doors will go into the water evenly.

Between shifts — the men work six hours on, six hours off, 24 hours a day at sea; although if the fish are running, they may actually end up working up to 18 hours a day — the men catch up on their sleep, read (the cook, a science-fiction fan, is just getting into a new book "about a guy who trades in his lungs for a set of fins," while one of the trawlermen is curling up with *The Horse Ranch*, a western by Earl Murray that he tells me "isn't bad to pass the time.") or watch pre-recorded movies on the ship's VCR (the fare this trip ranges all the way from *Hamburger Hill*, a Vietnam war movie, to *Teen Lust*, a soft-core porno flick).

Meals are served around the beginning and ending of each watch. Breakfast is from 5:30 to 6:30 a.m., dinner (as the noon meal is called) is from 11:30 to 12:30 and supper from 5:30 to 6:30 p.m. The fare tends to basic meat-and-potatoes dishes — hot dogs and french fries, Newfoundland steak (fried baloney), roast beef, macaroni — but that doesn't make the job of preparing it any easier. Arthur, who has previously worked as a cook in the Royal Canadian Navy and aboard National Sea's factory freezer trawler *Cape North*, starts his day at 4:00 each morning and is responsible for everything from selecting the menu to washing the dishes. The job, in fact, has changed very little in the 80 years since Frederick William Wallace described fishing-schooner cooks as "a very capable, hard-working class. They baked bread and had to prepare meals — 'three square meals a day' for crews numbering as many as 24 men, without any assistance. They set and cleared the table and washed up the dishes. It was their job to make out the list of stores required and keep account of the quantities consumed. The fresh water was in their charge and they looked after the oil lamps in cabin and forecastle, as well as the port and starboard sidelights, the anchor light and binnacle lamp.... When the vessel was on the grounds, the cook had to bear a hand on deck attending the dories coming and going until such time as there were crewmen available to take charge, and he frequently took the wheel and steered. In rough weather, his ability to prepare hot meals commanded one's admiration. At unearthly hours in the morning, he had to turn out and get the breakfast ready. To be rated as a good cook demanded the qualities of a superman, and most of them were good cooks, else they didn't last long aboard a fisherman."

When crew members aren't sleeping or reading, they tend to gravitate to the galley, where coffee is always available and where they can get what the fishermen call a "mug up" and a bit of conversation.

Today, there is a good deal of talk about items they've heard on the news during their brief time ashore, especially the recently announced Nova Scotia provincial election, which will take place four days after they're scheduled to arrive back home from this trip, but two days after they set sail for their next one.

"Will we be home at the right time to vote in the advance poll?" asks one.

"Don't matter," says another, "there's no one worth voting for anyway."

"The one to vote for," says Eric Nowe, "is the party that says it's going to raise the price of fish." There are nods and grunts of agreement before Nowe concludes. "Too bad none of 'em will." Unlike many of the old-fashioned fishing skippers who remain aloof from their crews, even taking their meals at sea in their cabin, Eric Nowe is very much part of the galley camaraderie. "I need to be with people," he says. "I can't imagine walking around all day with a long face and not talking to anybody." That probably shouldn't be surprising — Nowe is not only usually a mate rather than a captain but he himself also identifies very closely with the concerns of the fishermen. He was, in fact, the man most responsible for getting them union representation nearly 20 years ago. His concern then, as today, was with the price of fish.

There is also a good deal of discussion today of other news of a recent seizure of a significant number of marijuana plants in untended land in Nova Scotia's Annapolis Valley. "Got to watch out for that wacky tabacky," jokes one.

"I remember being on one ship," says the chief engineer, "and we had a couple of young fellows aboard this trip. They asked me if they could use the engine room for something. I said, 'Well, I don't see why not, just as long as you don't leave a mess.' And they said, 'Oh, don't worry, we won't leave no evidence.' I said — 'cause I finally figured out what they were up to — 'You won't leave no evidence because you ain't going to be smoking any of that stuff down here.'"

As usual, the fishermen can bring almost whatever subject is under discussion back to fishing and their own lives. Not surprisingly, they enjoy recalling shared stories about fishing trips past. "Remember the time with the frozen peas?" the chief engineer says. Everyone laughs without the story even having to be told. "We had this new fella out with us one trip," one of the fishermen explains later for my benefit, "a real greenhorn, and so we made him go aft with this bag of frozen peas. Told him the best way to get the fish to swim into the net was to drop these frozen peas off the stern. We told him that was his job and sent him back there to do it. We all had a great laugh, but didn't it beat all — that was the biggest bagful of fish we brought in all trip!"

Inevitably, whenever fishermen get together, most of the talk centres around the state of the fishing industry and what can — and should — be done, and soon, to set things right.

Not unlike most workers in most jobs anywhere, fishermen believe they don't get paid enough money for the work they do. But the problem for fishermen is complicated because they don't, in fact, get paid a wage for the work they do at all, but receive a share of the take from the fish they catch. They are what are known as "co-adventurers," sharing with the owners in the profits and risks of each trip. Under the complex system that has developed over the years, the fishermen's share of the catch is based on 37 percent of the gross value of the fish landed during a given trip, minus the costs of food and other provisions for the trip. All of the experienced crew members receive an equal share of the crew's portion of the "lay," as it is known. In addition, the ship's officers each receive an extra percentage of the total catch — ranging from a five-eighths-of-one percent share for the cook to a two percent share for the mate and the chief engineer — paid from the company share. The captain receives five percent for his work. Whatever is left after that goes to the company to pay for costs of operating and maintaining the vessel, as well as to make a profit.

The system works fine if there are plenty of fish available for the catching and if the fishermen can command top dollar for the fish they catch. Neither has been the case in recent years. Thanks to everything from previous years of overfishing to tighter government catch regulations to circumstances beyond their control, and even knowledge, fishermen say they've been catching fewer and fewer fish each year for about four years. "One year I took nine trips off and I still ended up with $65,000," Eric Nowe says, "and the men made $30,000,

$35,000 each. That was the good times. Now ... now, it isn't so good."

"I'll be lucky if I make $20,000 this year," one deckhand tells me, "and that's not taking off more than two or three trips all year. You know $20,000 might not sound too bad ashore, but I'll be at sea maybe 240 days in the year and when you're at sea and there's fish, you work straight through, 18 hours lots of times. Jesus, man, I'd hate to think what it would work out to if I tried to figure it out in hours."

To make matters worse for the fishermen on the *Ballard* and the company's other wetfish boats, fishermen who work aboard the factory freezer trawler receive a guaranteed daily wage as well as paid shore time and bonuses for short trips. "Why should the guys on the *North* get paid so much a day and we don't?" the deckhand wants to know. "I mean, they're out 30 [days] and in five, out 30 and then they get a whole trip off. What's so hard about that? We spend more time at sea in the run of a year and there's more isolation for us? Why don't we get paid like they do?"

Eric Nowe, for one, believes that the day will soon have to come when the fishing industry completely abandons its traditional "share-of-the-catch" system for paying fishermen and moves to an hourly or daily wage. "The co-adventurer thing might have been fine once," he says, "but how can we be co-adventurers when the company's the one setting all the rules about where to fish and what to catch and everything?"

To rub salt in the wound, the decline in fishermen's real incomes, Nowe tells me, has come about just exactly at the same time as National Sea Products Ltd. — their ostensible co-adventurers — has been proudly reporting record profits. In fairness, the fishermen add, they were making what they call "top dollar" in the midst of the company's financial traumas in the early 1980s.

The disparity is partly the result of a four-year collective agreement signed by the company and the fishermen's union, the Canadian Brotherhood of Railway Transport and General Workers, back in early 1985, when the company was still struggling to escape from its brush with nationalization. That contract — which provided for an increase of just one cent a pound over the entire four-year term of the contract in the price paid to fishermen for market cod, for example — could not have anticipated the dramatic turn around in the market price of fish or in the company's fortunes.

Regardless of the cause, however, the result has been that the fishermen watched with declining incomes and rising anger as the media touted National Sea's incredible resurrection and second coming. Today, some blame the union. "We give them $32 a month and what happens," complains a trawlerman, "they send $21 to Ottawa to pay staff and secretaries and such there. And the other

$11 goes to Halifax. What do we get for our money?"

Others blame the company. "If they were smart, they'd have reopened the contract a year ago and said, 'Okay, boys, things are going well and we want you to have your fair share.'"

Nobody is expecting that the next round of negotiations, scheduled to begin late this year, will be easy or that a settlement will come quickly. Few, however, expect there'll be a strike. "It's just not in the cards," says one.

Some of the fishermen say they'd quit fishing if they could, but many have tried. Most end up back on the ships, where many spend more time each year than they do ashore. "I left once, worked on the gypsum boats," a trawlerman tells me, "and when I left I vowed I'd never come back on one of these things again." Why did he? He shrugs. "There must be something about it I like, but I'll be goddamned if I can say what it is."

Bill Morrow won't be surprised. "When I went out on the boats as a young fellow," he had told me, "I used to listen to everyone griping, damning the company for this and damning the company for that. But then, when the fish were running and everybody was working flat out to get as much fish as quickly as possible and get back home, suddenly it was exciting and you couldn't imagine any job on shore that could be as satisfying." Morrow's own theory is that, in spite of their complaints, fishermen do enjoy the challenge involved in a job in which you are rewarded for your success at the task. "I'm not sure that's what they'll tell you, but I think it's the truth."

When I ask him why he's still fishing after more than 25 years, Eric Nowe begins by defining what he doesn't like about other jobs. "I don't like punching a clock," he tells me. "I worked in the plant once and I couldn't stand that. I was crazy to get back fishing." He pauses, realizes what he has just said. "Maybe you should ask me what I like about fishing someday when we're hauling back lots of fish and we're all out there on deck pulling together and thinking about getting enough fish to go home. Ask me then, because that's when I can't think of anything else I'd rather be doin'."

But that, unfortunately, is not a sight I'm about to see on the *Ballard*, at least not on this trip.

It's a little after three a.m. on the morning of August 25, 1988, and, with just a few hours to go before we rendezvous with the *Cape North*, Captain Nowe has decided to "try a couple of tows just to see. Everybody's gettin' itchy to get fishin'." Although the *Cape North* is also fishing for redfish, Nowe tells me that the conditions that make this a good area for the *North* — an abundance of redfish, but not in such huge concentrations as to overload its factory freezing capabilities, and an irregular ocean bottom that is especially well suited to the

North's mid-water trawling gear — make it all wrong for the *Ballard*.

Still, fishing remains an inexact science at the best of times and Nowe was not about to steam this far without at least giving it a try.

The first tow — a two-hour trawl that produced only 1,500 pounds of redfish — seemed to support his doubts. A second two-hour tow at daybreak produced identical results. "I think it's time we headed nor'west and got us some fish," Nowe said as we shook hands and I began to climb down a rope ladder to join the mail in the little inflatable Zodiac speedboat the *North* had sent over to pick us up. "Good luck," I called as the Zodiac pushed off from the *Ballard*. "Thanks, we'll need it," Eric Nowe called after me.

The *Cape North* is something else again. From the water it looks like nothing more than a larger version of the *Ballard*. In a sense, that's true. It's 105 feet longer than the *Ballard*, and its capacity is 500-600 tons of finished product versus 190 tons of headed and gutted fish for the *Ballard*. And the *North* also still appears to catch its fish in essentially the same way as its regular stern trawler counterparts — by dragging a trawl along behind it in the water and then hauling the net aboard and dumping its catch into a hold below deck.

Below deck, however, you suddenly begin to realize what makes the *Cape North* unique in the Canadian fishing industry. In the *Ballard* and other wetfish boats, the fish that get dumped down into the fish hold are simply headed and gutted and then covered with ice in order to preserve them until they can be taken to shore and transferred to a land-based processing plant for filleting or whatever final processing is required.

On the *North*, by contrast, the fish hold opens up into a full-fledged factory, not unlike a land-based processing plant. There are machines to head and gut the fish as well as fillet it. The fish are then quickly frozen in what are known as shatterpaks — individual fillets — or made into frozen blocks for use later in other products. There is even a fish-meal plant where the fish by-product — heads, tails, guts — can be turned into bags of premium fish meal.

The advantages of the system are obvious. Because the fish is frozen within hours of being caught, it is firmer and tastier, and therefore more likely to attract top prices in an increasingly quality-conscious international marketplace. At the same time, because the fish is processed and frozen rather than simply "iced," the ship itself can remain at sea indefinitely — or at least as long as its fuel and other provisions last. And again, because the fish is being frozen, the ship can range freely over great distances to fish in waters that would not otherwise be practical.

Those are just a few of the reasons why National Sea carried on a sometimes controversial eight-and-a-half-year battle during the 1970s and 1980s to convince

Ottawa to grant a license to operate a factory freezer trawler. The company ran into opposition along the way from everyone from a federal fisheries minister who believed that the fishermen rather than the company should own the vessel, to union leaders who feared the ship would wipe out shore-based jobs, to fishermen's wives who worried about the fact women were to be permitted to work aboard ship, to the premier of Newfoundland who didn't want any Nova Scotia-based company catching and processing fish he regarded as the property of his own province.

The company eventually overcame all those objections and its five-year license, which was ultimately granted in late 1985, will expire in 1991. After that, the company will have to convince federal policy-makers again that a factory freezer trawler not only helps the company but that it does so without harming other fishermen and land-based fishing communities.

Regardless of the outcome of that debate — and the company is confident there won't be nearly as much debate this time around — the mere existence of the vessel has already had a profound impact on what might be called the fishing lifestyle.

That becomes abundantly clear the moment you enter the wheelhouse. In contrast to the spare, almost spartan atmosphere aboard the *Ballard*, the *North*'s wheelhouse is decorated with hanging plants, and there's brewed coffee, fresh fruit and muffins on a table. You can even catch the faint sound of light-rock music coming from a radio that's tuned to a St. John's, Newfoundland, pop station.

Despite the fact that the wheelhouse is far more high tech than the one aboard the *Ballard* — the Furuno video depth sounders and fish finders boast color monitors, for example, that help the ship's officers find and catch fish hundreds of metres below the surface — the atmosphere here is easy-going, almost casual compared to the sense of urgency that pervades wetfish trawlers like the *Ballard*. That's probably because the *North*'s crew know they are here for the long haul — they may spend more than 60 days at sea on a single trip in an unvarying work-shift routine of six hours on and six hours off — and so they don't need to regard each tow or each shift as their last.

The officers themselves seem different as well. While Eric Nowe and the other senior officers aboard the *Ballard* are all men in their mid-40s to mid-50s, not one of the deck officers aboard the *North* is over 35. Perhaps not surprisingly, that creates a wheelhouse atmosphere that seems more in keeping with a college graduate class than a conventional fishing vessel.

Between their regular navigational and fishing duties, for example, the officers amuse themselves by fiddling with a Rubik's cube or collectively attempting to solve the weekly crossword puzzle from the *New York Times*. "What's a three-letter word for Tibetan Gazelle? Starts with the 'g.'"

In the mornings, they listen to — and gently mock — an open-line show from radio station VOCM in St. John's. "You'll have to listen," Captain Chris Morrow tells me, suddenly slipping into a heavy Newfoundland accent: "'Hello again, dis is Bill Rowe, da v'ice of da common man — *and woman* — in Newfoundland and Labrador. You call me up and you tell it like it is to our vast listening audience.'

"It's wonderful. They get the same people phoning in every day. One woman called the other day to complain: 'Now Bill, all you ever talk about is sex — you're always going on about them mammograms and abortions and homos in the church — you got to get off this sex, sex, sex.'" He laughs. "Someday, we're going to call him up on 'Free-for-All Friday,' and say we have a skidoo for sale."

And there are plenty of shipboard pranks to help pass the time too. Phony telexes informing crew members that their request for a trip off has been denied, for example. They've already told one of the other crew members that I'm a company psychologist sent out to prepare a report on the mental state of the ship's crew. Later, the crew member will show up nervously at my door. "You asked to see me," he says tentatively. I hadn't.

Don't let the jocularity fool you, however. Despite their banter and their relatively young ages, every one of the officers aboard the *North* is a bright, highly trained and seasoned fishermen.

Although he is the son of the company's chairman of the board, Chris Morrow began his career on deck like any other fisherman. That was 10 years ago. Today, he is one of just 15 fishermen in the entire company to possess a Fishing Master Class 1 license. That means he is certified to captain any sized fishing vessel anywhere in the world.

It is a tribute to the company's growing emphasis on training and certification to note that, despite Morrow's qualifications, he is still only the first mate and relieving skipper aboard the *North*. That's because Larry Mossman, the *North*'s regular master, who is off this trip, has had more years of fishing experience than Morrow and possesses a Class 1 license as well.

So does Terry Hayward, Eric Nowe's son-in-law and Morrow's first mate this time around. Hayward, an easy-going young man who began fishing with Nowe's brother, Morris, also comes from a seagoing family. His father was a seaman rather than a fisherman, and his uncle is a boat builder. During his off-hours, Hayward often reads fishing-industry publications in search of news about the latest developments in fishing technology and vessel design. "Look at this one," he says at one point, handing me a copy of a recent issue of *World*

Fishing, a fisheries-management trade magazine published in England. The story is about a newly built Irish fishing vessel, the *Veronica,* which will have a capacity of 2,000 tons of fish and will be capable of freezing 250 tons of fish every 24 hours. "Now they're not going to do any processing at sea, but still and all.... That is something else."

Third Mate Steve Comeau, from Bridgewater, joined the *North* two years ago as a deckhand and quickly worked his way up to the wheelhouse. During his seagoing career, Comeau has worked aboard an oil tanker — "I was making $750 a month and I remember waking up one day thinking I could be making better money fishing and be home every few weeks too" — and, ironically, aboard the *Ballard* before deciding he preferred the life aboard a factory freezer trawler. "There were a great bunch of guys on the *Ballard,*" he tells me, "but I found when I was on the wetfish boats, I'd end up coming home after a few weeks, and the first day I'd have a few, and then the second day I wouldn't feel much good for anything, and then the third day I'd be back at sea again."

He joined the *North* two years ago. "The first two trips," he remembers, "seemed like forever, but then came the trip off and by the time it was over, I felt better about coming back." Crew members aboard the *North* work two consecutive trips — with five days at home in between trips — and then get the vessel's third trip off entirely.

"I prefer to think of it as a day off for every two days you work," Tom Pittman says. "That makes it sound better." Pittman is the *North*'s second mate. He's also the grandson and namesake of one of Lunenburg's most famous fishermen. Although he is just 26, he has already spent a good deal of time in the fishing industry. He worked as a deckhand for his Uncle Mike, the skipper of National Sea's wetfish trawler the *Cape Briar,* for example, then did a stint as a small-boat fisherman aboard a 65-foot trawler and even spent some time as a processor in the Lunenburg fish plant before finally signing on with the *Cape North* two years ago.

Pittman says he has "a love-hate relationship with the sea. When I'm ashore I want to get out to sea but when I'm out here, I'm always thinking about getting home," Pittman tells me as he shows me to my cabin.

By contrast with the *Ballard,* where I shared a small cabin with one of the trawlermen, my quarters aboard the *North* seem almost luxurious.

It's a single cabin with a bunk, a couch, a table, a sink, carpeted floors and plenty of space for stowage. The sign above the door to the cabin says "Funken." Most of the signs throughout the ship, as I later discover, are also in German — even down to the one on the small bottle opener by the sink that boasts an advertisement for Holsten beer from Hamburg.

That's because the *North* actually spent the first nine years of its life as the *Scombrus,* fishing for German owners, before National Sea bought it. Then, for most of its first year as a National Sea vessel, the ship was actually still run by a German captain and a number of key officers that National Sea hired to train its own officers in the ways of factory freezer trawling.

"What we found out," Terry Hayward tells me later, "is that the Germans were ahead of us in some things but behind us in others. Quality was a problem. I remember we went up north and the Germans would load up the fish hold and then leave a bagful of fish out on the deck. The fish would freeze and they wouldn't be good for anything then. But you couldn't tell them anything. The Germans wanted to do things their way and not the company's way, and it caused a little bit of tension."

Most of the Germans have since left, although several did decide to stay and become Canadian citizens. Two of the 62 crew members on this trip, in fact, are from that original German group.

Of even more interest, perhaps, is the fact that five of the crew members — two stewards and three processors — are women.

Although there were some initial fears about the impact the presence of women might have on social relations in what has always been an all-male world (and in what is essentially a very small floating town where people must live and work together, sometimes for more than two months at a time), the concerns have proved groundless.

That's not to suggest there haven't been some shipboard romances, even the occasional marriage among crew members. "But if that happens, they both don't usually continue with the ship after that trip," Captain Chris Morrow tells me. "You couldn't maintain any sense of romance in a situation where you had to spend every moment — working, eating, relaxing, sleeping — with that other person for weeks and months at a time. And there's no escape out here."

For the most part, the women who work on the ship have simply earned the respect of their male colleagues for doing their jobs well. In fact, the person selected as the *Cape North*'s "crew member of the year" last year was a woman. Steward Shirley Baker is already a legend aboard the *North.* "I've never seen anyone work so hard," Terry Hayward tells me at one point. "It doesn't seem to matter what time of day or night, Shirley's out there working. She must shampoo the carpets twice a trip. And she doesn't just do her job. She's always volunteering to do the laundry for people or help out with this or that." Baker, a native of Bridgewater who joined the *North* a little over a year ago, says she loves the sense of camaraderie that is an integral part of the seagoing and fishing life. "It's a great place to work," she tells me.

As Tom Pittman takes me on a tour of the ship, my first sense is that the *North* — with its large officers' cabins, separate officers' and crew's messes, hospital, pharmacy, canteen and laundry room — is a far bigger and far more luxurious ship than the *Ballard*. When I suggest that to Pittman, however, he just laughs. "You ever been aboard any of the Norwegian boats? They put us to shame."

He also points out something that is only apparent as you go deeper into the bowels of the ship to the crew's quarters. Many of the cabins in this section of the vessel are, in fact, even smaller and more crowded than those aboard the *Ballard*. Some of the trawlermen and fish processors must sleep three to a cabin with no separate wash-up facilities at all.

"This ship was built for German officers and deckhands and a Portuguese processing crew," Terry Hayward will explain later. "That's why you see such a difference between the cabins we're in and the ones everybody else lives in. The Germans were only concerned about their own."

"Now *this*," Tom Pittman says as he leads me down a hallway, "I got to show you this, Stephen, because this sums up the German attitude exactly — this is *the jail!*" And it is, complete with steel bars. "I guess they used it to keep rowdies in when they were at sea." He laughs. "We use it for storage."

On our way back up to the wheelhouse, I ask Pittman about his famous grandfather. A few days earlier I'd visited with his grandmother to hear her recollections of the late skipper whose fish-finding prowess was legendary. "I don't really know much about him at all," he tells me. "He was long gone when I was growing up. So it's just what I hear — that he was very big, that he was the one who got the Lunenburgers into trawling, that stuff. But I'd like to know more.... Here, let me show you something," he says, stopping at his own cabin. He takes a small photo he has tacked to the wall beside his bunk. "Tom Pittman the third," he says proudly. "Seven months old." He laughs. "He was born January 4th. We sailed January 3rd. My wife was in labor when we left." Pittman didn't see his first-born son for nearly two months. When I ask him about that, he shrugs. "I wish I'd been there, but, you know, what can you do? That's just the way it is out here."

It is. It's difficult enough for those of us who live and work on land to imagine what any deep-sea fisherman's life must be like. But it becomes that much more difficult if you try to imagine a situation in which you spend two months — sometimes more — living in confined quarters, isolated from family and friends with no days off and little to do besides work, eat and sleep.

"You get used to it," Tom Pittman tells me.

Not everyone does, of course. Although there is now a core group of men and women who have chosen to make relatively permanent careers out of the *North*, there was also a good deal of turnover among crew members, especially in the early days. Even today, it is easy to find people aboard ship who are already actively looking for other jobs.

"What do you hear about the oil rigs?" Kay, one of the stewards, asks me soon after we are introduced. Newfoundland premier Brian Peckford and Prime Minister Brian Mulroney have recently announced a major new effort to develop the Hibernia oil fields off the coast of Newfoundland, and Kay thinks she'll apply for a job working on one of the supply boats servicing the offshore-drilling rigs as soon as exploration begins again. A Newfoundlander who worked on supply boats based out of St. John's until the offshore industry collapsed in the mid-1980s, she says she wants to get a job on a supply boat, partly because it would allow her to spend more time in her home province and partly because she finds the *North*'s long trips and close quarters confining.

"The money's steady and there's nothing to spend it on out here so you get a good cheque when you get home, but I don't like it because you don't have any privacy here," she tells me, "no place for moods and stuff. You can't really talk to people because if you tell somebody something, then everybody knows. But if you whisper, everybody wants to know why you're whispering."

On her last trip, she tells me, she and another steward "got into a row over who was supposed to do what and we ended up having to go see the captain and getting it straightened out. Things that wouldn't bother you on land, because you could go home at night and forget about them, become big deals out here because you can't escape from them."

And those ordinary, everyday problems become exacerbated, she says, when the ship isn't catching fish. "Like now," she tells me. "Everybody's on edge because we're not catching very many fish. If we were waiting for the last 100 tons or something, it'd be okay because everybody'd be anticipating going home. But we've been out here three weeks and we're still waiting just to reach the halfway point [in filling up the hold] so everyone is upset." By actual count, in fact, the *North* has hauled in over 600 tons of fish in order to produce 195 tons of finished product in three weeks.

As we sit in the officers' mess talking, four or five of the trawlermen wander past the door on their way out to the fish deck. The call has come down from the wheelhouse that it is time to "haul back" the net.

"Let's hope this one's a good one," Kay says.

It isn't.

Up in the wheelhouse, as Tom Pittman skillfully works the winches that will haul the *North*'s huge mile-long trawl from the sea bottom, 200 fathoms below, back up through the opening in the stern and onto the deck of the vessel, Chris

Morrow anxiously scans the blue-black water astern, looking for the telltale patch of boiling, foamy greenish water that will announce that a good-sized net full of fish is about to break through the surface.

This morning, unfortunately, there is no green spot, just a small, bobbing ball that looks red in the distance. For a few moments, no one says a word.

Finally, Morrow breaks the silence. "How much you figure?"

"Two, maybe, if we're lucky," Pittman answers.

Two tons of redfish is not much to report for a four-hour tow, not nearly enough to keep the processors down below busy for more than a few hours. For the factory workers, that will mean another afternoon of movie watching, card playing and waiting in the mess.

Down below in the factory area, Production Manager Paul Vandine takes the news in stride. There is little else to do but hope that the next tow will be better.

Like the other officers aboard the *North*, Vandine is young — just 26 — and from the Lunenburg area but, unlike them, he'd never worked on a fishing boat until he landed a job as a processor when the *North* began fishing for National Sea two years ago.

"I'd wanted to go fishing when I was a kid," Vandine tells me, "but unless your parents were fishermen or your father was friends with a captain or something, it was really hard to get a chance." He laughs. "When I was in high school, I wanted to become an optometrist, if you can believe that." But a botch-up in his student-loan application forced him to postpone his first year of university, and that put him on a course that he says led him almost straight to the *North*.

"A friend and I decided to go to Europe for five months. I ended up spending everything I'd saved for university, not to mention being $2,000 in debt to my friend by the time I got back to Lunenburg. I was really keen to find a job to pay back my friend, so I went back and got a job at the Foodmaster. That was a local grocery store where I'd worked as a kid."

The store was also, and not coincidentally, owned by National Sea Products. So when the company began looking around Lunenburg a short time later for bright young people to train for its new dockside grading program, the store's manager was quick to suggest Vandine's name. A few years later, when the company acquired the *Cape North*, Vandine decided it was his opportunity to use what he had learned about filleting and grading fish according to quality in a job where he could also pursue his boyhood dream of going to sea.

Vandine began as a processor himself but quickly worked his way up the ranks to production manager. "If you're looking for a comparison," he says of his current role, "this job is very much like being a hockey coach who's trying to put together his best lines. You try to match the people you have with the job they're best at — you want to have your best packers packing, that sort of thing. And there's lots of psychology involved too, especially out here, if you're going to keep everyone working at their best. If somebody's not doing well — if they're homesick or they got a bad letter from home or they're spending a lot of time off by themselves or whatever — you have to try and talk to them, joke with them, whatever you can. Because it's really a group effort out here. And everyone has to work together."

For his part, Vandine says he plans to stay with the ship, at least until the end of its current five-year license. "I like my job. It requires thought and it gives me responsibility. And I like the money and the time off." Vandine and a friend are already planning a five-week trip to Katmandu during one of his off-trips this winter. "But I'd be a liar if I said I wouldn't rather be home than out here," he's quick to add. "I really don't like being out here at all."

Based on the results of this morning's tow, he knows, he will be out here for a while yet.

Back in the wheelhouse, Morrow shakes his head in frustration. He says nothing.

Despite his relative youth, Morrow — like Eric Nowe — finds it easy to reminisce about those days "not that long ago when you could leave port, shoot away, haul back and not see the deck [for fish] all trip. In those days, you just caught what you caught and there wasn't that much concern about the quality of it either."

Although it is true to say that Morrow and his fellow officers aren't up against the kind of time pressures Eric Nowe and the wetfish-trawler captains face, that's not to suggest in any way that they are not under extreme pressure.

For starters, they aren't merely trying to catch fish but manage a factory too. That means they have to bring in enough fish each day to keep both the trawlermen and the factory's two shifts of processors working full tilt but, at the same time, they have to be careful not to catch more fish at one time than can reasonably be processed within five or six hours. After that, the fish will become less firm and consequently less valuable.

Partly because its license stipulates that a significant percentage of its catch must come from what are considered "under-utilized" fish species, and partly because of the way in which federal fishing quotas are now allocated, the *North*'s fishing options are even more circumscribed than those of the wetfish boats. Consider, for example, these complex fishing instructions telexed to the *North*'s skipper as he left port for one recent fishing trip:

You should direct for redfish in Area 3P [a federally designated fishing zone]. While directing for redfish in 3P, all other species should be limited to a 10 percent by-catch. If you are fishing in 3PS, you should make all attempts to avoid American Plaice because there is only a small amount remaining to cover by-catch for the remainder of the year.

You are also free to direct for redfish in 4VN with the same 10 percent by-catch applicable to other species. Please be reminded that the area of 4VN that is inside the line marking the Gulf of St. Lawrence is closed to *Cape North* for fishing as a condition of license. Redfish in 2 and 3K and 3LN is open to you as well....

If catch rates fall off substantially, you are permitted to direct for cod in 2J3KL. As you are aware our quota in 2J had been caught. We have only a small reserve remaining in 3K. If at all possible, cod fishing should be restricted to 3L where the company has the most quota remaining. If a decision is made to change from redfish to cod, you should contact us in Halifax so that we are kept informed of the vessel's activities and can advise on production priorities.

Your redfish production should be scheduled to ensure that H & G production is a number one priority.

If you have any questions at anytime during your trip, please feel free to contact us. Best wishes for a successful trip.

Regards
NATSEAHOMS HFX

And, of course, despite the fact the *North* can remain at sea for long periods without returning to port, they must deal with the reality that everyone still wants to fill the ship's holds and get back home as quickly as possible. A short successful trip may also mean more money in each crew member's pocket because, in addition to the per-day wages the crew members receive, there are additional bonuses for short trips.

For some of the fishermen, however, the bonus system is actually a sore point. The amount of the bonus relates to the type and value of the fish landed, as well as to the duration of the trip, and the fishermen say the result is that it's almost impossible for them to earn a bonus on a trip such as this one, when they are catching — on the company's instructions — redfish. "I was on a 42-day cod trip and I came back with a bonus of $1,300," one fisherman says. "I could come back from a shorter trip catching redfish and get no bonus. But the thing is, I work just as hard to catch one as the other. And I don't have the choice what we catch." He sighs. "There'll be no bonus on this trip, that's for sure."

This will not, everyone is beginning to realize, be a short trip either. And the frustration in the wheelhouse is becoming palpable. As the *North* begins another tow, Morrow carefully eyes the two color video screens in his master's "cockpit" area. The *North* has two separate devices designed to help him pinpoint and catch schools of fish.

The first is a traditional sonar sounder attached to the hull of the ship. It sends out beams of sound from the ship toward the ocean floor. Based on the echoes that bounce back to the sounding device, the captain can tell not only how deep the water is but also if there are any schools of fish in the vicinity.

At the same time, there's a second sounding device called a transducer attached to the opening of the net. It sends back signals about what is entering the net. That's designed to help the captain "aim" his trawl in order to catch the most fish possible.

As he watches the screens that translate the information from the sounders into colors and patterns, Chris Morrow keeps his left hand on the throttle, speeding up and slowing down the vessel to best position the net to not only catch the fish the sounding devices suggest are down there but also to avoid catching the net on the rough sea floor.

"That looks a little better," he says to no one in particular as bright, thick splashes of green begin to appear like drops of rain on one of the screens.

"There's something down there." Tom Pittman agrees. "I just wish we knew what."

Despite the increasing sophistication of fishing equipment, there are still no devices available that can tell a fishermen what type of fish — from valuable redfish to valueless jellyfish — is really going into his net. "I've seen some ads that *say* [their equipment] can," Terry Hayward tells me, "but none of them really do." And, of course, there still aren't any devices that can make fish magically appear when a fisherman lowers his net.

"We've been very lucky this year," Chris Morrow says. "We've had some good 35-day, 40-day trips. But you can't always be lucky." He looks back at the screens. "We need this one," he adds.

They get it. When the day's second four-hour tow is hauled aboard a few hours later, there are more than 15 tons of redfish fattening the net's cod end.

"That'll keep 'em busy for a few hours," Morrow says, referring to the men and women on standby in the fish factory below. But the relief is momentary. When your job is to catch 600 tons of finished fish products, it seems that there is always another tow to be made, another net to be hauled back.

Down in the crew's mess, a few of the trawlermen are drinking coffee and playing a game of backgammon while they wait for the inevitable instruction from the wheelhouse that will tell them it is time to "haul back" again.

Some of their fellow fishermen aboard the wetfish trawlers dismiss the trawlermen on the *North* as "members of the geriatric set" because they only work six-hours-on-six-hours-off shifts on deck instead of the up to 18 hours at a stretch that they must often do. And unlike their wetfish counterparts, they don't have to head, tail, gut and ice the fish themselves. To a certain extent, the complaint is legitimate. Like the officers in the wheelhouse, the deck crew changes every six hours, regardless of how much or how little fish is being caught. And they don't ordinarily have to worry about what happens to the fish after it is dumped into the fish holds. But, as with the officers, their work is not without its physical and emotional price. By the end of a trip, they may have been working 12 hours a day for more than 60 days without a single day off.

Few of them will concede that their jobs are actually any easier than those on the conventional trawlers either. "The work's no different than on a wetfish boat," one of them tells me. "The only thing is that the money's better. That's why I'm here."

"I been coming out for two years now and I can't say I like it yet," adds another, "but at least there's more money here than there is on the wetfish trawlers. I got a friend, he's on a wetfish boat and he made $20,000 last year. I couldn't live on that."

There are nods of agreement all around. "I got a wife and two kids," says another. "I used to fish wetfish, then I went shore fishing but there was no money in it either. So now my oldest kid is going to school and I need the money so here I am. This is my first trip and I never been away this long before but I just keep thinking about the money I'm making. I figure I can get used to a lot of things for the right money."

Later that day in the officers' mess down the hall, the talk is about money too, but in this case the discussion concerns investing money in the stock market — in National Sea stock, to be more precise.

The mail that the *Ballard* dropped off with me this morning included a stack of pamphlets and a videotape presentation from National Sea's head office outlining a new company program called "Employee Shareholder Program (ESP)," which is designed to make it easier — and cheaper — for employees to buy stock in their company.

Like many large far-flung corporations, National Sea has recently begun using its own slickly produced video programs to communicate with its employees. Given the ubiquitousness of video cassette recorders aboard National Sea's vessels, it's probably as good a way as any to get a message out to the men aboard the ships.

In this case, the video is especially popular because Terry Hayward is one of its stars. During his last trip ashore, Hayward was filmed asking a question about the company program — "Is my investment taxable?" — as part of a visual question-and-answer session involving employees from all parts of the company.

"Rewind it and let's watch it a couple of more times," Steve Comeau jokes as he and Hayward and I eat dinner in the mess.

The food aboard the *North* is far more varied and interesting than that served on the *Ballard*. Tonight, for example, there is a choice of honey-glazed chicken, lasagna with garlic bread or shrimp salad, as well as the usual assortment of accompaniments ranging from hash-browned potatoes to buttered carrots. Last night there was salt cod and pork scraps or bacon-wrapped beef tenderloin. The mess itself is also well-stocked with fresh fruit, bread, cakes and juices for between-meal snacks.

"So, what do you think?" Comeau asks Hayward. "Should I put my money into National Sea?"

"Now's the time," Hayward replies. "I mean, think about it. The ones who got in back in '82 or '83, when the price was just five dollars, they did okay for themselves, for sure. So, right now, the price is down to — what is it? — $11, $12? If you buy now, who knows, maybe in a year or two it might be worth something." He pauses. "I remember I thought about it the last time but then, you know, like everybody else I guess, I wasn't sure what was going to happen with the company and I didn't do it."

Laughs Steve Comeau: "I guess that means you'll have to work for a living then."

Comeau and Hayward have just finished their regular six-hour afternoon shift. After dinner, they may watch part of a movie on the mess VCR — because of their limited time between shifts, few crew members seem to see an entire movie in a single sitting, but satisfy themselves instead with catching half-hour snippets of the movie here and there until they eventually see it all — or retire to their cabin to read for an hour or so, then catch a few more hours sleep before returning to the wheelhouse for the midnight-to-6-a.m. shift.

Tonight, Hayward sifts through the mess's collection of video cassettes — "This has to be the worst selection yet" — before finally settling on something called *Bloody Birthday*, a not-very-good flick about three 10-year-old children who were born without any consciences in the middle of an eclipse. "This isn't going to keep me awake," Hayward announces after five minutes as he gets up to head back to his cabin. "How long you planning to stay with us?" he asks me before he leaves.

"Oh, probably another day or so and then I'll hitch a ride on another wetfish boat going back to Nova Scotia," I say.

Hayward looks at Comeau. They both laugh. "Good luck," says Hayward.

The extent of the luck I would need only really became apparent to me the next morning when I listened in to the radio-telephone conversations between the captains of National Sea's wetfish fleet and Linda Roxall back in Lunenburg. Each morning each of the company's trawlers is required to report its previous day's catch and current position to the fleet office. After a quick check of their coordinates, Chris Morrow informs me that there isn't another National Sea vessel within 100 miles of us.

The reason is simple. Even though the area on the edge of the Grand Banks where the *Cape North* is now fishing is regarded as prime redfish spawning grounds, the fishing zone itself isn't considered especially hospitable for the wetfish boats. That's largely because they use groundtrawls — trawls that drag along the ocean floor — to catch their fish. But the jagged, uneven ocean bottom in this area of the Grand Banks can easily tear or damage those trawls.

The *North*, by contrast, uses what is called a mid-water trawl that operates just above the sea bottom, and that, coupled with more sensitive electronic equipment that warns the skipper of the ocean floor's changing terrain, helps keep the vessel's expensive fish-catching gear from being damaged.

The end result is that other National Sea vessels steer clear of this area, which some fishermen refer to as "the hellhole," because, as one explained, "you can fish there for weeks at a time and never see another boat."

Chris Morrow is sympathetic to my desire to get back to shore — I've already lined up a week's worth of appointments for the following week and there's a long-planned family vacation looming on the horizon — but there's little he can do to help. It costs $30,000 a day to operate the *North,* so Morrow can't simply stop fishing for a day or two to ferry me to a wetfish trawler and then steam back to the fishing grounds again. And he can't very well ask one of the other wetfish trawlers to steam out of its way to pick me up either. "As you found out already," he reminds me, "most of the trawler captains aren't too kindly disposed to us now. Imagine what it would be like if we asked them to take a day off fishing to come out and get you?"

In the end, there is little to do except fall into a routine of eating, sleeping, reading, watching movies, wandering the ship and waiting. One evening, four dolphins swim by the ship, putting on a spectacular show as they frolic in the North Atlantic. "Too bad they weren't heading west," Tom Pittman jokes. "Maybe you could hitch a ride with them."

Each morning, I arrive at the wheelhouse in time to hear the trawlers report their position to Lunenburg. The closest any of the other vessels get to us is 75 miles. "If they get close enough so we could steam, maybe six hours over and back, we could probably do that," Morrow offers helpfully. "The only problem is that that ship just left port two days ago. Even if we get you aboard them, you won't be home for at least another week, maybe more."

I go back to the mess to watch *Bloody Birthday* for the third time. Later that day, I'm back in the mess again watching an old James Bond movie, *To Live and Let Die*, when Chris Morrow arrives.

"How badly do you want to get home?" he asks.

"Badly enough," I answer.

"There's a Portuguese trawler heading past us on its way to St. Pierre. I talked to the captain and he says he'll take you as far as St. Pierre. You'll get there the day after tomorrow but you'll have to find your own way home from there."

"Done," I said quickly. The day after tomorrow — a Thursday — was the day before I was supposed to be heading off on that long-planned vacation with my family. Within half an hour, I was packed and on deck waiting for the Zodiac to ferry me across to the waiting Portuguese side trawler. As I waited, crew members suddenly appeared from every part of the ship with letters and packages for me to mail for them from shore. "It beats waiting for the mail boat," Kay tells me as she hands me two letters and wishes me well. "Say hello to Newfoundland for me," she says.

My enthusiasm for the short journey by launch from the *North* to the Portuguese boat dims quickly when three 50- to 60-foot whales seem to materialize suddenly out of nowhere and begin to swim back and forth between the two vessels, surfacing now and again to breathe.

"Think of the story you'll have," Steve Comeau jokes as he encourages me into the Zodiac, "'Reporter swallowed by whale!'" Without a pause, he turns to the winch operator. "Lower away."

We aren't swallowed by a whale, of course, but we are almost swamped by the outflow from the Portuguese vessel's scuppers. The Portuguese crew is busily washing fish heads and guts off the decks, and the scuppers through which the water pours just happen to be located alongside the Jacob's ladder I have to climb up to get on deck. The Portuguese have apparently not thought to turn off the water flow and the two *North* crew members aren't able to make them understand their frantic hand signals. "Oh, the hell with it," says one finally. "Let's just do it quick."

As the oily, fishy water pours over me, my kit bag and the crew's mail — not to forget into the launch itself — the Zodiac pulls alongside, I scramble up the ladder and my luggage follows quickly after. The Zodiac's crew, not surprisingly, wastes no time getting out from under the scuppers and heading back to the comforts of the *Cape North*.

"This way, please," one of the ship's officers says, grabbing my bag and leading the way to the bridge.

The Portuguese ship is the *David Melgueiros*, a 38-year-old Dutch-built factory freezer trawler. It's "the largest side trawler in the world," Captain Antonio Fonseia says proudly, but then adds with a wry smile that "it's not too modern anymore."

Fonseia is an easy-going but thoughtful 19-year veteran of the international fishing business with a salt-and-pepper beard and glasses that hang from a chain around his neck. He tells me he has visited Canadian ports like Halifax and St. John's "maybe 40-50 times" and has many Canadian friends, especially in St. John's.

Fonseia speaks English fluently. Most of the officers also have a smattering of English — "We learn English and French in school," the radio operator tells me — and I quickly find I can communicate with most of the rest of the crew with a combination of rusty French and various gestures. It isn't difficult, for example, to understand what the young deckhand means when he does a happy finger-snapping dance. "St. Pierre," he says. "Two days. Plenty girls!"

The *Melgueiros* is owned by SNAB, a state-owned Portuguese fishing company that operates a fleet of fishing vessels that roam the world from the waters off Africa to the Falkland Islands to the North Atlantic.

The *Melgueiros*, which left the port of Aveiro on June 29, 1988, for what Fonseia says he expects will be a six-month North Atlantic fishing trip, is actually part of a small flotilla of four Portuguese vessels that are currently fishing in an area just to the east of Canada's territorial waters called the Flemish Cap. Like the *North*, they too are looking for redfish, which they hope to sell to the Japanese as well.

There is even a Japanese technician aboard ship for the trip, the captain tells me. His job is to inspect the catch each day to determine which fish will meet the high Japanese standards for color and texture and which must be rejected and sold to others at lower prices. Although this particular Japanese is "a nice enough fellow" who only rejects about 10 percent of the catch — "There was one fellow on another of our boats that was rejecting 35-40 percent of everything they caught" — the captain says the real problem (shades of his Canadian counterparts) is that there simply aren't enough fish out there to catch anymore.

"The fishing is hard," the captain says. "Three, four, maybe five tons a day. It's no way to make a living. And nothing like it used to be."

The Portuguese have been fishing on the Grand Banks for centuries —

before, in fact, there was even a Canada — but Canada's declaration of a 200-mile territorial limit in 1977, coupled with more recent accusations that the Portuguese have continued to ruthlessly overfish the grounds, has resulted in a Canadian decision to ban their ships from fishing anywhere inside Canada's territorial waters.

To make matters worse as far as Fonseia is concerned, Canadian authorities have also now forbidden the Portuguese to visit Canadian ports to take on supplies. That's why the *Melgueiros* must spend its 48 hours ashore in St. Pierre, picking up fresh fruit and other supplies, as well as giving its 55 sea-weary crew members a much deserved mid-trip break. Captain Fonseia shakes his head sadly. His ship's agent in St. Pierre, he says, will end up having to purchase the supplies the *Melgueiros* needs from a company in St. John's anyway, "so what's the point of keeping us out?" he asks.

Over the years, he tells me, he and other Portuguese fishermen have developed close friendships with people they've met in St. John's. "I'd like the chance to visit them again," he says.

He also knows all too well that his young crew members would much prefer the bustling night life of urban St. John's to the quainter style in tiny — population 6,300 — St. Pierre. But there is nothing he can do about that and he is resigned to the reality that the closest the *Melgueiros* will get to St. John's on this trip is the opportunity to listen to Bill Rowe's "V'ice of the Common Man and Woman" open-line show from VOCM Radio. Incredibly, it is playing in the wheelhouse here too, although no one seems to be listening.

After they leave St. Pierre the crew of the *Melgueiros* won't see land again until they return to Aveiro, probably just before Christmas. While at sea, they — or their families back home — are paid a small monthly salary and then, when they return, they receive their portion of the six-percent share of the total value of the catch that is set aside to be divided equally among all of the crew members.

For the officers, Captain Fonseia tells me, "fishing is not a bad living, but it's pretty terrible if you're a crew member." Some of the crew members, I suggest, seem very young. "We have one boy of 14," the captain says. "You know, I had some hard-core movies with me this trip, but I didn't bring them out." He laughs. "That boy, he's not much older than my own son."

While most of the fishermen aboard the *Melgueiros*, like their counterparts aboard Canadian fishing boats, seem to have gotten into the fish business directly from school and learned what skills they possess on the job, their chances for advancement to the wheelhouse are apparently far more limited than in Canada.

Most of the officers I talk to, in fact, have never actually been fishermen themselves, but are instead graduates of navigational schools. The captain, for example, tells me he was trained in a merchant-marine school and has never been a deckhand. And the pilot, who has worked on bulk carrier vessels and merchant ships, only finally switched to fishing a year ago because "merchant jobs hard to find." His first trip on a fishing vessel was for six months off the coast of Africa last year. "Awful trip. Money is shit. This," he adds with a gesture in the direction of the North Atlantic, "much better."

There are no women aboard the *Melgueiros* either. But there are plenty of pictures of them, mostly pinups from the Spanish edition of *Playboy*, which not only decorate one wall of the wheelhouse but are also tacked up on the walls beside many of the bunks in the crew's quarters.

My own quarters for this trip have more in common with some of the things I've read about the old-time Canadian fishing vessels than anything I've experienced on either the *Ballard* or the *North*. The un-airconditioned cabin at the stern of the *Melgueiros* contains sleeping accommodations for eight crew members, although only six of the bunks are currently in use. There is also a very small washroom with a sink — hot water only — a toilet and an overhead tap that the crewmen use as a shower. But since there is no shower stall, the water from the tap seems to wash not only the man taking the shower but also the toilet, sink and floor of the washroom. (Why the shower worked that way was one of those little mysteries that my inability to speak Portuguese prevented me from solving.) The cabin also contains one small sitting table, two chairs and enough lockers for the men to store their luggage and equipment. To get to their work stations or to the mess to eat, the crew members have to go outside along the deck. While that was no problem in the still, warm August air, it brought back memories of some of the conversations I had with some of National Sea Products' older skippers and the stories they'd told of having to battle the winds and the icy rain of a North Atlantic gale just to get from bunk to breakfast in midwinter.

During the 36-hour journey from the edge of the Grand Banks to St. Pierre, I ate with the captain and some of the other senior officers in the officers' mess. Dinner here is far more ritualized than it is aboard the *North,* where the officers would usually wander in just before or just after their shift, order their meal and then sit, alone or in groups of two or three, watching a movie on television while they ate. (There are pre-recorded movies aboard the *Melgueiros* too, of course, but the crew usually watch them together after a meal. As is the case aboard the Canadian fishing vessels, the fare tends to run to recent popular movies with the only real difference being that the movies — *Rocky III, Avenging Force, A Bridge Too Far* — all come with Portuguese subtitles.)

Aboard the *Melgueiros*, all of the officers from each watch eat together, and their meals are served to them by the stewards. "No wine aboard the *North?*" the first officer asks as he pours me a glass of red wine. "Here then, have some Portuguese Coca-Cola." There isn't just wine with dinner — which tonight features a Portuguese fish dish of cod bodies, boiled potatoes and vegetables in a tangy broth, served with fresh baked bread and an apple (which the Portuguese peel and quarter before eating) for dessert — but brandy and port afterwards as well.

"The *North?* What company she fish for?" the first officer asks as he takes a sip of his brandy.

"National Sea. From Halifax," I offer.

"Oh, National Sea," replies the captain, as if he'd just suddenly realized what the words meant, and then adds, as if translating for others in the crew: "N–S–P. NSP!"

"Ah! NSP!" There are nods and smiles from all around the table, then laughter as the officers — including even Abe Ryoichi, the Japanese quality-control officer who doesn't speak either Portuguese or English — raise their glasses in a toast in my direction. "NSP!"

Incredibly, it turns out that the officers of the *Melgueiros* know of National's international sales network. The company has had success in the lucrative Japanese market and now has a sales office in Tokyo. National's sales office in Lisbon, Portugal, purchases fish in markets in Portugal that end up in Japan. Abe Ryoichi pulls out a piece of paper and hands it to me. On National Sea's Halifax letterhead, it lists telephone numbers and addresses for company contacts in Halifax in case he needs them. "NSP!" he says, smiles broadly and raises his glass again.

Tomorrow at 8 a.m., the *Melgueiros* will arrive in St. Pierre. With the nets now completely stowed, and the decks — and even the walls and ceiling of the wheelhouse — completely scrubbed and polished in preparation for landing, there is little to do but enjoy what is left of our last night at sea and to prepare for the partying ahead.

Up in the captain's quarters — unlike the crew's spartan cabin, the captain's quarters boasts a bedroom, a sitting room, a full bathroom with bath and bidet as well as a private television and video cassette recorder — Captain Fonseia is pouring tumblers of homemade cherry brandy for me and his officers. "My sister made it," he tells us. "The cherries are from the cherry tree in front of my house."

My conversations aboard the *Melgueiros* — like those aboard the *North* and the *Ballard* earlier — eventually get around to fishing and to what Tom Pittman had called the "love-hate" relationship with the sea that all fishermen seem to share. They may complain about wages that are too low for work that is too hard and about the time they must spend away from family and friends, but most of them find it impossible to imagine themselves living any other sort of life.

The captain, for example, tells me that he would like to quit his job, stay home and spend more time with his wife and family but, unfortunately, there are no shore-based jobs that will pay him as much as he can make as a fishing captain. What would he do on land, I ask him? "Oh, I don't know," he says. He laughs. "Probably wish I was back at sea." He pours another drink. "Isn't that the truth," he says to no one in particular.

Back in my cabin, a less sedate party is already well under way. Music — American pop, Portuguese folk — blasts from several "boom boxes" in different parts of the cabin, each competing for attention with each other and with the laughter and loud conversation of about a dozen crew members who have crowded into our cabin from other parts of the ship to join in the celebration tonight.

"Drink?" One of my cabinmates is already filling my coffee cup with anisette. "To shore!" he says and we all take a drink. "To women!" toasts another. More drinks. More laughter.

One of the crew members, who has turned his bunk into a makeshift ironing board, sings — in a heavy Portuguese accent — "Get ready, 'cause here I come,'" as he irons the clothes he will wear ashore tomorrow.

"Tomorrow, first thing, I call my wife," another crew member says. He's a Mozambiquan-born fisherman who married a Portuguese woman and moved to Portugal 17 years ago. "Here, let me show you." He hauls out a weathered photo album to show me pictures of his wife — "very pretty, you see" — and his son. He invites me to visit him if I'm ever in Portugal. "I been to Halifax. Many times. Nice place. Nice people. Maybe next time Halifax again." He smiles and raises his glass. "Good fishing! Good friends!"

We all take a drink.

The next morning, shortly after dawn, the rocky outlines of St. Pierre finally come into view. With the exception of those involved in the docking routine, most of the ship's crew appear on deck already dressed in their best clothes, with their cameras over their shoulders. Although even after the ship docks, there are inevitable delays before they are cleared by French customs to go ashore, few seem to mind. The ship's agent has already arrived and begun distributing bagsful of mail from home that's been collecting in his office while they've been at sea. Most grab their letters and packages and hurry back to their cabins to find out the news from home in private before beginning their all-too-few hours of freedom ashore.

As I wait for my own clearances from St. Pierre immigration officials, I thank the captain again for his kindness and hospitality. He waves me off. "If we had asked your captain to take one of our people, he would have done the same for us. That's just the way it is at sea. We help each other." He shakes my hand. "Good luck with your book."

By the end of the day — after a two-hour ferry ride from St. Pierre to Fortune, Newfoundland, and a four-hour bus trip from Fortune to the St. John's airport — I'm winging my way back to Halifax in time to begin my own family vacation the next day.

"No, it didn't get no better, no better at all." It's two weeks later, and I'm calling Eric Nowe to find out how the *Ballard* fared after I left to board the *North*. "We ended up with 135,000 pounds, mostly codfish, very little of redfish," he says. "Four hundred and fifty-some dollars gross. That was the share. A pretty poor showing, that." The *North* fared no better. "It was so bad out there," Bill Morrow tells me later, "they couldn't even fill the hold."

But most fishermen, including Chris Morrow and Eric Nowe, have had their share of bad trips before. "There's nothing to be done about that now," Eric Nowe says flatly. "You just have to go back out and hope it gets better next trip. That's just the way it is."

When I try to thank him again for his help, Nowe just laughs. "So, Stevie, did you learn anything out there?"

A little, Eric, a little. Thanks.

Part IV
Back on Course

16
The Private-Sector Solution

MICHAEL KIRBY'S job, as he saw it, was to keep the fishing industry, and the 44,000 jobs it represented, afloat. Kirby was a pragmatist. While he was quick to point out that his job wasn't necessarily to preserve the five large east coast fishing companies — National Sea Products Ltd., H.B. Nickerson & Sons Ltd., Fishery Products Ltd., the Lake Group and John Penny and Sons Ltd. — or to maintain their existing managements in their positions, neither, he said, was it his function to get rid of them.

Many in the fishing industry aren't convinced, even today, that the motives of Pierre DeBané, the new fisheries minister, were nearly as pure. DeBané, a Quebec lawyer and former aide to Pierre Trudeau, had succeeded Romeo LeBlanc as fisheries minister in a September 1982 cabinet shuffle.[1] Like his predecessor, DeBané was considered to be a member of the Liberal party's left wing, and many fish-company executives believed DeBané was always ideologically more interested in nationalizing their companies than he was in saving them.

Kirby, a technocrat who prided himself on an ability to analyze problems logically, had arrived at a similar belief in the need for a government takeover of the fishing industry, but he'd gotten there by a different route. Having concluded that the fish companies would need a massive injection of several hundred million dollars in new capital in order to survive — and, more importantly, to become profitable in the future — and having decided that there was no private entrepreneur rich enough, or foolish enough, to risk that kind of money on a chancy proposition like the fishing industry, Kirby quite logically decided that government would have to step in and become the owner of last resort.

In theory, the corporate restructuring should have followed smoothly from that assumption. After getting the banks to agree to terms for the settlement of

---
1. LeBlanc became a senator.

their outstanding debts, the task force would negotiate with the affected provinces to see how much of the financial burden they each could be persuaded to assume and then they, the two levels of government and the banks, would all go to the managements of the existing companies with a "done-deal" already in place. But the real-life negotiations dragged on through the spring and summer of 1983. The Bank of Nova Scotia, recognizing that the federal government couldn't simply walk away from the industry and allow it, and the jobs it creates, to disappear, played fiscal hardball with the restructuring team, while the Nova Scotia and Newfoundland governments each used the fishery's problems to advance their own political agendas.

Part of the problem, as Kirby outlined it in a speech after the restructuring was complete, was that he was attempting to deal with two very different cultures. "Politicians hesitate to make firm decisions, unlike businessmen, and the two mix very badly," Kirby said. "If the same deal could have been done solely through private-sector negotiations, a settlement probably could have been reached in a matter of weeks or, at most, a couple of months."

In the end, it took Kirby's restructuring group until June 24 to hammer out the rough edges of the first deal with the Bank of Nova Scotia. That agreement provided for folding the existing fish companies into two new super-companies — one in Nova Scotia and one in Newfoundland — that would be jointly owned by the federal government and the bank. Over the course of five years, the government would pay off most of the companies' $276.9-million worth of bank loans, after which either party could exercise an option to force the other to buy it out completely if it so wished.

Two months later, in late September, the restructuring group convinced mercurial Newfoundland premier Brian Peckford to go along with a plan that would see his province convert $31.5 million of company debt to equity in a new super-company. The Bank of Nova Scotia would do the same with $44.1 million of its outstanding loans, while the federal government agreed to inject $75 million worth of equity into the company, which would be 60 percent owned by Ottawa, 25 percent by Newfoundland and 15 percent by the Bank of Nova Scotia.[2]

A week after that, the restructuring team wrangled what turned out to be not much more than a lukewarm agreement-in-principle from John Buchanan for a similar arrangement in Nova Scotia. Under the terms of this deal, Ottawa, the

---

2. That company eventually became known as Fishery Products International (FPI). In the beginning, says the current chairman, Victor Young, the government put seven or eight bankrupt companies together into "one giant bankrupt company." Under the leadership of Young, a former Newfoundland power company executive, FPI eventually downsized the company, turned it into a profit-maker and, in 1987, the firm was privatized.

federal government and the bank would create a holding company to buy out the Nickersons' 56.5 percent interest in National Sea, and then Ottawa would buy up $45 million worth of new common shares that the company would issue, thus giving the consortium a 93 percent ownership of the company.

Despite the time it had taken, and the difficulty involved in winning agreement from the major government and banking players, Pierre DeBané was delighted with the outcome. On October 17, the same day that the terms of the deal were being outlined to National Sea directors in Halifax, DeBané was telling reporters in Ottawa that he hoped the new government-controlled fishing super-companies would be in operation by the beginning of 1984. Federal and provincial officials, he said, were "already examining a list of candidates for the top executive posts with the two companies."

In answer to a question, DeBané said the federal cabinet's restructuring committee had searched first for a suitable private investor to rescue National Sea Products Ltd., and even though it had hired MacLeod Young Weir, a nationally known investment firm, to help them find that private-sector savior, the search proved fruitless.

"That," says David Hennigar, "is just because they weren't looking for one."

Hennigar, who ultimately almost had to literally force himself into the restructuring process, says his interest in National Sea was not only long-standing but had also only recently been reiterated in conversations with representatives of the Bank of Nova Scotia.

Hennigar — the grandson of legendary Nova Scotia industrialist Roy Jodrey — and his uncle John Jodrey are the current keepers of one of Canada's largest family fortunes. Hennigar would seem to have been a logical candidate for the restructuring team to approach about investing in the company. His family had held shares in National Sea since the company was formed in the 1940s. In 1974, it had acquired additional shares to bring its total holdings to 12.5 percent and had held on to them despite several offers from "emissaries of the Nickersons" to buy them out in the early 1980s. By the time of what Hennigar calls "the troubles," the family's holdings in National Sea — as required by the Ontario Securities Commission — were all on the public record.

Hennigar was anything but a passive investor. At one point during the early stages of the company's problems, he approached the Bank of Nova Scotia's George Hitchman with a proposal — "which was very similar to the final deal we reached" — to take over the company. But Hitchman said such a decision wasn't then up to the bank to make and referred him to Jerry Nickerson instead. At a meeting at Halifax's Airport Hotel, Nickerson rejected the offer. "He had his own agenda," Hennigar says today.

At the company's 1983 annual general meeting, shareholder Hennigar was also very much in evidence. He complained about the company's decision to switch its auditors from Clarkson Gordon to Thorne Riddell, also H.B. Nickerson's auditor, because he was concerned "about getting stiffed with Nickerson's assets. I wanted to put them on notice, so I sent a letter to all the directors reminding them of their responsibilities and then I sent my lawyer [Robert Granger of Toronto's Aird and Berlis] to the meeting to reiterate my points."

Despite his earlier offer to buy the company and his high profile as a shareholder, Hennigar says, no one from the restructuring team or from MacLeod Young Weir ever approached him to ask if he'd be interested in buying National Sea. Hennigar is convinced that's because "any professional advisor tends to come up with the solution that his principal is hoping to hear." Hennigar believes that the "principal" in this instance — the federal government — was simply looking for an excuse to nationalize the fishery.

When he first heard the announcement of the government-bank deal to take over the company, Hennigar says now, "It got my blood up. My grandfather used to say: 'Government couldn't run a gravity-run water-feed system at a profit.' It seemed clear to me that having another basic industry owned by government would not be in the best interests of Nova Scotia."

Hennigar's decision to make a stand against the government takeover, Michael Kirby believes, was partly ideological, partly the logical outgrowth of his own Nova Scotia patriotism and partly an effort to "demonstrate that he was cut from the same cloth as his grandfather." During the 1950s, Hennigar's grandfather, Roy Jodrey, had staged a remarkable public campaign to prevent the takeover of DOSCO. "I think David saw an opportunity to play a bit of the same role his grandfather had played in the DOSCO situation," Kirby says today.

Hennigar's interest was heightened after he read newspaper reports about a hearing on the restructuring proposal held by the federal parliamentary committee on fisheries. Nova Scotia's negotiators — Resources Loan Board chairman Joe Zatzman, Fisheries Minister John Leefe and Deputy Fisheries Minister Sandy MacLean — had gone to Ottawa to make the province's case against the deal to the committee. But the session in the hearing room of the Ottawa Railway Station building did not go well.

"It looked to me like we were losing the battle to the Bank of Nova Scotia and the feds," Zatzman recalled later. "So I decided to have my say. I blasted the whole concept." Although the outburst was cathartic, Zatzman says he left the meeting "discouraged. I thought we'd lost the deal."

When he arrived back in Halifax, however, there was a phone message for him from David Hennigar. That same evening, Zatzman met at his home with a representative from Hennigar's Burns Fry office in Toronto who proceeded to question him closely about the status of the two Nova Scotia fish companies.

"Hennigar told me he was interested in getting in on the restructuring, but he didn't think he had a chance until after he read what I had to say," Zatzman recalls. "I remember thinking, 'Why does anyone wait until the 11th minute of the 11th hour of the 11th day to come forward?' But what did it matter? He did come forward." After that, in fact, Zatzman became deeply involved in discussions with Hennigar over the future of National Sea.

After reading earlier reports about government nationalization plans in the spring of 1983, Hennigar had already tentatively approached Bill Morrow at National Sea to find out what was going on and to see what he could do to help. Prior to striking up their alliance in the fall of 1983, Hennigar says he and Morrow were not close personally. "I was the one asking all these embarrassing questions at the annual meetings every year, so I'm not even sure Bill liked me very much at that point. But I was the only game in town at the time." Morrow himself says he doesn't remember it that way — "I actually appreciated his questions" — but he does agree that the two would not have been regarded as friends before they began talking about the company's future.

By the time of the October 16, 1983, meeting in Halifax, when the restructuring committee finally presented the details of its proposal to National's Sea's executive committee, the two were already informal allies. When Morrow telephoned Hennigar after the meeting to let him know what had happened, Hennigar, like Morrow, was shocked by how badly the private shareholders, whose ownership of the company would be reduced to just 6.8 percent, and almost certainly "locked-in" permanently, would be treated under the government's plan. "What Bill told me," Hennigar allows with ironic understatement, "didn't make me very happy."

At the next day's meeting of the company's full board, the directors agreed to appoint a restructuring committee to begin negotiations with Ottawa and the banks, but Morrow refused to serve on it. He told puzzled fellow directors he wanted to be "free to pursue other options." In the end, board chairman Bill Mingo[3] was appointed to head up the committee, and the directors also agreed to ask that trading in National Sea shares be suspended. Almost as an afterthought, Michael Kirby, who had presented the federal proposal that day, informed the directors that he had scheduled a meeting for later that afternoon with "a

---

3. Mingo, a prominent Halifax lawyer and partner in the firm of Stewart, MacKeen & Covert had become chairman of the board in 1980 largely to referee between the Nickersons and the Morrows, according to Jim Morrow. "Mingo did an able job," he says, "of keeping the Nickersons and the Morrows from each other's throats."

minority shareholder" who was interested in discussing the restructuring.

That minority shareholder, of course, was David Hennigar.

Although their first meeting was inconclusive, one important outcome of it was that the two men discovered they liked and respected one another.[4] And that, says Kirby, was important. "I've always been convinced of the importance of personal relationships in making tough deals work," he says. "If it hadn't been for the personal relationship I developed with Cedric Ritchie and George Hitchman, we couldn't have made a deal with the banks. And if it wasn't for the personal relationship between David and myself, that end wouldn't have worked either."

In the beginning, it didn't. The sticking point was the amount of new investment that would be required to make it fly.

As part of his own assessment of National Sea's worth, Hennigar had asked Rod McCulloch, Clarkson Gordon's senior partner in Halifax, to prepare some financial projections for him. McCulloch's figures — like those done for the federal restructuring group by Price Waterhouse's Jack Hart — showed that National Sea could indeed be profitable again. But the two sets of numbers were dramatically different when it came to the question of how much new money would be needed to make the company viable. Largely because he projected that the company would have to replace two of its vessels every second year, Hart predicted the company would need close to $100 million worth of new investment. Hennigar calls that "a humungous amount of money," and says it was more, certainly, than he or any other investor would reasonably be prepared to put forward. But, he adds quickly, it was also far more than the company really needed.

Because Kirby believed Hart's figures were correct and because the restructuring committee itself was reluctant to endorse anything that smacked of what Peter John Nicholson had described as a "chewing-gum and bailing-wire solution that would fall apart again in a few years," Kirby initially didn't take Hennigar's proposal all that seriously.

Neither did Jerry Nickerson. When the board met again on November 2, 1983, against the backdrop of the release of the company's third-quarter financial results, which showed that National Sea had lost another $7.6 million,

---

4. Ironically, although the two men had travelled for years in the same social, business and economic circles, Kirby and Hennigar had never met before. Today, they see each other at least once a month, says Kirby, who adds that he developed enormous respect for Hennigar during the negotiating process. "If he gives you his word, you can depend on him without question," Kirby says. At one point, Hennigar's lawyers pointed out a section of the deal that would have a negative financial impact on him that Hennigar hadn't previously realized. Still, Hennigar refused to allow them to make changes to the draft deal. "I gave my word on this," he told them.

Nickerson told the directors that the deal with the bank and the federal and provincial governments, for all practical purposes, was done and that it was now just a matter of ironing out the details. As if to second that thought, the board approved the appointment of Richardson Greenshields to come up with a fairness evaluation on the worth of the company's shares.

Later that month, Ottawa even shepherded a bill through Parliament authorizing it to spend $455 million — in the form of cash, loan guarantees and conversion of debt to equity — to restructure the east coast fishery and create two huge new super-companies in Nova Scotia and Newfoundland in which the main shareholders would be the federal and provincial governments and the Bank of Nova Scotia.

When he was asked in an interview with a reporter during the parliamentary debates whether the government had ever seriously considering selling National Sea to a private investor, Pierre DeBané said there simply wasn't anyone interested. "We couldn't find any [investor] and we were told it would be a minimum of three years before there would be," he told one reporter.

Despite that, David Hennigar pressed forward. He was a past master at the art of making difficult deals and he began to piece together the elements of an alliance against the federal plan.

With company management — and a small but important group of directors,[5] including both Bill and Jim Morrow, Fred Russell, Hal Connor and Cal Pratt — already clearly in support of his efforts, Hennigar approached Nova Scotia premier John Buchanan "to try to get him on-side as well." Although he was able to appeal to the premier's own well-known preference for private over public ownership, Hennigar had a far more potent argument to offer as well. "I was able to show him that there was no downside for the province in a private-sector solution," Hennigar explains. Unlike Ottawa's proposal, which would have forced the province to ante up actual dollars for new investment as well as forgive outstanding loans, Hennigar wasn't asking for anything at all from the provincial government. In fact, the province, which stood to lose $25 million after the Nickersons defaulted on their payments on the Canso plant, would now get "full value for the plant."

After the province's support was assured, Hennigar "started to make some noise, to kick a few tires, to see if I could get a reaction." Initially, the only federal reaction was a stony silence. John Buchanan finally managed to arrange what was supposed to have been a face-to-face meeting between Hennigar and federal

---

5. The board itself had become far less a sure bet to support Hennigar's efforts. Bloated by the presence of so many outside directors representing different interests, it had become "unwieldy," recalls Hal Connor. "They were good people, but they didn't understand the fish business."

fisheries minister Pierre DeBané, but DeBané didn't even bother to show up for the session.

"We ended up in Ottawa in the biggest conference room I'd ever been in," Hennigar remembers, "but when we sat down to talk, the people across the table from us were [the restructuring committee's Michael] Kirby and [David] Mann. When they suggested we get started, I said, 'Listen, we came to see the minister and we don't intend to start until he gets here.'

"'Well,' they said, 'We don't know where he is.' I said I came to see the minister and I have no intention of starting without him.

"About 15 minutes later, DeBané finally walks in carrying this big sheaf of pink telephone messages. He went through this routine. He just said, basically, 'Thank you for your interest, but we're very sorry. It's too late. There's nothing to be done now,' and started to leave."

But Hennigar halted his retreat with an angry threat: "If you walk out of here," he informed the minister coldly, "I'm going to go talk to the press and tell them that we were prepared to make you an offer and you refused to listen."

DeBané stayed.

"There are a few things I want to say," Hennigar began. Two-and-a-half hours later, he had laid all his cards on the table. He repeated his contention that the government's analysis of the economics of restructuring was based on faulty assumptions and said that he had his own figures to show the company could be saved for far less money than the committee thought.

More importantly, he was prepared to make a concrete offer to save it. But he also had a warning for the minister and his team. If the government and the banks thought they could get away with cutting a private deal that didn't take into account the interests of the minority shareholders, he said, they'd better think again. He would fight any attempt to nationalize the company and might even launch legal action on the grounds that a bank-government deal would dilute the value of the holdings of the minority shareholders.

Hennigar could see by the reactions on the faces of the minister and his aides around the table that day that he had, indeed, kicked a few tires. Hard.

A few days later, Hennigar was back in his office in Halifax when one of DeBané's aides telephoned him — the minister wanted to meet with Hennigar and Morrow that afternoon at 3 p.m. at the Clipper Cay, a well-known waterfront restaurant in Halifax. "I knew when they called that we were making some progress," Hennigar recalled later, "although I still wasn't sure what vital organs we'd hit."

At the beginning of the meeting, the answer seemed to be none. "Now Mr. Hennigar," DeBané began, "let's be reasonable. How much would you accept for your shares?"

It is not a question of price, Hennigar cut him off, it is a matter of principle. "What we had here," he says now, "was a deal in which the bank was going to be made whole again and the government was going to walk in and run the company — there were bureaucrats already measuring rug sizes — and I just said, 'That's not right and I'm not going to let it happen.'"

By the end of what Hennigar now describes as "a real donnybrook," the two sides did agree to at least exchange feasibility studies.

After he looked carefully at the government's figures, Hennigar became more convinced than ever that McCulloch's projections were the accurate ones and that, as a result, there really was a possibility "we could do a deal."

The news of Hennigar's interest finally leaked out to the press in mid-December, ironically on the same day that John Buchanan and Pierre DeBané were scheduled to meet in Halifax to try and "cross the t's and dot the i's" in the final wording on their previously agreed deal-in-principle to restructure National Sea.

Although he was quick to claim to reporters that he had always favored the idea of private rather than public investment in the company, DeBané was equally quick to add that the Hennigar proposal — which involved an investment of only $10 million by the private sector group[6] —"was substantially less than what the government had in mind for the restructuring plan." Still DeBané promised that his staff — as well as that of Nova Scotia fisheries minister John Leefe — were more than willing to meet with the Hennigar group to see if a deal could be reached.

DeBané's pre-conditions were simple enough. The proposal couldn't be based on getting government grants or loan guarantees, and it couldn't be done in such a way as to affect the restructuring plan already in place in Newfoundland. "Hopefully," DeBané told reporters, "they will come back with a proposal that fits those parameters and if they do come with one, even at this late date, we will be very satisfied."

That clearly wasn't going to be true of the Bank of Nova Scotia. Two days before Christmas, 1983, Hennigar flew to Toronto to meet with the Bank's chairman, Cedric Ritchie, and its president, Gordon Bell. At that session, Hennigar suggested converting $75 million worth of the bank's debt into "difficulty-term-preferred-shares,"[7] with the shares to be redeemed in three equal installments of $25 million between 1987 and 1989. But the bank offi-

---

6. The original Hennigar group included Hennigar himself, Bill Morrow and former National Sea chairman Hal Connor.
7. Term-preferred shares are issued at approximately half the prime interest rate but their dividends are tax-free. The finance minister can authorize such a share issue under a special section of the Revenue Canada Act if he decides that a company is in severe financial difficulties.

cials weren't interested. "Again we got stonewalled," Hennigar complains. "They had what they considered a good deal and they didn't want to look at anything else."

The Royal Bank, which had less to lose, was far more amenable to a private-sector proposal. After securing the support of the bank's Halifax-based regional vice president, George Buckrell, Hennigar flew off to the bank's Montreal head office on January 4, 1984, with a delegation that included Bill Morrow, Rod McCulloch and — not coincidentally — Nova Scotia fisheries minister John Leefe. "After they had a chance to look at our forecasts — and to see that the province was in support — the bank agreed [in principle] to support us," Hennigar says.

However, the Bank of Nova Scotia appeared to make that gesture irrelevant just two days later when its own formal response to the Hennigar proposal was made public in a telegram to Deputy Prime Minister Allan MacEachen. Bank president Gordon Bell declared that the bank wasn't prepared to accept the Hennigar proposal "or any variation of it which is at all similar." And he warned that unless an acceptable deal was achieved — and soon — the bank would move to recover $75 million in outstanding loans. "The Bank of Nova Scotia has only continued to provide credit to National Sea because of the initiatives taken by the Government of Canada to resolve the severe problems of the Atlantic fishing industry," Bell wrote. "If it had not been for this initiative, the bank would have called its loans to National Sea long since." The bank gave the company until January 12, 1984, to come up with an acceptable arrangement for paying off its debts.

As if the bank's rejection wasn't bad enough, the new chairman of National Sea's restructuring committee also weighed in with a public putdown of the Hennigar proposal.

Prominent Halifax lawyer Frank Covert, who had replaced Bill Mingo as chairman of the committee to avoid a possible conflict-of-interest situation involving Mingo[8], claimed in a newspaper interview that the private-sector group's proposal would simply drive the company deeper into debt. "I say I would like to see free enterprise take it over," Covert explained to a reporter from the Halifax *Chronicle-Herald*. "The province says it would like to see free enterprise. The federal government would like to see free enterprise. But free enterprise has not come up with a viable offer and, until they do, the only thing we have is an offer from the [bank-government] consortium."

"Covert was a real mystery man during all of this," remembers Hal Connor.

---

8. Given that Covert and Mingo were both from the same Halifax law firm, Stewart, MacKeen & Covert, and that both men were well-connected Liberals generally supportive of the federal position, some wags around National began describing their firm as Stewart, MacKeen & Conflict.

"At the start he was with us in support of the free-enterprise solution, but he seemed to lose faith later on. I don't think that either he or Mingo ever really understood the mercurial nature of the fishing industry, that as sure as you went down, you would come back up again."

To complicate problems for the private-sector group, a "federal spokesman" suddenly turned the screw another revolution when he told a reporter from the *Globe and Mail* that if the Nova Scotia government — which was now very openly in the Hennigar private-sector-solution corner — refused to participate in the previously agreed federal restructuring package, "'there is a 50-50 chance that the federal cabinet will simply do nothing,' setting the stage for the possible bankruptcy of the east coast corporate giant."

By this point, the whole issue had become something more than just another news story. It became a *cause célèbre*. The Halifax *Chronicle-Herald*, for example, ran a series of five front-page editorials in which it cast the dispute almost as a holy war between the forces of godless government and those of divinely ordained free enterprise.

The man who was probably most responsible for generating those *Herald* editorials was Bill Morrow himself. After one inaccurate article about the affair in the newspaper, Morrow telephoned *Herald* publisher Graham Dennis to set the record straight. Dennis, a long-time foe of the federal Liberals and a staunch defender of private enterprise — whose newspapers two most notable editorial campaigns of the 1970s involved battles against the imposition of estate taxes and the provincial takeover of the province's private electric utility — was more than a trifle interested in what was happening to National Sea. Morrow briefed Dennis on the situation as he saw it, and shortly after that, the editorial series began.

"More than a company is at stake," thundered the *Herald* in one editorial. "A way of life, and one which can be described without exaggeration as noble and fulfilling, is at stake. What will replace it, if the private sector fails to survive this crisis, will in all probability be a collectivization on the Soviet or Chinese model.... Certainly, the federal government is a culprit and stands to be suspected, if not accused ... of a calculated decision to nationalize the industry.

"The conclusion is irresistible," claimed the editorial's writer, "that in formulating its game plan, the federal government ignored its true mandate and pursued a solution which would facilitate if not ensure a nationalization, and for that purpose purchased the concurrence of the other party [the Bank of Nova Scotia] holding most of the cards."

As if to emphasize the newspaper's perceived connection between the federal government and the socialist hordes, another editorial pointedly noted that Fisheries Minister DeBané was out of the country in January "attending celebrations of the 25th anniversary of the Castro revolution." The source of that tidbit of information was none other than Bill Morrow himself.

Although Michael Kirby later argued that the *Herald* editorials "generated more heat than light because the objective background stories had not been written and because it was clear to any unbiased observer that the tone of the editorials was grossly overstated," he admits that they were effective. By characterizing the issue as a "struggle to save the fishery from nationalization," Kirby wrote later, the *Herald* touched an instinctive chord among its readers, because nationalization "is still snake oil in most of Nova Scotia."

These editorials were only one element in what was becoming a more and more complicated and confusing media spectacle. It got to the point where there were so many contradictory stories and unattributed quotes from "authoritative" spokesmen appearing in the media each day, Hennigar recalls now, "that Mike [Kirby] and I agreed to talk to each other each morning before we looked at the newspapers."

Hennigar was actually too busy to spend much time reading newspapers. "I brought my suitcase with me to work each morning," he says, "because I was never sure where I was going to end up by nightfall."

He was working on several fronts at once trying to come up with a deal that would work. On the one hand, he and Kirby — joined occasionally by John Leefe — haggled over how much new investment would be needed to put together a "do-able deal."

"I remember one meeting late one Friday night in the provincial cabinet room," Kirby says. "Here I was back in my old office using my old phone. It felt very strange. Hennigar, Leefe and I were all there trying to work out a deal. We talked on the phone with Buchanan, who was home with the flu, but it didn't work. It became very ideological. You had three guys all arguing the same issue from different ideological viewpoints."

At the same time that Hennigar was negotiating with Kirby, he was also busily trying to find another private-sector investor willing to join him in his quest to save National Sea. He finally found that investor in Donald Sobey, the president of Stellarton-based Empire Company Ltd.

While that might have seemed puzzling at first blush — given that the 1974 Jodrey investment in National Sea had been seen as a counterweight to the then-unwelcome presence of the Sobeys and given that it was the Sobeys, whose sale of its shares to the Nickersons back in 1977 launched the company on its long and slippery slide toward financial collapse — the simple truth was that the Sobeys and Jodreys were already natural allies.

"Over the years, the Jodrey-Sobey association became so close that, when

Nova Scotians talked of the families that dominated bluenose business life, they inevitably mentioned Jodreys and Sobeys in the same breath," the *Globe and Mail* explained. "Roy Jodrey and [Sobey family patriarch] Frank Sobey were directors on each other's boards and worked closely on various deals. They also shared a disdain for governments, suffered fools badly and, most important, liked each other. Both were cut from the same free-enterprise tartan, and there was nothing either liked better than talking business."

The Sobeys and the Jodreys, arguably the two richest and most powerful business families in the province, already jointly controlled a sizeable chunk of Halifax's most valuable real estate — five large office towers, two major hotels, three prime apartment towers and two shopping centres — through a development company known as Halifax Developments Ltd. Halifax Developments, led by Hennigar and Donald Sobey, was also then involved in a battle with two men who were considered outsiders in the Nova Scotia business establishment — Moncton financier Reuben Cohen and his Montreal-based partner Leonard Ellen — for control of Nova Scotia Savings and Loan Company.[9]

Perhaps more significant than their joint investments, however, was the fact that Hennigar, a third-generation Jodrey, and Donald Sobey, a second-generation Sobey, shared their families' profound distaste for government intervention in private enterprise and equally profound sense of parochial provincial patriotism.

In December 1983, as Donald Sobey later described events to author Harry Bruce, "I was talking to Hennigar and I said we might be interested in joining their effort to privatize National Sea. I said maybe we can get Empire to take some [shares], and we might put in some Halifax Developments." While the practical implications of the scheme were that Hennigar would have "additional impetus to put it across to the public and banks that this was a serious proposal," Sobey admitted that his real interest in the deal was to keep the government out. "We simply felt it would be a disaster for Nova Scotia to have National Sea in government hands."

So did his father, Frank Sobey. In a rare and extraordinary letter to the editor of the Halifax *Chronicle-Herald,* the family patriarch, then in his 80s, made an impassioned plea for a private-sector solution.

"It would be a disaster for Nova Scotia and the fishing industry in general if

---

9. The directors of Nova Scotia Savings and Loan recruited Halifax Developments to act as a white knight to protect them from the advances of Cohen and Ellen in 1980, but that move touched off a bitter six-year legal battle. According to a report in the *Globe and Mail*'s *Report on Business Magazine,* David Hennigar "quarterbacked the Halifax establishment team's fight against Cohen and Ellen." The battle finally ended in 1987, when the Supreme Court of Nova Scotia ruled in favor of Cohen and Ellen, and described NSSL's directors as functioning as "a sort of benevolent junta," whose actions "breached their fiduciary duties."

National Sea became a part of a Crown corporation," he wrote. "It would be in the best interest for the employees, the suppliers and the shareholders of National Sea if they remained in the hands of private interests.

"They have by far the best processing and cooking plant, and the largest, on the Eastern seaboard. They have the best facilities to sell and move fish into the U.S. and foreign markets.

"The Bank of Nova Scotia is run by big boys; I can't see why they should expect the government to pay off a collateral loan made to a shareholder and not to National Sea. I know the Bank put up the money for these shares and the loan was made to a shareholder and not to National Sea.

"It is bad for the people of Canada and will be bad for Nova Scotia if the government starts to operate National Sea. There are tremendous assets in National Sea and it is the backbone of the fishing operation in Nova Scotia, and the largest market for inshore fishermen.

"The government of Canada has never been successful in operating any company that I know of. They have made a mess of the two airplane manufacturing companies they took over.

"Even their bellwether Canada Development Corporation is in trouble and losing money.

"All that would happen is that like all government-operated companies, National Sea will end up with a larger percentage of executives and management people and a smaller percentage of labor in their plants."

Perhaps not surprisingly — given the source of the remarks and their import — the editors at the *Herald* didn't publish Sobey's letter in its usual letters-to-the-editor section but in a prominent place on page three of the newspaper. But even the addition of the Sobey name and resources wasn't enough to immediately swing the support of National Sea's directors to their proposal. The directors considered it — as well as the federal government-Bank of Nova Scotia proposal — during an 11-hour meeting in a downtown Halifax hotel on January 9, 1984. While the directors met in one room, Hennigar and Sobey rented another room nearby and shuttled in and out of the directors' meeting discussions.

How long would the negotiations last? a reporter asked David Hennigar at one point. "It should keep you fellows fully employed," Hennigar joked.

At the beginning of the meeting, as part of its own pre-arranged agreement with Ottawa, the Nickerson brothers, along with their brother-in-law, Eric Shibler, who was H.B. Nickerson's vice president of finance, resigned their positions on the board. Thus ended — with far more whimper than bang — Jerry Nickerson's business dream. "Jerry Nickerson was a very aggressive guy," Joe Zatzman says today. "He had a vision and he moved on it. Unfortunately for him, he missed it by a year. If he'd been able to hang on and the industry had turned around, he might be looked upon as a genius today." He stops. "Luck and timing are important in any business. Jerry's just ran out too soon."

The Nickerson interests on the board were replaced by three federal nominees — Jim Baillie, Petro-Canada's Joel Bell and restructuring-committee member David Mann.

When David Hennigar asked to be permitted to also name three directors — himself, Donald Sobey and lawyer Robert Granger — to act as a counterweight to the federal presence on the board, the directors offered him only one position. Hennigar rejected that offer and Granger — speaking on behalf of Hennigar — warned the federal board members that he would be watching carefully to ensure there was no "self-dealing" involved in any votes taken that day.

After a break for lunch the board heard details of both the Hennigar-Sobey proposal and the federal version.

The Hennigar-Sobey proposal still called for the private investors to put up about $10 million in new equity while the province converted $23 million in debt into preferred equity and the federal government provided a $75 million loan guarantee as well as several million dollars worth of tax concessions to the new private ownership. Many directors, even those sympathetic to a private-sector solution, believed the proposal didn't involve nearly enough private money. Their more important concern, however, was that the proposal was conditional on gaining an agreement from the federal government to allow the company to issue more shares to Hennigar so that Ottawa's and the Bank of Nova Scotia's current holding of 56 percent could be reduced to just 34 percent.

The federal proposal, which involved the Bank of Nova Scotia and the provincial government rolling over more than $100 million of debt into equity and Ottawa coming up with another $90 million worth of new money, was now conditional too. The original proposal had been put forward on the understanding that the province supported it. Now that support seemed less sure, and Ottawa said it would only continue to participate if the province agreed to go along.

During the board's discussion of the federal proposal, Bill Morrow slipped out of the room and placed a hasty call to provincial fisheries minister John Leefe. A short time later, a courier hand-delivered a letter from Leefe to the board, which declared that the government of Nova Scotia was no longer supporting the federal proposal.

That left the board in a quandary. In the end the directors decided to reject both proposals as "less than adequate" even as they urged the parties to continue working on new or modified proposals that would be acceptable.

At the request of the Hennigar-Sobey group, the National Sea board also sent a telex to the Bank of Nova Scotia, asking for a 48-hour extension on its January 12 deadline.

The bank refused. On January 12, the bank notified the company that it would require repayment of its $75 million in loans to the company by January 26 and, if the company failed to meet that deadline, that it would "exercise its security" on February 9. Those were, in fact, the minimum requirements under the terms of the loan.

With hopes for a solution to the company's problems seemingly unravelling, the various combatants began attempting to make sure they weren't blamed for the failure.

"We are in a position where the problem can be solved tomorrow if the province agrees to the agreement it signed with DeBané on September 30," Michael Kirby argued. Claiming that the federal government's hands were tied — "Our proposal is blocked by the province, and we can't deliver on the [private sector-proposal]" — Kirby told a reporter for the *Financial Post* that if the company was forced into bankruptcy, "there is absolutely no question which level of government is responsible — let's be crystal clear on that point — and it isn't the federal government."

The province, for its part, claimed that its original support had only been conditional. Although earlier reports indicated that the province originally had three conditions — that the company's redfish quota be increased, that its northern cod quota be increased and that the government commit itself to returning the company to private investors within five years — provincial negotiator Joe Zatzman now added what he said had been a fourth condition: that no private investors were available. Given that there now was a private investor, Zatzman said, the province was not obligated to go ahead with the original agreement.

At the same time, another provincial official leaked word that Ottawa had threatened to withhold approval of provincial requests on other federal-provincial issues — including the offshore, the Cape Breton Development Corporation and the Sydney Steel Corporation — if Nova Scotia didn't go along with the federal plan. "All we know is that MacEachen and Regan were pretty tough on Buchanan and threatened him with some things," an unnamed source told the Halifax *Chronicle-Herald*. "And there was talk of some transfer payments."

Even the Bank of Nova Scotia weighed in with a defense of its position. Bank president Bell, in Halifax for the bank's annual meeting,[10] handed reporters an eight-page statement outlining the bank's view that "the crucial issue is a viable restructuring solution ... [to] provide the environment in which longer term ownership and strategy issues can then be adequately addressed." The bank, his statement said, could have saved itself a lot of heartache and much of its potential loss if it had called its loan in 1981 when the Nickersons first got into trouble, but "that would have been terribly disruptive and, in our judgement, inconsistent with our social responsibility and with our ultimate faith in the fishery. So we hung in." Having released its statement, however, Bell refused to answer any other questions about National Sea because of what he described as "client confidentiality." This provoked "an enraged reaction from the reporters," Hennigar remembers with a laugh. "They'd been waiting since morning for this special press conference, and then that was all the bank was prepared to say. I think it's fair to say that that lost the bank any remaining sympathy it had in the Halifax media."

Behind the bickering, the frantic negotiating continued. But by this time, says Hennigar, "there were also an incredible number of byplays to deal with and there were always wild cards coming out of left field."[11] Suppliers began to demand cash on delivery for goods, for example, then Air Canada cut off the company's credit altogether. "We had people stuck all over the place with credit cards that Air Canada wouldn't honor," Hennigar remembers.[12]

There was also concern that the Bank of Nova Scotia, which had already instructed the company not to make any more payments on its loans to the provinces of Nova Scotia and Newfoundland, might move in on the company's payroll-deduction account as well.[13] Because the directors could be held personally liable if those withholdings weren't paid, they agreed to set up a special trust fund at Central Trust to hold those funds. That provoked a nasty letter from the bank warning the directors not to put their own interests ahead of those of the company's creditors.

"May we have your reply today," the letter demanded.

To try and salvage what could still be salvaged from the deteriorating situation, the federal cabinet committee on restructuring finally decided to convene an

---

10. Ironically, that annual meeting also marked the end of a long Jodrey-family tradition of direct involvement with the Bank of Nova Scotia. Hennigar's uncle, John Jodrey, who had been a member of the bank's board since 1964 and latterly a vice president and a member of its executive committee, had reached mandatory retirement age and stepped down during the meeting. He was named an honorary director.

11. Although it didn't ultimately have any real impact on the outcome of the negotiations, one of those wild cards was the announcement on January 13, 1984, that Michael Kirby was being appointed to the Canadian senate as a reward for his work in restructuring the fishery.

12. Later, just before Hennigar was scheduled to fly to Ottawa for a meeting with the federal cabinet's restructuring committee, Liberal minister Gerald Regan called him to ask if he could be of any assistance. "You sure can, Gerry," Hennigar told him. "You can get Air Canada to turn on our credit cards again."

13. The bank's demands were keeping company officials busy. In late December, the company management had been forced to scramble to find redundant assets it could sell off in order to maintain their working capital within the percentage of debt required to satisfy the bank. At the last moment, they managed to come up with a parcel of Halifax land that had once been part of the company's head office. The provincial government quickly agreed to buy it.

all-day session in Ottawa to meet with all of the parties individually once again. "Everyone got 20 minutes," remembers David Hennigar, who made his presentation to the committee early in the morning in an amphitheatre in the external affairs department complex. The session, says Hennigar, "felt like beating your head against the wall." But then, late that afternoon, he was called to a second meeting in Deputy Prime Minister Allan MacEachen's office, where Gerald Regan, John Buchanan and Nova Scotia development minister Roland Thornhill were also gathered. "That meeting was the turning point," says Hennigar, who told the politicians that he still planned to follow up with legal action if his proposal was rejected.

"I think they realized at that point that I had a resolve about this thing and I was going to see it through. I think it was MacEachen who probably made the decision: 'Hey, these guys really are serious and they want to have a run at it, so let's let them.' Things moved pretty fast after that."

During another round of intense negotiating between Hennigar and Kirby, Hennigar agreed that the private-sector group would put up additional capital. "He [Kirby] jacked me up a bit on how much cash I would put in," Hennigar admits. "He got me up to $20 million and then he quit. But that still wasn't a bad deal," he adds with a laugh, "considering I started with none."

On January 18 the Royal Bank, which had been present in Ottawa to support the Hennigar group's proposal, issued a public statement acknowledging that it had agreed "in general terms" to finance a restructured National Sea.

With that next-to-last hurdle in place, the final step was to find a bank willing to buy the company's so-called difficulty-term-preferred shares. The Royal Bank already had tax losses and therefore didn't need the tax write-off advantages such shares offered. The only other bank that had the capital and the need was the Toronto Dominion, which conveniently also happened to be the bank on which Donald Sobey served as a director.

As soon as Hennigar suggested the Toronto Dominion possibility to Donald Sobey, he arranged a meeting for later that same day so that he, Hennigar and National Sea's senior vice president of finance, Malcolm Pitman, could outline the company's proposal to bank president Dick Thomson in Toronto. "It was in the middle of this awful snowstorm, so we grabbed a cab [in downtown Halifax] and took off for the airport where we just made the plane," Hennigar says. The National Sea group had brought along briefcases of documents to support its arguments and Hennigar remembers "spending what must have been four hours in this TD storeroom making Xerox copies of all the documents." A special committee at the bank was convened to go over the material as it was being generated and, by the end of the day, the bank had agreed to take up the difficulty-term-preferred shares.

With all of that already accomplished, there was little left for National Sea Products' board of directors to do at its February 6 meeting but to approve a deal that now carried the endorsement of both the provincial and federal governments, as well as the financial support of the Royal Bank and the Toronto Dominion Bank.

Speaking on behalf of Ottawa, Michael Kirby told the board that the new proposal had "the complete support of the federal government," while Nova Scotia fisheries minister John Leefe added that the province was satisfied with it as well. So was the board's own restructuring committee, which unanimously recommended approval of the complicated deal. It took Hennigar's lawyer, Robert Granger, one hour and eight minutes to read the whole thing. Under its terms:

— Scotia Investments Ltd. (the Jodrey family's investment arm), Empire Co. (the Sobeys) and Isleview Investments Ltd. (the Morrow family investment company) agreed to provide $20 million in new investment in return for $15 million worth of the company's common and $5 million in preferred shares.
— The Nova Scotia government agreed to convert about $25 million of a total of $34 million in debt owed it by National Sea and H.B. Nickerson & Sons into equity. Five million dollars of that was to be taken up as National Sea preferred shares, while the remaining $20 million was in the form of preferred shares in a National Sea subsidiary operating the Canso fish plant.
— The Toronto Dominion Bank agreed to buy $75 million worth of financial difficulty-term-preferred shares, the proceeds of which would be used to pay off the company's debt to the Bank of Nova Scotia.
— The Royal Bank agreed to become the main banker to the restructured company and provide it with a $100-million line of credit.
— And the federal government — which still wasn't convinced that National Sea could be viable without even more new investment than the private investors were prepared to put in — offered to put in $10 million more to buy non-voting preferred shares after agreeing to pay the Bank of Nova Scotia another $80 million so National Sea and the restructured Newfoundland fish company could acquire H.B. Nickerson & Sons' assets free of debt.

When all was said and done, the Hennigar group — which included not only the Jodrey, Morrow and Sobey families' holdings but also those of other key private investors, including Hal Connor — held 47 percent of the shares in the restructured National Sea, the federal government 20 percent, the Bank of Nova Scotia 14 percent; there was a common float of 19 percent.

The board elected David Hennigar as chairman and added the two other appointees — Donald Sobey and Robert Granger — that Hennigar had earlier unsuccessfully requested.

National Sea had been saved. And at post-board-meeting press conferences, everyone involved was quick to claim credit for its survival.

At his briefing, Fisheries Minister Pierre DeBané said that Ottawa had taken the lead in saving the company because "Canada needs some very big entities" to compete in international fish markets. A relieved Michael Kirby's analysis was that "it was the first time a government in Canada ever did what the U.S. did in terms of the Chrysler situation."

For his part, Nova Scotia premier John Buchanan made a point of emphasizing how small the percentage of government ownership had become. That, he said, had been Nova Scotia's aim all along. "We are not socialists," he said.

At his press conference, David Hennigar — as if to emphasize his own distaste for government and his own confidence in the future of National Sea — announced that Scotia Investments had obtained first rights to buy up Ottawa's share whenever the federal government was ready to sell.

Did David Hennigar save National Sea from the clutches of government socialists or did Ottawa bail out the banks and the company with taxpayers' dollars?

Although the simplest and most reasonable answer may be Joe Zatzman's homey suggestion that "if you want water you have to prime the pump, and that's all that government's involvement was supposed to do in this case," the question itself has been the subject of endless argument and speculation since the day the deal was announced.

After *Atlantic Insight* ran a laudatory article on the company's success following the restructuring, for example, one reader wrote to the magazine to complain. Pointing out that the federal government had retired Nickerson's debts to the Bank of Nova Scotia, allowing National Sea to acquire some of the Nickerson assets while avoiding its debts, as well as the fact of provincial conversion of debts to equity and the federal investment of $10 million in new money, the writer says: "With all due credit to the work by [new National Sea president] Gordon Cummings and National Sea Products ... it is less-than-accurate to paint NSP's new profitability as totally a private sector achievement."

Another letter writer suggested to readers of the Halifax *Chronicle-Herald* that the provincial government could improve its financial position by requesting National Sea to "return some of the millions that the province contributed in rescuing this company."

In their replies to such letters to the editor as well as in their speeches to local service clubs and other groups, company officials go to great lengths to correct what they call "misapprehensions that ... like some corporate Lazarus, National

Sea was brought back from beyond the grave by massive infusions of government money, by forgiveness of debt, and by written off interest."

Marshalling its arguments for the other side, company officials pointed out that National Sea was the only one of the five east coast fishing companies involved in the restructuring that did not ever default on an interest payment and that did not have to resort to bankruptcy or government takeover in order to survive.

While it is true that the federal government invested $10 million, company officials are quick to note that the company didn't ask for that investment. "[The federal] government doubted the private investors' numbers and insisted on the $10 million, a highly unusual (if not unique) situation." And the federal government, like the provincial government, ultimately benefited significantly from their investments in the company.

In the case of the Province, company officials explain, National Sea in effect paid $20 million to buy the Canso plant, which the Province owned as a result of the Nickerson collapse. The Nickersons had defaulted on a $13-million loan and the government hadn't collected a penny in interest on that loan since 1981. So the government ended up making a $7-million profit on the transaction. The remainder of the so-called provincial contribution — $5 million — was debt that the government converted to equity and for which it was once again handsomely rewarded when the company's fortunes turned around.

While there is still disagreement about the respective roles of the private investors and the governments in National Sea's turnaround, there was virtually no disagreement with the argument that the main immediate winner from the restructuring was the Bank of Nova Scotia. The bank received $80 million from Ottawa to pay off its bad loans to the Nickerson group and got 14 percent of the restructured company as well.[14] At the same time, it also received the $75-million proceeds from the difficulty-term-preferred shares purchased by the Toronto Dominion Bank.

On February 6, however, there were more parties than post-mortems. It was Bill Morrow's wife's birthday, and before going out for dinner, Morrow and Hennigar dropped in on a celebration the company's office staff were staging at the Billy Club, a private nightclub in Dartmouth.

"When we walked in," Morrow remembers, "there was a big cheer."

When the cheering stopped, everyone realized there were still plenty of questions left to answer. And plenty of work to do.

---

14. When the federal fisheries minister claimed that Ottawa had contributed $90 million to the Nova Scotia fishery rather than primarily to the Bank of Nova Scotia, Bill Morrow quipped to a reporter: "I've been looking around my office trying to find bags of money but I can't find it."

17
Rescue at (National) Sea

LOOKING back on it later, David Hennigar would joke that he slept like a baby that night in June 1984: "I'd sleep for an hour, wake up and cry for an hour, sleep for an hour...."

At the time, though, it was no joke.

Hennigar had called on every resource and connection he had to save National Sea Products Ltd. from the embrace of public ownership. And he had succeeded. But just four months after he gained control of the company, a Bay Street consultant named Gordon Eric Myles Cummings, a senior partner in the management consulting firm of Woods Gordon Inc., had spent the day telling him that he might as well have let the federal government nationalize the business. After three days of going over National Sea's books and quizzing its managers — who openly predicted losses of $5 million that year — Cummings had even worse news: "Management will succeed beyond their wildest dreams," he told Hennigar. "Fifteen million is more likely than $5 million."

"When we told him he could lose $15 million," Cummings recalled later, "you could really see that we had his attention."

On the one hand David Hennigar shouldn't have been surprised. Although the amount of the losses Cummings was predicting were far greater than he had expected, Hennigar had known from the beginning that there could be transitional problems at National Sea. Bill Morrow himself had pointed out that one result of the internal strife the company had endured since the Nickerson takeover was that almost no new blood had been brought into the senior management ranks since 1977. "Jerry and I were never able to agree on who to hire, so nothing could be done," Morrow had explained.

At the same time, the uncertainties of the last few years had exacted a physical and psychic toll on many of the executives and directors who remained. "I could never get any sleep, I was always thinking about the problems we were going through," Hal Connor remembers today. "I went to my doctor and he said to me, 'Your blood pressure is 200 over 100, Hal. What are you involved in anyway?'" He laughs. "I guess he didn't read the papers. Anyway, I said, 'Look, I've not only lost all my money, I've lost everything I worked for all my life. And my friends and my colleagues are in the same situation.' And you know, at some points, that's just how I felt."

Connor was not alone. Many of the company's loyal, longtime employees were so exhausted — and so relieved by the mere fact that their threatened company was still in existence — that they found it difficult to gear up for the immediate and ultimately far more important job of turning the company's fortunes around again.

Although some veteran observers of the industry, such as Bill Morrow, were convinced — rightly, as it turned out — that the company's fortunes would soon improve, the turnaround was six months later in beginning than he'd expected and that, he admits, "added further discouragement to many."

For his part, David Hennigar knew that the restructured company soon would have to begin making a number of tough, unpleasant decisions. Some uneconomic plants would have to be closed, some departments reorganized, even some people fired. Hennigar had been wondering for some time if he should dump that nasty job in Bill Morrow's lap. Morrow is an easy-going, friendly man who, although he had certainly fired people from time to time in his career, found the task painful. He'd also grown up in the company and lived with its employees through the many corporate highs as well as the occasional lows, and he'd developed natural personal and corporate loyalties in the process that transcended simple economics. Perhaps most importantly from Hennigar's point of view was the reality that Bill Morrow had already paid a personal price for his tireless efforts to save his company — his blood pressure was way up after almost three years of unrelieved stress.

Did David Hennigar really have the right to make Morrow the point man for a new round of inevitably brutal cost-cutting measures that might even make his health worse? At the same time, David Hennigar very much wanted Bill Morrow to continue to be involved in the company. He carried around in his head more knowledge about the fishery — and more contacts and connections within it — than anyone else in the entire industry. Hennigar wanted, and knew he still needed, Bill Morrow at the helm to help navigate National Sea through the still stormy seas of an extremely complex, heavily regulated industry.

Perhaps ...

He appraised the lanky six-foot consultant sitting across from him in his Halifax office this morning. Though Toronto-based, Gordon Cummings probably knew more about the fishing industry's finances than anyone else in the country.

He had done consulting work for the industry on both coasts for 15 years and had crunched the numbers that served as the basis for the Kirby Task Force's original recommendations about reorganizing the industry. Cummings had also been invited — and would have been delighted — to join Kirby's restructuring team when it began trying to put together a final deal among the Bank of Nova Scotia, the federal and provincial governments and the troubled east coast fishing companies. But federal officials hastily withdrew their invitation after they realized Woods Gordon's other corporate arm — Clarkson Gordon, the chartered accountants — numbered both the Bank of Nova Scotia and National Sea Products Ltd. among its recent clients. They feared that having one of Woods Gordon's senior partners as an advisor to their restructuring committee would spark conflict-of-interest charges from the Opposition and the press, so they had hired Jack Hart of Price Waterhouse to prepare their projections instead. (His figures were the ones that had been the subject of so much controversy during the negotiations between Hennigar and Kirby.)

In the end, Cummings had been involved in the restructuring process anyway. He'd acted as a sounding board and provider of second opinions for Rod McCulloch while McCulloch, Bill Morrow and David Hennigar put together the private-sector deal to buy National Sea. Although most of his work was done by phone from Toronto, Cummings had flown into Halifax for a few meetings with the private-sector group, and Hennigar had been impressed by both Cummings' grasp of the industry and his clear-headed way with numbers.

He also found that he and Cummings agreed on most things and, perhaps even more importantly, that they liked one another. There was, Cummings says now, a personal chemistry at work between them — at least partly the result of their mutual devotion to profit. Explains Cummings: "I remember at one point David said to me, 'You're so simple to deal with, Gordon. All you think about is profit.'"

That was one reason why Hennigar had quickly agreed when McCulloch suggested Cummings be part of a post-takeover assessment of the company's short-term problems and prospects. But there was another reason as well. From the beginning, Hennigar had a sense that Cummings might very well fit in with his own future plans for National Sea. Why? "Gut instinct," Hennigar allows with a laugh. "I don't want to take away the mystery of the thing, but it was as simple as that."

A week after Cummings delivered his bad-news assessment to Hennigar, Cummings was in Winnipeg working on another job when Rod McCulloch telephoned him. David Hennigar, McCulloch explained, wanted him to come down to Halifax and work for National Sea on a three-month assignment. "I said, 'Now come on, Rod, you know that partners don't go on assignments for three months.'" But McCulloch was insistent: Hennigar was an important client for Clarkson Gordon, and he could be an even more important one in the future. Finally, after what Cummings says now was "a lot of gnashing of teeth," he agreed to spend four to five days a week during August, September and October working for National Sea.

It was an especially difficult time for the company. Because the restructuring had not produced an instant and dramatic turnaround in National Sea's fortunes, its future continued to be the subject of intense speculation. In August, Bill Morrow was even forced to publicly deny published reports that the company was on the brink of bankruptcy.

Cummings, meanwhile, worked diligently to make sure that that wouldn't happen. He helped the corporation's senior management committee improve its overall decision-making process as well as formulate a new mission statement and strategic plan. And he helped Sandy Roche — a former Newfoundland deputy minister who'd recently been promoted from running the company's Newfoundland plants to overseeing its Canadian operations — to come up with a plan for deciding how to reduce the number of company-owned production facilities.

As Cummings worked, David Hennigar discreetly observed from a distance. Finally, during a meeting a few weeks after Cummings arrived, Hennigar obliquely broached the subject of hiring him. How did he like Halifax, Hennigar wanted to know? What did he think of the idea of he and his family living here? Although Cummings says he quickly realized what Hennigar was driving at, he remained coy.

"Well," he said, "it's a very nice place and all, but Woods Gordon isn't going to open an office here, so it wouldn't make any difference whether I wanted to live here or not."

"Well, maybe it's not Woods Gordon I'm thinking about," Hennigar allowed.

Cummings said he was "flattered" by Hennigar's offer, but added quickly that he was already on a contract with the company for two more months anyway. "Why don't we just go along until near the end, and that way you'll get a better chance to see whether you're really interested. If you are, we can still talk then."

At first the 43-year-old Cummings had no intention of leaving his 15-year career and senior partnership at Woods Gordon to join what very well might still be a sinking ship at National Sea. "When you're in consulting and you do turnaround work, you often get asked to join the company," Cummings explains. "In fact, if you don't get asked you feel like you must have failed. That's why I always kept stock answers on hand for just such offers."

In early October, after August's operating results showed a profit based on that month's operations, Hennigar increased his pressure on Cummings.

"The easiest way to fix a problem like this," Hennigar told Cummings during a dinner at his home one night, "is to hire the guy who told you you have the problem, and tell him to fix it. And that's what I'm going to do."

Cummings offered his usual pat refusals, but Hennigar kept pushing. When Cummings finally tried to beg off with the argument that Hennigar couldn't afford him, Hennigar says now, "I knew I had him then. It was just a matter of how much it was going to cost me."

Before any final commitment was made on either side, however, Cummings insisted that Hennigar talk to John Wilson, the chairman of the board of Woods Gordon, to find out if Wilson thought Cummings had the right stuff for the National Sea job. If he did, Cummings said, then the final hurdle would be for Cummings' wife, Barbara, to fly down to Halifax to spend a weekend with Hennigar and his wife, Carolyn. He and his wife always made important career decisions together, Cummings told Hennigar. If they all got along, and if Barbara agreed, then he would take the job.

Hennigar flew to Toronto the next week and had lunch with Wilson. "It was a typical David lunch," Cummings jokes. "John not only ended up paying for lunch but, after it was over, he had to lend David a subway token as well." Wilson told Hennigar that while Cummings had never been in charge of a group of more than 15 people, let alone run a major international company before, he believed the odds were "better than 50 percent" that Cummings could successfully make the transition to chief executive officer.

While that might not exactly sound like a ringing endorsement, it was — given the circumstances — a daring prediction. As Cummings himself is the first to admit: "If I had gone through the *Globe and Mail* and applied for 100 CEO jobs advertised there at the time, I probably wouldn't have even gotten shortlisted for one of them.

"What I offered National Sea," Cummings suggests, "was not experience so much as a fresh start."

Having successfully passed his first "test" — as Hennigar jokingly described it in a telephone call to Cummings after his meeting with John Wilson — he was ready for Barbara Cummings' final inspection. She flew to Halifax from Toronto during the Thanksgiving weekend in 1984. The two couples spent the day together in the Annapolis Valley, closing up the Hennigars' summer cottage for winter and then, on the drive back to Halifax, stopped at the Blomidon Inn, a country inn in Wolfville, to have dinner. After the meal, Barbara Cummings confided to her husband, "You can work with him. I think you should take it."

Cummings did, but he insisted that the final terms of his contract be worked out with both Hennigar *and* Bill Morrow. "Bill and I had to understand what our respective roles in the company were going to be," Cummings explains. "Inevitably, there were going to be differences and it was important that we deal with the whole issue straight up and from the beginning."

Essentially, the arrangement they reached was that Cummings would become National Sea's executive vice president and chief operating officer and assume responsibility for the internal, operating side of the company, while Morrow would continue as president and chief executive officer and represent the company's interests in the larger world of business and government.

Although their respective roles have since changed — Cummings became president and Morrow chairman of the board (David Hennigar became chairman of the board's executive committee) in the summer of 1985 — the initial rapport they developed has lasted.

"Contrary to the expectations that might be on the street, the relationship isn't wearing thin at all," says National Sea vice president Robbie Shaw. "In fact it's getting better and better. What you have is a situation in which Gordon's aggressiveness and creativity is disciplined by Bill Morrow's experience. I'm in awe of how well it's worked out."

"When I came in in 1984, it would have only been reasonable to expect that Bill might be a bit resentful," Cummings says today, "but no one could have handled the transition better than Bill did. One of the first things he did, in fact, was to make sure I got an Air Canada 'Gold Card' so it would be easy for me to get around. He's done everything possible to make the situation work — for us and for the company. Because our strengths are not the same, there really isn't any competition between us. And because we both want National Sea to work, we recognize that — even when we do disagree over something, and inevitably we do from time to time — we're working for a common cause."

That common cause, as Cummings saw it when he arrived at his new job in November 1984, was nothing less than making National Sea Products Ltd. "a winner again." As he later explained in a 1986 speech: "The overriding purpose of my mission was to prove that the necessary natural, human and creative resources still existed to keep this country's largest fisheries-based firm profitably within the private sector."

At first glance, the Montreal-raised, Toronto-based Cummings is the least likely person you'd expect to end up running an international fish company. The product of a broken home in a working-class district of Montreal, Cummings overcame a childhood bout with polio only to drop out of high school at 16 because, as he admits today, he had fallen madly in love with a girl he'd been going out with for two weeks, and he wanted a job so that he could make lots of money to impress her.

When they broke up two weeks later, Cummings refocused his energies on what he decided was a far more important goal—making something of himself. A depressing two-year stint as a lowly Canadian National Railways junior mail clerk persuaded him he would need more than simple ambition to get ahead, so he doggedly filled his spare time over the next few years with night courses to upgrade his education: he received his Bachelor of Commerce degree in 1964; a Registered Industrial Accountant's designation in 1966; his MBA in 1969.

"People say, 'Jeez, wasn't it a great sacrifice going to school and working at the same time?' But it wasn't at all," Cummings insists. "I knew I wanted to succeed, I knew this would help and I was enjoying it. And, of course, I had the support of my wife too. [They met in 1960.] I don't think you could do those things without a wife who was supportive. But Barb and I wanted the same things. Her dad had worked for the railways, for CP, and he'd never risen above a clerical position. We knew that if we were going to get ahead, I'd have to get a better education and that I'd have to work hard to get it." He pauses. "Canada truly is a land of opportunity if you want to bust your butt to get there. Anyone who says you can't get ahead if you try in Canada is going to have a hard time convincing me."

Even as he was polishing his educational credentials, Cummings was also slowly but steadily climbing the corporate ladder too — moving from CN to Gillette of Canada in 1960, and from there to an accounting job at Continental Can in 1962, to a controller's job at Bundy of Canada in 1968 and then, finally, to Woods Gordon as a consultant in 1969.

Cummings opened Woods Gordon's financial planning and control practice in Montreal in 1970 and, by 1974, was a partner in the firm. "In the beginning, it was just a one-person practice," Cummings recalls. "When I left for Toronto, it was a 12-person practice."

His decision to move to Toronto in 1981 had a good deal to do with political events in Quebec during the 1970s. Although almost apolitical himself until the 1976 provincial election campaign that brought the separatist Parti Québécois to power, Cummings says the separatist threat convinced him he had to do his part "to make Canada work."

"I was driving home from work one evening and I was listening to a radio broadcast of a speech [federal Liberal cabinet minister turned provincial Liberal candidate] Bryce Mackasey was giving at a rally in Dorval. What he was really saying was, 'Look, if you really love your country, now's the time to get the rag out of your backside and do something.' I came home all enthused, and when I got there, my wife said, 'Listen, have you heard the radio? We've got to do something.'"

Cummings became president of his Montreal-area Liberal-riding association — "You could have held our nominating convention in 1976 in a telephone booth" — and later was one of only two Anglophone strategists on the provincial "*non*" campaign committee for the 1980 provincial referendum on separation. "We delivered over 40,000 '*non*' votes in our own district," Cummings says proudly. "We had a party that night."

But by then, however, it had become clear that in the highly charged atmosphere of Quebec political and business life, Woods Gordon's Montreal operation should now be run by Francophones. In 1981, after helping train French-speaking successors, Cummings moved to Toronto "fully expecting to spend the rest of my life there."

Instead, three years later, he was in Halifax starting a new life and a new job. That job, as Cummings describes it now, was straightforward if daunting. He needed to get National Sea's management working as a team again, but first he had to stop the financial hemorrhaging.

His first act was to sell off six of National Sea's 21 small processing plants, mainly to local owner-operators he believed could run them more efficiently. He transferred some employees, fired others (largely in the production areas) and — as a symbolic gesture — agreed to an earlier decision by company management to put a hold on plans to order a $50,000 sign for the company's new corporate head office. He announced that the company's administrative offices would occupy two lower floors instead of the prestigious top floor of the 17-storey office tower because, as he put it in an early interview: "We want no ivory towers."

The personnel changes were most dramatic on the marketing side. "Take a look at a corporate organizational chart before and after Cummings' arrival," Michael Kirby,[1] who, as a federal senator, has continued to monitor National Sea's progress, suggested to a reporter in 1986. "You'll find a lot of the players,

---

1. Interestingly, shortly after the restructuring was completed, David Hennigar nominated both Kirby and fellow restructuring-committee member David Mann to serve on National Sea's board of directors. He wanted Kirby on the board, Hennigar explained to incredulous reporters, "because of his abilities and background, and the knowledge he could bring to the board." Although both Kirby and Mann initially accepted the offer, there was such an uproar in the House of Commons over possible conflict of interest that both men quickly withdrew their names from consideration.

especially in marketing, are different since Cummings took over." The company's Tampa-based U.S. marketing headquarters, for example, was known for spending rather than making money. Cummings moved the entire operation to Portsmouth, New Hampshire, where it would be easier to control from Halifax, and then set about building a new, aggressive sales team under the direction of John P. MacNeil, who became vice president of marketing in 1984.

Cummings' fine-tuning of the company's decision-making structure began with that crucial management tool, the annual budget. Asked to present the already prepared 1985 budget to the board of directors, he refused. He candidly told the board he didn't think the projections worth bothering with and asked for a month's extension to get the budget right. Cummings says the process was a "great opportunity to deal with a lot of people in the organization on results and on plans and activities—to have them tell me why they couldn't do something and for me to say that's not good enough. It was a chance to force a new attitude down through the organization and then to start building on it."

He held weekly operating meetings so that he and every one of his nine top executives would know what was going on in the company at all times. Then he added monthly-results reviews so they could compare their budgeted targets with actual numbers. "Some managers found it terrible," Cummings admits, "because that sort of management technique, which isn't all that fancy, had never been done here before."

Interestingly, however, as Cummings himself is quick to point out, there were very few personnel changes in the company's top ranks. "We didn't change the people so much as we changed the attitudes," Cummings says. But the new additions were significant.

One was Rod McCulloch, the Clarkson Gordon senior partner in Halifax who'd been so instrumental in Cummings' own decision to join National Sea. "Rod had been thinking about making a change anyway because he and his wife liked Halifax and they wanted to raise their kids here. We had lunch one day and I was talking with him about that as a friend, as someone who'd just gone through a mid-life career change myself. After lunch we both went back to our own offices and then I called him up and said, 'Look, Rod, I'm now calling you wearing my other hat. Would you consider joining National Sea?'" In what was an almost uncanny repeat of Cummings' own earlier conversation with David Hennigar, McCulloch began by joking that National Sea couldn't afford him. "But the discussion," Cummings says now, "went very quickly from a theoretical discussion, to 'Hey, this turkey's serious.'" McCulloch joined the firm in the summer of 1986 as executive vice president, finance and administration.

The other key addition was Robbie Shaw, who became a vice president with responsibility for human and government relations as well as for developing a long-range corporate strategy. Shaw's background for that job was appropriately eclectic: he'd been a federal civil servant, the principal assistant to Gerald Regan from 1974 to 1978 while Regan was the Liberal premier of Nova Scotia, and a vice president at Halifax's Dalhousie University.

Shaw, a native Nova Scotian, says he had long been intrigued by the fishing industry, which he describes as "the most relevant industry there is for an Atlantic Canadian." Shaw first discussed the possibility of joining National Sea with Bill Morrow in 1978 after the Liberals were defeated in that year's provincial election, but the Nickersons had just gained control of the company and there were no positions available. Two years later, the company did try to hire Shaw, but he'd just joined Dalhousie University. Finally, in early 1986, with Shaw looking for a new challenge and National Sea beginning its turnaround, the timing was right.

But Cummings insists that he didn't impose Shaw or McCulloch on a reluctant management team. "In fact, it was quite the opposite. I remember I went to people and said, 'Look, we've been talking to Robbie Shaw and he's available. What do you think?' Their reaction wasn't that this was some sort of threat or anything. They said, 'Gee, can we really get him? That would be great.'"

Cummings himself believes the most important change he brought to the company at the beginning was a change in focus. Under Cummings, National Sea became what he calls a "market-driven corporation." In many ways, of course, as Cummings is the first to admit, that new focus only became possible as a result of changes in the industry spawned by the Kirby Task Force report.

Kirby had finally convinced Ottawa policy-makers to stop using the fishery as a political weapon and accept the industry's long-standing argument for a more rational allocation of fish quotas. The result was a new, five-year Enterprise Allocation arrangement.

Under Enterprise Allocations — or EAs as they became known in the industry — the fishing grounds were divided into zones and each company was assigned a pre-determined share of that zone's quota for each species of fish. It was then allowed to harvest the fish when and as it saw fit. What that did, in effect, was to turn the ocean into a huge — and free — holding tank for the company's live fresh-fish inventory.

Instead of asking the fleet to catch all the fish it can as fast as it can, the introduction of EAs allowed the company to direct the National Sea fleet to harvest more selectively, bringing the catch into line with market demand. This strategy eased the firm's perennial problem of bloated inventory and attendant high carrying costs.

To make EAs work even better, the company developed what became known as the Fishing Plan, essentially a communications network that enabled the company's trawler captains, plant managers and sales executives to maintain such close daily contact with one another that — to take an admittedly simplistic example — if a fish buyer in Minnesota suddenly requested a particular quantity of a particular kind of fish, a trawler captain in the North Atlantic could be directed to alter course, change gear, adjust his fishing schedule and port of arrival in order to meet that demand, and do it within the constraints of Enterprise Allocations.

National Sea made a concerted effort to implement some of the other of the key recommendations of the Kirby Task Force report too. The company's European competitors had already begun using new technologies to improve fish quality by reducing the number of times and ways in which fish are handled between net and processing line. In 1985, National Sea followed suit and began converting its traditional bulk-storage trawling fleet into modern containerized vessels.

Interestingly, it was Fisheries Resource Development Ltd., the research and development company set up by National Sea and Nickerson in the optimistic early days of their union and then quietly absorbed by National Sea in March 1983 after the Nickersons found themselves in financial difficulty, that was largely responsible for enabling National Sea to begin playing quick technological catch-up in the mid-1980s.

"I give full credit to Bill Morrow for that," says John Maloney, the head of FRD, which is now a division of National Sea. "I remember in the worst days of the financial problems him saying to me that in times of adversity, the last things you want to cut are your spending on advertising and on research and development because when the crisis is over, you're going to need to have those parts of your company working at full power. And he was right."

Shortly after Maloney arrived at FRD in the summer of 1980, he began to realize that the east coast fishing industry had fallen behind its European counterparts in fish-handling technology.

The result was that eastern Canadian fish, which suffered through a good deal of rough handling between the ocean and the dining-room table — "If you can imagine it, we were actually sucking the fish out of the ship's hold with machines that were driving these fish into each other, smashing and banging them into each other at speeds up to 100 miles an hour" — could not command the premium prices European fishermen were getting for their catches in the lucrative American market. "At the time of the downturn," Maloney points out, "Icelandic fish was commanding a 50-cent-a-pound premium over ours."

If everyone agreed that something needed to be done, there was little consensus on what that something should be. "The fleet people said, Look, we do our job. We get the fish, we bring it in. What happens after that is your problem. What we had to do was demonstrate to them that we needed to have a system that would work all the way from the sea all the way through the plant. And then we had to demonstrate to the senior executives in the company — and remember that this process was going on while the company was going through all its financial problems — that what we wanted to do would produce more benefits than costs."

Maloney and his materials'-handling experts developed several prototypes, but it was Earl Demone, the company's veteran fleet vice president, who ultimately came up with the novel and ultimately practical notion of quite literally cutting some of the company's trawlers in two and then adding 22 feet of new hull in the middle to accommodate more efficient fish-storage containers. That way the company could dramatically reduce the number of times the fish was handled between vessel and plant, but without reducing valuable shipboard storage space. "What we had to do was develop a system for retrofitting the ships in an innovative way and at the least possible cost," Maloney explains. "Once we'd done the work, we were able to show that we not only could produce the quality we needed, but that we couldn't afford *not* to do these things."

At the same time, to further improve the quality of its product, National Sea introduced its own system of dockside grading of landed fish and paid a premium to crews who delivered better-quality fish.

Inside the plant, FRD was instrumental in convincing the company to switch from hand-filleting its fish to machine filleting. "The machines had been around for years but they were ineffective for redfish, which accounted for a good deal of our catch," Maloney points out. "In order to make it practical to get machine filleting for the whole operation, we needed to overcome the problems with the redfish machines, so we worked very closely with two different companies for almost two years to develop just the right equipment for our own needs."

Although there was initially some opposition to the new equipment from plant workers who feared it would lead to a loss of jobs, Maloney insists that was never the intention. "It's simply that machine filleting gives you a higher-quality product and that higher quality means it will command a higher price and be more in demand. In the end, machine filleting generated more jobs than it cost because it opened up new opportunities for us to sell to higher-quality markets."

By the time Fisheries Resource Development Ltd. was finally able to put together the technology and the systems to allow the company to containerize and mechanize its operations, National Sea had recovered sufficiently to be in a position to commit the cash necessary to upgrade its facilities.

After far too many years of worrying about its future and even its survival, National Sea was finally in a position again to look to the future.

The most significant event in making that clear to those in the company — as well as to investors and the public — was the company's swift success (after 10 fruitless years of trying) in persuading Ottawa to permit the company to operate a high-tech deep-sea factory freezer trawler capable of processing and freezing fish at sea.

18
The Factory Freezer Trawler

THE COMPLEX up-and-down, on-and-off story of how National Sea Products Ltd. managed to win that factory freezer trawler license actually begins way back in the mid-1970s when Jack Davis was the federal minister of fisheries.

At the time, Canada was involved in the International Law of the Sea Conference, but its ultimate outcome was in such doubt that federal officials decided it would be politic for Canada to establish a presence in its own northern waters. As part of that show-the-flag effort, federal deputy minister of fisheries Ken Lucas suggested to Bill Morrow that National Sea take one of its wetfish trawlers for a fishing trip to the northern tip of Labrador.

"We told him it wouldn't be economical for us," Morrow recalls. "If we were going to fish up there, we said, we'd need to have a factory freezer trawler. He said, 'Fine, why don't you get one then?'"

It didn't turn out to be that simple.

The company itself had been interested in acquiring at-sea freezing capability for some time, and had even assigned fleet captain Earl Demone to find a design for such a vessel. Initially, the company considered building a ship modelled on a British freezer trawler. They were simple vessels, designed only to freeze groundfish in blocks while the ship was at sea. Final processing was still done on land.

Before deciding to build or acquire, however, Demone decided to talk to fish-company officials in West Germany. The West Germans were the world's most technologically sophisticated fishing nation. By the mid-1970s, in fact, the Germans were well into the production of their third generation of factory freezer trawlers, and the latest incarnations not only included on-board freezing but also filleting capacity, meal plants and huge storage facilities. The German boats were also already ice-strengthened, which made them practical for use in

Canadian North Atlantic waters as well.

During his days as a vessel captain, Demone had struck up a friendship with some of the skippers from Nordstern, a mid-sized West German fish company, and he decided to ask them what they thought of using the British freezer-trawler technology.

"I went squid fishing with a few of them off New York and I told them what we were thinking about," Demone recalls. "They said, 'Look, Earl, we don't want to interfere in your business, but the freezer trawler is just the wrong way to go. There's no money it.'"

Demone began to look more closely at the newer-style German factory ships instead. As a result, National Sea — with the federal government's blessing — chartered the four-year-old West German factory freezer trawler *Frederick Busse* (named after a famous German fish entrepreneur and industrialist) for a six-month trial period in May 1977. To undercut objections from other fish companies and inshore fishermen, National Sea agreed to limit its catch primarily to non-traditional species of fish.

At the time, however, National Sea was so uncertain about the outcome of the experiment that it made its agreement with Ottawa contingent on the federal government agreeing to share equally in any losses the vessel incurred over and above $300,000. Almost incidentally, the company and the federal government also agreed to split any profit that might result from the venture.

But the new technology — coupled with an unusually good squid-fishing season — transformed the company's anticipated losses into a $500,000 profit. That created an embarrassment for the government, Bill Morrow recalls now with a laugh. "We wrote them out a cheque for their share of the profits," he says, "but they weren't set up to deal with the idea of a profit and nobody knew what to do with our cheque."

The success of the venture convinced both National Sea and federal fisheries department officials that the company should get its own factory freezer vessel. Says Bill Morrow: "I remember Ken Lucas coming into my office one day in August of 1977 and saying to me, 'Okay, you've had all this success, so when are you going to get a ship?' And I said to him, 'Well, Ken, I just signed a letter applying for the license.' And I showed it to him. He said, 'That's great. Canada should have had that years ago.'"

Bill Morrow laughs. "A little while after that, Jack Davis was out, Romeo LeBlanc was in, and we never even got a reply to our application."

Later, when he went to Ottawa to personally press the case for a factory-freezer-trawler license, Morrow recalls, "I went to see Romeo and he gave me this lecture on who should own the boat. He said it should be the fishermen themselves. I said, 'Well, you know, that's all very well but they're not interested in owning the ship. And besides, who's going to raise the money for them to get it?' But those arguments didn't make much difference to Romeo and we couldn't even get a decent hearing from him."

But the company continued to press its case. Over the next eight years, in fact, National Sea applied for a license to operate a factory freezer trawler on four more occasions. That was done, Morrow says today, in spite of the fact the firm's majority shareholders for much of that period were never more than lukewarm about the project. "The Nickersons didn't want to spend the money," Morrow says, "and they still questioned whether we should be looking at a factory freezer trawler or whether it didn't make more sense to just get a freezer trawler."

During the short-lived Conservative government of Joe Clark, the company's application finally seemed to at least be getting sympathetic consideration. "The fisheries minister, Jim McGrath, gave us a good hearing, but he was from Newfoundland and so he was under a lot of pressure from his provincial counterparts. The Newfoundland government didn't want to see us getting a license because they worried about what it would do to their fishery."

In the end, that mattered less than the fact that the Tory minority government was defeated on a vote in the House of Commons and then lost the subsequent federal election to the Liberals. Newly re-elected prime minister Pierre Trudeau appointed a Quebec lawyer, Pierre DeBané, to the fisheries portfolio. "He was hopeless," says Morrow. "And then we got into the problems of the early eighties and ..."

After the company was restructured in 1984, the need for a factory freezer trawler became even more clear to everyone, including Gordon Cummings who made getting a license one of his top priorities.

Using some of the political skills he'd picked up during the Quebec referendum battle, Cummings out-maneuvered political, union and community rivals to win the license in less than six months of lobbying. National Sea's swift success this time was remarkable, and not just because similar National Sea requests to operate the trawler had been turned down on five other occasions in the past eight years. What made it even more remarkable was the fact that John Fraser, the federal fisheries minister at the time the application was filed, was forced to resign soon after in the infamous "tainted-tuna" scandal. Even though his successor, Eric Neilsen, was only holding the job temporarily, he agreed to National Sea's application.

Ottawa's about-face on the issue, Nova Scotia fisheries minister John Leefe declared admiringly at the time, was largely the result of a masterful demonstration of lobbying skills by Gordon Cummings.

Although foreign fleets have been using factory freezer trawlers — essentially floating fish factories — in Canadian waters since the 1950s,[1] Ottawa had rejected past company applications on the strength of impassioned pleas from inshore fishermen and land-based fish processors. They argued that factory trawlers would eliminate many onshore jobs and further disrupt the traditional way of life in hundreds of small Atlantic fishing communities.

Cummings carefully attempted to counter those arguments at a series of meetings with regional and federal politicians even before National Sea officially filed its application in the late spring of 1985. Then, after the application was officially filed, Cummings and a group of key executives—including Bill Morrow, Jim Morrow, Earl Demone and Sandy Roche — fanned out across the region to talk up the cause among local plant workers, who were worried about the possibility that the new trawler would eliminate their jobs, and to lobby local politicians, who fretted about the effect such a ship might have on their economies.

In many communities National Sea's traditional reputation for honesty helped sway the uncommitted. "When the Lockeport plant burned, no one believed we'd ever rebuild it," Bill Morrow explains, "but we said we would and we did. So when it came to the factory freezer trawler, people there remembered that we had a reputation for coming through for the community."

At the same time, Cummings assured both the politicians and those in the local communities that the new technology was necessary just to get the product National Sea wanted, not to get more fish. He insisted it would result in a net loss of only 25 jobs in the whole Atlantic region. To underline how vital the license was to the company's future, Cummings pointed out that Skipper's Restaurants Inc., one of the largest American fast-food chains, had recently decided to transfer an $8-million fish contract from National Sea to an Alaskan company because that firm employed factory freezer trawlers. (Skipper's likes its fish to be frozen at sea because it remains firmer and then can be sliced more thinly.)

While Cummings' pitch won converts in the Nova Scotia government as well as among many local town councils and boards of trade, Newfoundland was another story. In a province where hundreds of small coastal communities still depended on their local fish-processing plants for work, the company not only ran up against hostility to the proposal itself but also prejudice against National Sea—a mainland company that was headquartered in Nova Scotia and that was planning to exploit what Newfoundlanders considered a provincial resource.

Cummings says he tried to be as diplomatic as possible, telling Newfound-

---
1. The first factory freezer trawler was the *Fairtry*, launched in England in 1953.

land fisheries minister Tom Rideout, "Look, we don't expect you to support us on this now but, if this thing works, you might find that a year or two from now FPI [the Newfoundland fish company owned by the province and Ottawa] might want to apply for one, too. All we're suggesting is that you consider that before you may lay too many land mines you might end up walking across yourself."

Brian Peckford, Newfoundland's unpredictable premier, was slow to get the message. Accusing National Sea of planning to "rape us clean...[by] promoting a technology that has the potential to spell ruin" for the Newfoundland inshore fishery, Peckford launched a national campaign against the application. After Ottawa granted the license in November 1985, he threatened to challenge the decision in the courts. Cummings went out of his way to be conciliatory. He told reporters the company would "make every effort to repair any rift that may have occurred" even as he popped champagne at an impromptu company victory celebration. In fact, Cummings viewed Peckford's threat of court action as a "good way for him to defuse things. It's not in his nature to say, 'I lost.' I mean, jeez, we'd have all fainted if he'd done that." A few weeks later, Peckford quietly abandoned his appeal.

By then, National Sea officials were already in Hamburg, Germany, making arrangements to purchase a used but serviceable 11-year-old 270-foot factory freezer trawler named the *Scombrus* for $8 million.

"The license was granted on a Thursday or Friday," Bill Morrow recalls, "and by Sunday Earl [Demone] and I were on a plane to Hamburg, Germany."

Morrow and Demone, in fact, were interested in acquiring the *Scombrus* — the name means mackerel — from the start. "It was the right size for what we were after," says Demone, "and it was still relatively new." They'd first seen it in operation in 1977 during National Sea's own experimental charter of another German factory freezer trawler, the *Frederick Busse*. Because the terms of that charter required National Sea to fish for non-traditional species, the real market for much of the fish being caught was in Europe and Japan. National Sea was so successful in peddling its catch to the Japanese that the owners of several other German factory freezer trawlers — including the *Scombrus* — asked the company for technical assistance in preparing fish for that market and even offered them a commission to sell their catches there.

But that wasn't National Sea's only connection with the vessel's owners, the Pickenpack family in Germany. "When I was in sales," Bill Morrow says, "Mr. Pickenpack wrote and asked us if we had room for one of his boys to spend six months in our North American operations." In fact, two of Pickenpack's sons — Jan, who worked in National Sea's U.S. sales office, and Theis, who spent time at the company's Lunenburg cooked-fish plant — ended up getting their introduction to the North American fish business through National Sea.

When Morrow and Demone first contacted them, the Pickenpacks weren't interested in selling the ship, but added that if they changed their minds, National Sea could have first call on the vessel.

Even before they left Halifax, Morrow and Demone had come up with a contingency plan in case they couldn't acquire the *Scombrus*— they would visit other fish companies in Germany, then try their luck in Norway and France. If they couldn't buy the kind of ship they were looking for, they would visit some shipyards that had their own architects to discuss designs for a new vessel.

But they'd only gotten as far as Bremerhaven when they got a call from the Pickenpacks. The family had been thinking about Bill Morrow's argument that the quota situation for foreign vessels operating in the North Atlantic was unlikely to improve in the foreseeable future and had decided that if National Sea would agree to sweeten its initial offer by $500,000, well, they'd be willing to take the matter to their board of directors for approval.

How soon could they get the approval of their board? Morrow wanted to know.

When do you go back to North America, they were asked in response.

Ultimately, it was agreed that the Pickenpacks would contact Morrow and Demone in Norway with their answer. By then, it was clear to Morrow and Demone that the *Scombrus* was their only hope for a quick fix for their factory freezer trawler requirement. "There was nothing else available," Morrow explains. "The Koreans and the Chinese had been there before us and bought everything up."

When the Pickenpack family finally reached them at the Parkin Hotel in Alesund, Norway, they had good news. If National Sea would agree to the extra half-million, they had a deal. Bill Morrow quickly agreed and arranged to meet Jan Pickenpack in London a few days later to finalize the deal. Just in case the deal collapsed at the last minute, Demone went on to Spain to see what vessels might be available there.

In the end, Morrow and Pickenpack needed just a few hours — and a lot of long-distance phone calls between London and National Sea's Halifax lawyers — to finalize the deal. "The next morning, we went to the Royal Bank in London at nine. The manager gave us his office and by 11:30 we had it all wrapped up."

Less than two months later, a 12-man crew from National Sea (which included the future skipper, Larry Mossman) flew from Halifax to Germany to join Captain Hans Kruger and an equal number of highly skilled German fishermen, engineers, electricians, mechanics and fish-meal operators who were already experienced in the operation of factory ships and who would — with the Canadians — make up the initial crew of the newly renamed *Cape North*.

"We had permission to keep the Germans for up to three years," Morrow explains, "but by the end of the first year, most of them had gone home and we were left with an almost totally Canadian crew."

Although no one would ever describe it as among "the most beautiful vessels in the world" and no artist is ever likely to be so taken with its beauty that he paints a portrait of it, the steel-hulled 270-foot-long factory freezer trawler is still much more than just another fishing vessel.

National Sea's *Cape North*, in fact, is symbolic of the continuation of a fine old Lunenburg tradition of marrying the most advanced fish-catching technology of the day with the accumulated skills of generations of men — and now women too — who go down to the sea in ships.

To the casual observer, there is little to distinguish the German-built *Cape North* from the other 58 vessels in National Sea Products Ltd.'s deep-sea fishing fleet until you go below deck. There, you'll find a scene that would have amazed Ben Smith and the crew of his turn-of-the-century *Gladys B. Smith*.

Deep in the bowels of the *Cape North*, there is a brightly lit, modern floating fish factory, a huge room full of conveyor belts, stainless steel mechanical boners,

Cape North, *1986* (KNICKLE'S STUDIO PHOTO)

headers and gutters, a host of Japanese and German filleting machines, along with about a dozen men and women who are quietly, efficiently going about their business of preparing several tons of freshly caught fish — cod, redfish, pollock — for flash-freezing.

The *Cape North* is Canada's first real factory freezer trawler,[2] and it is difficult to remember now — two years after it began operations — why it once aroused such controversy. A recent study has shown that it not only did not result in the loss of shore-based jobs in its home port of Lunenburg, but that there are actually more shore workers employed now than there were when the vessel first arrived in the winter of 1986. And those who work aboard the *Cape North* in its processing plant earn nearly $6,000 more a year than their landlubber colleagues.

Of course, they work hard for their money. About 90 people work aboard the *Cape North*, with two of the three 30-person shifts on board ship for any single trip. A trip can last anywhere from six to nine weeks. The per-trip complement includes four officers, 10 trawlermen, three engineers, two oilers, a bosun, a netmaker, four cooks and stewards, two electricians, two fish-meal plant operators, two Baader (filleting machine) mechanics, two processing managers and 26 processors, several of them women.

At sea, their routine is relentless and unvarying — two six-hours shifts every day seven days a week. When they are not working, the crew members are sleeping, eating — the vessel's provisions include up to three tons of meat per trip, not to mention 1,000 gallons of coffee — watching one of the 60 or so movies on one of the ship's videotape machines, playing cards or just resting up for the next shift.

During their six-hour shift, the deck crew will put out and then haul in the huge trawl net, filled with several tons of fish, every two to three hours.

From the net the fish are dumped into the hold where they are separated into species and sped on their way through the shipboard processing plant where they are headed, gutted, tailed and flash-frozen, all within four hours of having been scooped from the sea. The ship has a capacity of up to 740 tonnes of finished product.

Because they are frozen so quickly, the $15 million worth of fish the *Cape North* catches and processes — about 11,000 tonnes each year — is more desirable and more efficiently processed than that caught, stored and then

---

2. There was one other vessel on the west coast, the *Kalastratus*, which Morrow refers to as a "so-called" factory freezer trawler. National Sea noted its existence, in fact, to support its successful FFT application. Remembers Morrow: "As a matter of fact, some federal government officials suggested we take it over, but a West German factory-ship owner took a look at it and advised Demone and I to 'stay away from it,' that it was 'still-born' and 'doomed to failure.'"

processed on land in the normal way. For example, the redfish the *Cape North* catches — about a quarter of its total haul — can be sold at premium prices to the Japanese, who prize its red color. That color used to be lost during the up-to-one week it would take a regular trawler to make it back to port for on-land processing. At the same time, the *Cape North*'s cod blocks sell for the top price on the United States market, where they are often now served in trendy restaurants. And nothing is wasted — what can't be used for human consumption is turned into premium meal and sent to the Far East for use in its fish-farming operations.

Because of bonuses for full holds and fast turnarounds, the crew's earnings depend on how much they catch and how fast. There can be bonuses of $2,000 and more for each crew member, depending on the success of the trip.

Because the crew works on a rotation system — one-third of them are ashore on any given trip — their lifestyles are totally different than those of their schooner and wetfish predecessors.

"If you're going to fish," Earl Demone offers enthusiastically, "this is the way to do it." Demone, whose own career spans all the way from the last days of schooner fishing to today's ultra-modern factory ships, says some wetfish fishermen sneeringly call their factory-ship colleagues "geriatrics" because it appears to be so much easier than conventional fishing.

For starters, of course, there are the creature comforts — the movies, the more modern living quarters — offered on board the factory ships. For another, there is the regularity of the work. Those aboard the factory ships work regular shifts, while those on conventional fishing vessels must often work day and night without a break when they're actually fishing. That's because wetfish trawling involves a race against time — the trawler must fill its holds and get back to port before the first fish caught deteriorate too badly to be worth anything. Because it has its own on-board processing facilities, the factory ship is under no such pressure.

But that's not to suggest there isn't pressure, especially on the vessel's captain who is still ultimately responsible for making sure that every trip is as quick and as successful as humanly possible.

As George Matteson, a one-time schooner captain and poet who wrote a book about fishing on Georges Bank in the late 1970s, put it: "Although the actual routine of each [type of] vessel is different, they all have one thing in common: each is organized so that while at sea the most possible fish will be caught in the least possible time. Most fishermen," he noted simply, "prefer to spend as little time as possible at sea."

But there are constraints on that conventional wisdom when you're dealing

Larry Mossman, Skipper, and Chris Morrow, Mate

with a factory ship. While the captain must make sure his vessel catches enough fish to keep the processing line operating efficiently, he has to be just as careful to make sure that the boat doesn't haul in so much fish at any one time that it can't all be processed within five or six hours of being caught. "It's a constant balancing act," says Earl Demone. And carried out, of course, against the backdrop of the reality that the men and women aboard the ship want to fill their hold and get back to port as quickly as they can.

All of that means extra pressure for the ruggedly handsome 30-year-old Lunenburger who captains the *Cape North*. Larry Mossman is, in many ways, a throwback to the days of Ben Smith. An almost instinctive sailor who began working on trawlers as a deckhand when he was just 17, Mossman joined National Sea Products Ltd. as a mate in 1977 and became master of the *Cape Bauld* at the incredibly young age of 21.

Mossman's leadership, as well as his almost uncanny ability to find fish for catching — shades of Ben Smith — made him the logical choice to take command of the *Cape North* after the company bought it in 1985. Before he took over, Mossman spent close to a year learning the vessel's ins and outs under the

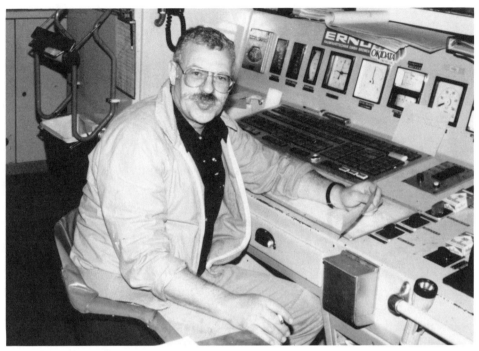

Rolf Munt, Chief Engineer

direction of some of its original German crew and other experienced factory-freezer-trawler officers. During that same year, Mossman also found time to earn his Fishing Masters Class 1 ticket, one of only eight Canadian fishermen to hold that distinction. (One of the others is Bill Morrow's son, Chris, who is first mate and relieving skipper aboard the *Cape North*.)

On Mossman's first official trip as captain of the *Cape North* — in the winter of 1987 — the vessel made its shortest trip ever to that point, just 41 days, and caught more fish than it ever had before on a single trip. "We had excellent fishing," Mossman allowed modestly on his return. "We had more fish than we could handle almost every day."

Perhaps that was one reason why Mossman was named National Sea Products Ltd.'s "Outstanding Individual" at the first annual President's Awards for Outstanding Achievement in 1986. Although the title is slightly different than Ben Smith's designation as a highline skipper, the meaning is the same.

But the factory-freezer-trawler license, which Cummings estimated would add $4 million to the company's bottom line in 1986, was just one element of a much broader strategy to increase profits quickly. And the trawler, of course, wasn't even a factor in the company's incredible 1985 performance. That performance was so unbelievable it even provoked a call in January 1986 from a worried official at the Toronto Stock Exchange. The TSE wanted Gordon Cummings to explain why there'd been a run on National Sea's stock. The stock, which had traded for less than five dollars before the Hennigar takeover, had suddenly jumped to $19.50 from $13 in less than a month.

The short answer to the question, as Cummings proudly told the official, was that National Sea—Canada's largest fish-processing company and one of the world's largest fishing enterprises, with annual sales of $454 million, 7,000 employees, operations in all four Atlantic provinces and three U.S. plants and interests in fish-processing plants as far afield as Uruguay and Australia—was back in business and building for the future.

And it was.

After two straight years of huge losses — a record $25.5 million[3] in 1983 followed by a still painful $11 million in 1984 — David Hennigar was finally able — with more than a little relief — to report to long-suffering shareholders attending the company's annual meeting in April 1986 that National Sea had actually made $7 million in 1985! To make sure no one missed the point, that year's annual report was chock full of colorful graphs with such titles as "Sales Growth Back on Track" and "Road to Recovery."

There were any number of reasonable explanations for the turnaround. There was the fact, for example, that fish consumption in the United States, where National Sea sells two-thirds of its product, was up to 14.3 pounds per person a year from 13.6 pounds just a year earlier. That was in no small part attributable to published reports in such prestigious publications as the *New England Journal of Medicine* in the spring of 1985 that showed a relationship between eating seafood and low rates of heart disease. That article described the results of a Danish experiment in which 852 men experienced a reduction of about 50 percent in the incidence of heart disease as a result of eating a minimum of one ounce of fish a week.

Although the federal department of consumer and corporate affairs in Canada refused National Sea permission to build an advertising campaign around those findings or even refer to them on supermarket coupons, Cummings lost few opportunities in his speeches and public appearances to mention the studies.

Even without being allowed to use the study findings in its sales pitches, however, National Sea had been able to take advantage of a growing North American obsession for low-calorie foods by introducing new and improved

---

3. The figures quoted represent net income before taxes and extraordinary items are included.

entrées and lighter-batter frozen seafood and by expanding its market for more profitable fresh fish.

At the same time, the company's first venture into non-fish food—frozen processed-chicken products bearing the Captain's Chicken label and touted on television by the avuncular Captain High Liner—was so successful that National Sea claimed 25 percent of the Canadian market after just five months on the supermarket shelves. Given its success with chicken, Cummings told reporters after the annual meeting, "I think it's safe to say that, as far as the non-fish market goes, we've really only just begun."

Cummings was more than happy to savor the sweetness of the company's newly found success. "In 1984 if you told anyone you worked for National Sea, they'd pat you on the head and feel sorry for you," he said. "Now we can walk down the street with our heads held high. We're winning." But he was equally quick to point out that the company was only beginning to get back on a profitable track, and that its performance was still far from satisfactory.

"I would not hold out $7 million in profit on $450 million in sales as a big bag of money," says Cummings. "It's only a one-and-a-half percent return. We want to make 10 cents on every sales dollar."

That may help to explain why, even after its 1985 success, Cummings refused to ease up. He constantly demanded of his executives: "Are you on team B or team P?" Team B, he explained, stood for breaking even and team P for making a profit. "Once you stop losing barrels of money, there's a tendency to breathe a sigh of relief and relax," Cummings told them. "But you've got to be in business for more than breaking even. I regard keeping the momentum going, breeding success and a winning attitude as one of my most significant jobs."

Cummings, who was a competitive distance runner in high school, says he doesn't believe in jogging — in life, or in business. "People today jog and find it wonderful to listen to the birds," Cummings told a reporter from Canadian Press in 1987. "My idea of running is only to win."

19

High on the High Liner

Name the Halifax-based fish firm which, with help from Ottawa and its bankers, survived a brush with bankruptcy in the early 1980s and now, with an ad character named Captain High Liner as its mascot, flourishes as North America's leading producer and exporter of fish products?
—From a quiz on "Canada's Business World-Beaters" in the 1987 *Report on Business 1000*

GORDON CUMMINGS is winning. And so is National Sea. The company's annual report for 1987 shows sales nudging $550 million, an increase of seven percent over 1986, and overall income before extraordinary items up 27 percent, to $27.6 million from $21.8 million a year earlier.

For someone who likes to win, the news — and the job — couldn't be better. "I don't know how the hell you could have a better job than this one," Cummings says, sitting in his large corner office on the sixth floor of the Purdy's Wharf office complex in downtown Halifax and contemplating the ships moving in the harbor beyond his window. It is a late afternoon in December 1987, and Cummings is in an expansive mood. And why not? "I've got one of the best jobs in Canada — in North America. I'm the president of a growing company in a growing market, and I have owners who say, 'Go for it.'"

Those owners, he notes, not only willingly invested close to $100 million in new capital expenditures in 1986 and 1987, but they also paid off many of the company's long-term restructuring debts before they were even due. (National Sea bought up the Toronto Dominion Bank's $75 million worth of difficulty-term-preferred shares, for example, a full two years ahead of schedule.) "The majority shareholders made clear from the beginning that they were looking to management to maximize the long-run potential of our company. Their focus wasn't just on the next quarter alone." He smiles. "What more could any chief executive officer want in an owner? What more could anyone want in a job?"

What more indeed? But Gordon Cummings' National Sea Products Ltd. has become so successful so quickly that by late 1987, some people are already asking what Cummings would do next? Would he abandon the company for another turnaround challenge? Would he try and trade on his growing reputation as one of Canada's best-known and most outspoken corporate executives to become the politician he'd almost become back in Quebec?

There was no disputing the fact that Cummings had developed a high public profile during his two and a half years at the helm of National Sea. *Canadian Business* magazine, for example, credited him with masterminding "one of the most remarkable corporate turnarounds of 1985." A headline writer at the Halifax *Daily News*, comparing him to Chrysler Corporation's popular and spectacularly successful chairman — also rumored to be interested in a political second career — dubbed him "the Iacocca of Nova Scotia." Toronto-based *Influence* magazine selected him as one of its top 50 Canadian "Men of Influence." And *Atlantic Insight* magazine named him one of its "Atlantic Innovators of the Year."

Despite his growing involvement in political issues — he was becoming one

Gordon Cummings, President and Chief Executive Officer

of the country's most quoted corporate supporters of the federal Conservative government's free-trade deal with the United States, for example — Cummings was always careful to steer clear of becoming identified with one political party. "It would be very inappropriate for me to be involved politically with one party," he explains. "We are a highly regulated industry. We have a lot of dealings with government, and I don't think it would be fair to those we deal with in government or fair to the employees or the shareholders of National Sea if I partook in partisan politics."

Cummings is quick to make it clear he has no plans to leave the company to indulge his interest in politics either. There is still far too much to accomplish at National Sea. The first — and most important — goal, he says, is to overcome the inexplicable but seemingly inevitable cycles of boom and bust that have dogged the company almost from the day it was founded nearly 90 years ago.

Many in and outside the industry — even those who applauded National Sea's incredible success since 1984 — remain skeptical about how the company will fare if fish prices suddenly dive to the bottom again or if interest rates go up like a rocket or if the international currency market does a back flip. Even Bill Morrow, who has lived through and survived industry ups and downs for more than 40 years, isn't sure anyone will ever completely tame all the many and different variables that make the fishery so fascinatingly — and frustratingly — unpredictable.

Still, Gordon Cummings intends to give it his best shot.

During the first days of his term in office, he launched an intensive multi-faceted strategic-planning process designed to make the company's future more predictable, and more profitable. Although executives at the company had long been concerned about the industry's boom-bust cycles and had, in fact, begun a program of formal strategic planning back in 1968, that process got sidetracked during the industry's troubles in the early 1980s. Cummings wanted to get it back on the rails again.

Robbie Shaw, who was hired partly to oversee the effort, admits "a lot of the basics still weren't in place [when he joined the company]. We didn't really have a grasp of what the market is, for instance, or who we're serving or how well we're doing it."

The first major step in the new planning process occurred in February 1985, when executives got together for a one-day brainstorming session to look at potential business opportunities. "We came up with 135 different opportunities," Cummings recalls. "We put them all up on the board and everybody left feeling great. But we didn't set any priorities and there was no follow-up, so nothing actually ended up being done about them. Later, we put together our

'B' team [a group of about a dozen up-and-coming young executives in their 30s whom management expects will one day hold senior positions in the company] and got them working with Robbie to narrow things down."

"At first," says Shaw, "we simply blue-skyed it. We talked in directionless terms and just let it happen. When you get enough bright, imaginative people in a room, you're bound to come up with something. At the end of each blue-sky session, we had lists of hundreds of opportunities. Then, after much gnashing of teeth and disagreement, we narrowed them down. In that process, we began to discover a set of common values that can provide the direction for the company in the future."

Surprisingly, one of the first things they decided was that, with the exception of the chicken line it was already selling successfully, the company should stick to the fish business for the foreseeable future.

"We identified a ton of opportunities, and some of them were outside the fish business," Cummings says. "But it became more and more apparent during the process that there were still lots of opportunities for us within the fish business. Tuna, for example. Tuna is the largest-selling fish in the world, but no one in this company really knows anything about tuna. And that's just one possibility."

Another, of course, is shrimp, one of the fastest-growing segments of the seafood business. Although National Sea had long been active in the shrimp market through its small Tampa operation, company executives knew they would have to expand their efforts dramatically in order to become a significant factor in the extremely competitive U.S. market. Because their existing Tampa subsidiary was in cramped waterfront quarters with little room for expansion, the company decided the only practical, quick way to take advantage of the potential opportunities on the shrimp side of the business was to buy one of its Tampa competitors — Treasure Isle, a family-owned Tampa business that operated the second largest shrimp-processing facility in the United States. The purchase price of all of Treasure Isle's assets was $28.6 million.

The Treasure Isle purchase reflected another decision made during the strategic-planning process. If the company was to remain in the fish business, Shaw's group also realized it would have to look outside its traditional Atlantic home base for new sources of supply. Despite the introduction of the 200-mile limit a decade ago and expectations that that would mean more fish for Canadian fish companies, the reality was that annual quota allocations and fish catches were actually dropping. "Fish is a valuable resource that's in short supply, and other companies are after the same fish as we are," Shaw concedes, "so we have to become smarter and broader in our scope in order to achieve our goals."

Part of that broadening of the company's scope involved an aggressive approach to acquisitions, mergers and joint ventures all over the world. To help it grab an even bigger share of the U.S. market, for example, National Sea spent $7 million to acquire the Chicago-based Booth and Fisher Boy retail labels, the country's fourth largest seafood sellers. Those labels already had well-established metropolitan markets in Chicago, Memphis, Dallas, Houston and Milwaukee. National Sea's aim, Cummings told reporters when announcing the purchase, was to triple Booth's $30 million in annual sales within three to four years.

On the world scene, National Sea spent $8 million to acquire French-based Bretagne Export S.A., one of the largest seafood brokers in western Europe. At the same time, company officials began holding preliminary discussions with fishing and trading officials in a number of other countries in attempts to acquire an interest in a major new fishing firm to be based in Eastern Europe, to launch a shrimp-fishing operation off the coast of Africa and even to establish a joint venture with the Chinese government. To increase the company's knowledge of the potentially huge Southeast Asian fishery — by 1987, National Sea was buying close to $8 million worth of fish products each year in Hong Kong — National Sea officials assigned a newly hired Masters in Business Administration graduate to spend time in Bangkok working with a major Thailand fish company as part of an executive-exchange program.

National Sea's strategic planners also began to seriously consider the once-fanciful idea of actually growing their own fish. "For years, we've simply taken from the sea what the sea produces," Gordon Cummings explains. "The only modern management technique that we use is conservation. Remember the Club of Rome in the 1960s and how they predicted that the world would run out of food? Well, mass starvation hasn't happened. Why not? Because of technology, that's why. The food industry is producing more food per acre, more food per ton of seed, than it did in the sixties. And yet the fishery is still operating today the same way it operated 500 years ago. We've done nothing to enhance the stock.

"We want to find out what makes the oceans tick," Cummings says. "When we know that, we want to know how to manipulate the oceans to produce more and better supplies — did you know that the female cod lays 2 million-3 million eggs? But only four or five of them live to be adults. If we could increase those numbers even a little, we would greatly increase the amount of stock available. But can we? Should we? Those cod are part of the food chain in the oceans. We don't know how all the parts of that food chain interact with one another. We don't even know if it was a good idea to sell silver hake, a species we don't sell much of in Canada, to the Russians. What will that mean for the future of the fish that we do catch that feed on those hake?"

In an effort to find out the answers to those and other questions — and not incidentally to learn how to better harvest what it hoped would ultimately be an enhanced stock — National Sea, along with Newfoundland's Fishery Products International, agreed to jointly fund a new chair in oceanography at Memorial University in St. John's, Newfoundland.

At the same time, National Sea spent $4 million to buy a 49-percent interest in Pafcon Investments Ltd., a British Columbia holding company that controls Pacific Aqua Foods Ltd., one of the largest fish-farming companies in British Columbia's thriving aquaculture industry. And it hired Bud Kirshner, the executive it considered the aquaculture industry's best and brightest talent, to run it.

The deal was a good one for all concerned. "National Sea's involvement gives the [aquaculture] industry an extra aura of credibility," Kirshner told the Toronto *Globe and Mail*, while Gordon Cummings made it clear he saw the investment as an entry point for National Sea's growing interest in aquaculture. "We're getting in, if not on the ground floor, then on the second floor of the B.C. aquaculture business," Cummings told reporters when the company's investment was announced. "This," he declared confidently, "will be the premier B.C. salmon-aquaculture operation."

While most aquaculture ventures to date have focused on growing expensive species like shrimp and salmon — a B.C.-farmed salmon, which costs $15 to grow to about nine pounds, can fetch anywhere from $43 to $50 during the winter and spring, when fresh wild salmon is unavailable — Cummings says its real potential may ultimately be in more conventional species of fish, such as halibut and even cod. "There's a fish-farm operation in Newfoundland," Cummings points out, "where a guy trapped codfish and then kept them in cages and fed them. Six months later, they'd doubled their weight. We take that very seriously."

The company's decision to try and find more and more new sources of supply through every avenue from acquisition to aquaculture is, of course, all part of Cummings' plan to finally break free of the industry's boom-bust cycles. "We're not there yet," he concedes, "but we've put the right pieces in place. We're very close."

On this December 1987 afternoon — with National Sea heading for another year of record profits and the future looking even more promising — Gordon Cummings can be forgiven for feeling a little smug about the future. "Nineteen eighty-five was the year of turning around, of selling off assets on the one side and of getting the factory-freezer license on the other," he explains. "That set the stage for 1986, which was the year of doing things right, of opening up offices and making acquisitions. And 1987 was the year of getting aggressive, of moving forward."

By 1992, Cummings confidently predicts, National Sea will not only almost certainly reach its target of becoming a $1-billion-a-year company, but it will also have finally put itself in a position where it will be insulated from the boom-bust cycles of the past.

If Cummings — as Canadian author Peter C. Newman put it in a column in *Maclean's* at the time — is "chronically bullish" about the future of National Sea Products Ltd., company chairman Bill Morrow seems almost downbeat by contrast. In his office down the hall from Cummings, Morrow strikes an optimistic but cautious tone as he talks about the company's future. After more than 40 years in the fish business, the wily Morrow has become inured to the vagaries of the industry. "If you go back over the years, you'll find that every seven or eight years, the industry seems to just go bust," he says. "There's always a good reason, but it's never the same reason. One time, the cause might be high interest rates. The next time, it might be poor catches." He smiles. "The only thing that seems certain is that just when you start feeling good about everything, that's the time you should learn to duck."

At National Sea, it soon became clear, the time had come to start ducking.

"NATSEA WORKERS STRIKE IN NFLD."
Halifax *Chronicle-Herald,* January 31, 1989
"COD QUOTA RUMORS FORCE TRADING HALT BY FPI, NATSEA"
Globe and Mail, February 3, 1989
"SCIENTISTS ADVISE 50 PER CENT CUT IN NORTHERN COD TAC"
St. John's *Sunday Express,* February 5, 1989
"ROUGH SEAS AHEAD FOR FISHERY FIRMS FPI AND NATSEA"
Financial Post, February 24, 1989
"NATSEA POSTS $5.8M LOSS FOR '88"
Halifax *Chronicle-Herald,* March 3, 1989
"NATSEA RIDES OUT WAVES OF PRICES, LABOR TROUBLES"
Cape Breton Post, March 30, 1989
"NATSEA EMPLOYEES ACCEPT CONTRACT TO END STRIKE"
St. John's *Evening Telegram,* April 10, 1989
"FORECAST PLANT CLOSINGS CAST NOVA SCOTIA FISHERY INTO NEW TURMOIL"
Globe and Mail, April 10, 1989
"TRAWLER SINKS AFTER COLLISION WITH CARRIER; 17 CREW RESCUED"
Halifax *Daily News,* May 4, 1989
"LOCKEPORT TERMINATED; SEVEN PLANTS FACING TEMPORARY SHUTDOWNS"
Halifax *Chronicle-Herald,* May 12, 1989

"I can't say that this has been the most fun year I've ever spent," Gordon Cummings allows with a laugh as he slumps down into an easy chair in his office. Although the office still commands a magnificent view of Halifax harbor, Cummings seems not to notice it this afternoon. It is 18 months later, and the confident predictions of December 1987 now seem almost naive in their optimism. The company Gordon Cummings heads has taken a dramatic downturn, and the newspaper headlines offer mute testimony to that.

National Sea's 1987 profit of $27.6 million turned into a $5.8-million loss in 1988. As a harbinger of even worse to come, the fourth-quarter loss alone was $7.9 million. Stock prices, which had topped $25 in 1987, collapsed to as low as $7.50 by late 1988.

To make future prospects even worse, the federal government released a dismal scientific reassessment of east coast fish stocks in February 1989. That report said that scientists had been mistaken in their estimates of fish stocks for close to a decade, and it called for reductions of more than 50 percent in the amount of fish east coast fishermen could harvest during 1989 and beyond. "It would basically mean you could kiss off the Canadian offshore fisheries," one fishing-industry official suggested to a reporter after word of the recommendation leaked out. Agreed a federal government official, who requested anonymity: "Your next recommendation would have to be to set up an immigration program and move the east coast to Toronto."

Given the fishing industry's continuing importance in Atlantic Canada — it still provides 40,000 direct and indirect jobs — and the potentially devastating impact of such quota cuts on everyone in the industry, Prime Minister Brian Mulroney assigned his chief of staff, Stanley Hartt, to handle the issue personally.

Although Atlantic Canadian lobby groups eventually persuaded Ottawa to reduce the quota by only 12 percent for the rest of 1989, Fisheries Minister Tom Siddon coupled that announcement with the news that he was setting up a special task force to take another look at the scientific basis for the recommendations. If the task force decided they were reasonable, he said, next year's quotas would have to reflect that reality.

Even without those possible additional cuts, things had already become so bad in the fishery by late spring 1989 that National Sea was forced to announce dramatic cutbacks in its own operations.

"Atlantic Canada is facing one of the toughest challenges in recent memory," a grim-faced Gordon Cummings told reporters on May 10, 1989, as he announced that the company's Lockeport fish plant — which had been completely rebuilt just seven years ago after a fire in 1980 — would be closed for good, putting 220 employees out of work. In addition, he said, seven other plants in Newfoundland and Nova Scotia would be closed temporarily, for periods ranging from one and a half months to four months, resulting in layoffs for close to 3,500 more workers. Four trawlers would be tied up, eliminating another 60 jobs, and 10 percent of the company's 100-strong Halifax head office would be let go as well.

What went wrong?

"What went wrong?" Gordon Cummings repeats the question, then muses for a moment. "Let's just say, 'What's changed?' What's changed is that there's been a drop in per-capita consumption of fish in the United States. It went from 15.4 pounds per person in 1987 to 15 pounds in 1988. Combine that with a drop in prices and the rising value of the Canadian dollar, and you've got a serious problem. But then when you add in the reduction in our fish quotas — in 1985, our quota was 280,000 tons of fish; in 1989, it's just 200,000 tons — well...." He pauses. "You know, if you could unroll the film and go back to the picture you had a year and a half ago, well, of course, there'd be things you'd do differently."

In fact, however, the roots of the current crisis at National Sea — and in the entire Atlantic fishery — have far less to do with any recent corporate decisions at National Sea and far more to do with a series of government, industry and scientific decisions made following the declaration of the 200-mile limit in 1977.

After decades of overfishing by ruthlessly efficient foreign fleets, Canada's fish stocks had been badly decimated by the mid-1970s. In 1959, for example, a small number of foreign fishing vessels harvested 200,000 tons of northern cod. Ten years later, far more foreign fishing boats were involved, and that figure had jumped to 800,000 tons. By 1975, however, even more vessels scouring the ocean floor managed to harvest only 337,000 tons of northern cod.

In order to allow the embattled stocks time to rebuild, the Canadian government decided to set annual quotas based on an ongoing scientific reassessment of how much fish was actually in the North Atlantic's swimming inventory and how much of it could be safely caught in order to allow fish numbers to increase. To calculate that, the scientists compared the catch rates — the number of hours required to catch a certain tonnage of a certain species of fish — reported by government observers aboard commercial trawlers with the results of annual surveys conducted by department of fisheries and oceans vessels. Based on their analysis of that data, the scientists determined that fish stocks were increasing rapidly — northern-cod stocks, for example, were thought to have increased fivefold between 1977 and 1987 — and the result was that quotas were increased accordingly, from just 7,000 tons of northern cod in 1977 to 293,000 tons in 1988.

But the scientific findings were based largely on the catch rates reported by commercial vessels rather than on the data collected by DFO vessels. The seemingly logical rationale for that was, the commercial vessels were actively fishing for much of the year, while the DFO boats made only occasional surveying forays into the fishing grounds. Although that may have seemed logical, scientists finally figured out that looking at the commercial-catch rates failed to take into account one important variable — the ever-increasing efficiency of the offshore trawlers. Thanks to improving technology, the trawlers were able to catch more fish in a shorter period of time each year, thus making it appear as if there were more fish available than there really may have been.

Unlike the optimistic reports of the commercial vessels, the DFO's surveys indicated that the size of the fish stock was actually declining. If that was correct, it meant Canadian quotas had been set artificially high for many years, and drastic cuts would now be needed in order to protect the long-term future of the industry.

To complicate the quota confusion, some local fishermen and some foreign vessels were continuing to catch more fish than they were allowed anyway. Some foreign fishing nations, for example, were deliberately overfishing just outside Canada's 200-mile limit. While there were agreed-on international quotas in those areas, some countries — notably, Spain and Portugal — simply ignored the agreements and did so with impunity because no country had jurisdiction to enforce quotas in the oceans beyond 200 miles.

Although Cummings was critical of both foreign overfishing and of cheating by some Canadian small-boat fishermen — "it's almost inbred in some parts of Nova Scotia to cheat on groundfish quotas" — he is quick to concede that "there's enough blame for all of us in this. We're not above blame and fault either. We've all just assumed for too long that the resource would always be there for us. If you go back to as late as last September [1988] and look at what was happening, you'll see that we were very busy politically at that time trying to make sure we didn't get shafted on getting our share of what we believed were going to be *increased* quotas."

In fact, National Sea's share of the increasing east coast fish quotas had actually been declining for several years as Ottawa responded to political pressure from inshore fishermen for a bigger slice of the quota pie and concluded a treaty with France that allowed French fishermen to take more formerly "Canadian" fish in disputed territory around St. Pierre and Miquelon.

But the impact of those quota reductions on National Sea's revenues had been offset — and ignored — because of a combination of increasing consumer demand for fish in the United States and what appeared to be ever-escalating fish prices.

But then the Canadian dollar began gaining strength against the U.S. dollar, making National Sea's fish less competitive in the American marketplace. At the same time, overall U.S. groundfish consumption suddenly took a nosedive. The cause — frightening media reports about medical wastes being dumped at sea and washing up on beaches along the U.S. eastern seaboard — really had nothing to do with National Sea's products, because most of its fish are caught in the relatively pristine waters of the North Atlantic. But skittish consumers didn't differentiate between sources of fish or pause to consider the real likelihood of contamination: they simply gave up buying groundfish entirely.

At that point, says Cummings, "prices dropped like a rock." A cod block, which had been selling for $2.30 in 1987, fetched only $1.20 by late 1988. Cummings estimates that that collapse in price cost the company $30 million in pre-tax revenues, while the strengthening Canadian dollar sliced another $15 million before taxes from the company's 1988 revenues.

To exacerbate all of those external factors, Cummings admits National Sea was also having internal problems digesting some of its much-touted recent acquisitions. Its purchase of Treasure Isle's shrimp plant, for example, had got tangled up in what Cummings calls a "significant ongoing dispute" with the sellers over the value of the operation's inventory at the time of the sale. "Trying to solve that is still taking up a lot of time for the people who are supposed to be trying to turn that operation around for us," Cummings says today. The result, he adds, is that Treasure Isle has already racked up a $1.5-million loss in the first four months of 1989.

While the company's other acquisitions have turned out to be less troublesome — "Pacific Aqua is already doing far better than we were expecting" — Cummings concedes that the net effect of all of the purchases has been to add significantly to the company's debt load at a time when sales are suddenly contracting. "If we had known what was coming, we might not have been as aggressive in our acquisitions or spent as much money to develop the Booth label or...."

Cummings pauses. "I'm not going to try to kid you," he says. "It was a hell of a lot more fun and a lot more personally satisfying when we were in an up market and doing well — it's more fun opening a new plant in Louisbourg than it is shutting one down in Lockeport. But what you have to do is forget that and say to yourself, 'Now is normal.' This is where we're at, and we have to deal with it. Until you can convince yourself of that, you can't get on with doing what has to be done."

They had to go back to the drawing board. "We did the [1989] budget in October," Cummings remembers, "and then we redid it again in November."

After the November budget revisions, Cummings says, "we knew we were going to have to take some plant closings. Originally, we'd planned to make them January 1, but we decided to wait for the outcome of labor negotiations to see what effect that might have." He shakes his head. "Given the circumstances, I really didn't expect a strike."

But National Sea's 1,200 Newfoundland plant workers did vote to strike early in 1989. While that two-month dispute delayed the company's first cutback announcement until early May, Cummings says today that he isn't sure it was the last such announcement he will have to make.

The task force set up by the federal government to reassess the scientists' recommendations for quota cuts has now concluded that the scientists' revised assessments were right, implying that there may now be huge reductions in next year's quotas. And that would mean even more reductions in National Sea's Atlantic Canadian operations.

"We've had to let some very good, competent people go because of all of this," Cummings says sadly. "But there isn't any choice. You do what you have to do."

For all of that, Cummings says he still believes the company is on the right track — "No one here believes that the things that have to be done aren't doable" — and that it will emerge from this latest downturn "leaner and meaner. The thing is you can never go through one of these downturns and come out the same company at the other end. In tough times, you can make some necessary tough decisions — matching your capacity with your ability to process the product, for example — and people are more willing to accept them. You have to learn from this kind of situation not to ever allow yourself to become fat and lazy."

His own long-term forecast is upbeat. Although Cummings says he has begun to realize that it may never be possible to completely eliminate the swings in the fortunes of a company in such an uncertain industry, "the key will be to change where the bottom is. If you look at a graph, you'll see that we've gone from relatively profitable years to big losses. What we need to do is to move the bottom of the curve to a spot that's above zero. Then the swings will be easier to take because you'll know things are not going to fall through the bottom every time. We were in the process of getting to that point with our strategic planning when we got hit with this downturn. But we were making the right decisions — the acquisitions, the decision to get into aquaculture, the decision to stick with seafood — and so when this is over, we'll be up and running again, better and faster than ever."

As if to underscore that point, there is a small news story on page 18 of the Halifax *Chronicle-Herald* on May 19, 1989. The article is entitled "National Sea stake raised" but is almost totally ignored amid the ongoing controversy over National's Sea's plant closure and layoffs — the main news that day was a request by Nova Scotia's Liberal leader for an emergency debate on the crisis in the east coast fishery.

"While stock market analysts are steering investors away from National Sea Products Ltd.," the story begins, "Scotia Investments, a Jodrey-owned company, has raised its stake in the fish company." Through a subsidiary, the company had just purchased 170,000 common shares in National Sea, increasing its total interest to "2.35 million common shares, 2.2 million non-voting equity shares and 23,488 second preference shares."

Explains George Bishop, the president of Scotia Investments: "We felt it was an opportunity to buy the shares at a good price. We believe in the company. It's still a good, sound company."

David Hennigar, the key figure behind Scotia Investments and the largest shareholder in National Sea, couldn't agree more. Today, as he sits in his small corner office in a downtown building overlooking both the Purdy's Wharf tower, where Gordon Cummings and his executives are quartered, and Halifax harbor beyond that, Hennigar is ruminating on the future of the company he bought just four years ago.

For David Hennigar, National Sea is more than just another company. Like Hennigar himself, National Sea is a company that is deeply rooted in the Maritimes. It is also a company, he believes, with the potential to put the Maritimes on the world map once again.

"National Sea," he says, "is one of the key companies in the Maritimes and one of the few that has the potential to be a world-class competitor.

"It is going to take time, it's going to take effort, it's going to take money," Hennigar allows. "Money is the least of it when you have the people and the effort. And we do. There's a spirit there now, a sense that if you've got the will, you can make things happen, you can make anything happen."

Although they would undoubtedly be shocked to realize what has happened to the company they launched as a humble little grocery store for fishermen 90 years ago, old W.C. Smith and his seafaring brothers and their fellow seamen and investors would certainly understand — and agree with — that sentiment.